THE LINCOLN BATTALION

The Lincoln Battalion

THE STORY OF THE AMERICANS WHO FOUGHT IN SPAIN IN THE INTERNATIONAL BRIGADES

BY EDWIN ROLFE

HASKELL HOUSE PUBLISHERS LTD.
Publishers of Scarce Scholarly Books
NEW YORK, N. Y. 10012
1974

HASKELL HOUSE PUBLISHERS Ltd.
Publishers of Scarce Scholarly Books
280 LAFAYETTE STREET
NEW YORK, N. Y. 10012

Library of Congress Cataloging in Publication Data

Rolfe, Edwin, 1909-1954.
  The Lincoln battalion.

  Reprint of the ed. published by Random House, New York.
  1. Spain--History--Civil War, 1936-1939--Foreign participation--American. 2. Spain--History--Civil War, 1936-1939--Personal narratives. I. Title.
DP269.47.U6R57 1974   946.082   74-651
ISBN 0-8383-1762-6

SEP 16 '74

Printed in the United States of America

Honor for them in this lies: that theirs is no special strange plot of alien earth. Men of all lands here lie side by side, at peace now after the crucial torture of combat, bullet and bayonet gone, fear conquered forever. Yes, knowing it well, they were willing despite it to clothe their vision with flesh....

Madrid

"What the hell are they trying to do! Kill us?"
  —American Volunteer at Jarama, January 16, 1937

"They learned to fight before they had time to learn to march."
  —Herbert L. Matthews

"The world will little note, nor long remember, what we say here, but it can never forget what they did here."
  —Abraham Lincoln

"If the world has a future they have preserved it."
  —Vincent Sheean

CONTENTS

1. Those Who Fought — 3
2. New York to Jarama — 18
3. Trench Vigil — 58
4. Bruneté: When the Rivers Went Dry — 89
5. The Aragon Offensive — 107
6. Breathing Spell — 140
7. Teruel: Spain's Valley Forge — 158
8. The Pressure No Man Can Withstand — 181
9. "Waiting, Waiting, Waiting . . ." — 226
10. The Ebro Offensive — 258
11. Last Days in Spain — 294

Index — 313

MAPS AND ILLUSTRATIONS

The Tom Mooney Machine-gun Company at Jarama;
  Major Robert H. Merriman, Chief of Staff   36
The best soldier in the brigade, Joe Bianca; A cave-
  dweller reads a letter from home   37
Map of Jarama   39
A front-line monument at Jarama; An interview with
  Col. Fuqua, U. S. Military Attaché; Major Merri-
  man, J. B. S. Haldane and Lt.-Col. Copic   52
Robert Steck, Transport Commissar, speaks; Lt. Bill
  Wheeler and Sgt. Joe Taylor; José María Sastré,
  35th Division Commissar   53
Map of the Bruneté offensive   93
Map of the Aragon offensive   115
A war casualty near Quinto; Belchité after its cap-
  ture by the Americans   132
Officers of the Mackenzie-Papineau Battalion (A)
  Frank Rogers, Commissar (B) Robert Thompson,

MAPS AND ILLUSTRATIONS

Commander (C) Saul Wellman, Commissar, and
Edward Cecil-Smith, Commander — 133
Four Commanders of the Lincoln Battalion (A) Milton Wolff (B) Leonard Lamb (C) Philip Detro (D) Hans Amlie — 148
Commissar John Gates, Lt. Melvin Offsink and Capt. Wolff; Lincoln sniper at Teruel — 149
Map of Teruel — 163
Map of the retreats — 185
Ernest Hemingway talks with Hugh Slater and Matthew Mattison (left) outside HQ — 212
A bath in an irrigation ditch; A detail at rest — 213
Barricades in Madrid; Sandbags for Madrid Telephone Building — 228
Herman Klein and Vaughn Love; James Lardner, third from left — 229
Map of the Ebro offensive — 261
George Watt and Abad Garcia; Yale Stuart; Paul MacEachron; John Gates — 276
A wall newspaper; A group of Americans, April, 1938 — 277
American survivors of the Lincoln Battalion; Officers after the last action — 292
Top-ranking officers in the last parade. Barcelona; Final review of the 35th Division. Marsa — 293

The photographs, many of them taken under fire, are by Harry Randall, Benjamin Katine and Robert Capa.

THE LINCOLN BATTALION

1
THOSE WHO FOUGHT

AN HOUR BEFORE DAWN, ON A COLD MID-FEBRUARY DAY IN 1937, a convoy of army trucks wound slowly up a narrow mountain road in Central Spain. All lights were out. A savage battle raged a few miles away and the road was under enemy observation. Halfway up the strange hill the order was given: stop.

Four hundred figures tumbled out of the trucks, spread out on both sides of the road, waiting for further orders. The rifles they carried felt strange to their hands. The guns were still swathed in slimy packing-grease.

"First you have to clean 'em, get the grease off," somebody said.

"With what?"

"You've got shirts, haven't you? Use them."

Belts were unbuckled, shirts pulled up and long strips torn off. Clumsily the men removed the bolts of the rifles, but few dared to take them apart. With fumbling, unaccustomed fingers they wound the bits of cloth around the cleaning rods, working them laboriously up and down the barrels.

"How do you know when it's clean?" a nineteen-year-old student asked.

"In the daytime," somebody said, "you peep down the barrel, and when it shines you know it's clean."

But it was still dark.

A few minutes later dawn began to streak the sky.

The order came in a muffled voice which carried far in the hills:

"Battalion attention!

"Company commanders, see that every man fires five rounds against the hill from the right side of the road. Five rounds, no more.

"Proceed in order, by companies."

The shots cracked out, in bursts, and the echoes amplified them till they sounded like a hundred machine-guns, all firing together. Company One, Company Two, Company Three lined up in quick succession and fired the allotted five rounds per man against the flank of the hill. Then came the riflemen in the machine-gun company, and the scattered members of the battalion staff. In a few minutes it was over. When daybreak came only the distant sounds of the battle reached the hills.

Of the four hundred men who fired against the hills that night, perhaps fifty had used rifles before. To the others they were strange and new.

THOSE WHO FOUGHT

Yet these men—most of them less than twenty-five years old—were within a few days to face a crack army in one of the most sanguinary battles of modern history. They were to launch an attack over open, unprotected terrain against some of the best soldiers in the world—Franco's expert and ferocious Moors—and to stop them.

These youngsters were Americans. They moved up to the front under the banner and the name of an American President. By unanimous vote they called themselves the Abraham Lincoln Battalion.

After two attacks under deadly enemy cross-fire, only a hundred and fifty men remained of the four hundred who had fired their five rounds against the Castilian hills. But Franco's offensive, which had aimed to cut the Madrid-Valencia motor highway and thus isolate Madrid from the rest of Loyalist Spain, had been so decisively stopped that never again, until the day the Spanish war ended, were the enemy to advance a single pace on this vital sector.

In the year and a half that followed, more than 2,000 other young Americans followed the original volunteers into Spain. They came from every State in the Union, climbing the perilous snow-covered Pyrenees in the darkness of night, crowding the holds of small fishing boats on the Mediterranean. Some were imprisoned by the French police, others were stopped by the non-intervention patrols, a dozen went down with the *Ciudad de Barcelona* when that steamer was torpedoed off the Catalan coast in the spring of 1937. Yet, despite the many hazards, 2,800 Americans succeeded in reaching Spain.

They fought in the Lincoln Battalion at Jarama in February, and held the trenches on this front for four long and soul-trying months. In the Loyalists' Bruneté offensive of July, 1937, there were two American battalions—the Lincoln and the newly formed George Washington Battalion —and after a week of fighting the casualties were so great that the remnants of the two units were combined to form the Lincoln-Washington Battalion.

In the Aragon offensive of August, September and October, the Americans stormed and captured the fortified strategic citadel towns of Quinto and Belchité, fighting at close range in the streets, throwing grenades and glycerin bottles with arms trained by pitching baseballs.

From there, after a short rest period, they entered the fighting at Teruel, and captured the heights of Segura de los Baños in a swift assault described later by army corps officers who observed it as a "perfect operation." They fought on until late February in 1938.

Then followed the inhuman retreats of March and early April, when the remnants of the Government forces, outflanked by enemy tanks, strafed and bombed by huge fleets of Fiats, Messerschmidts, Junkers and Savoia-Marchettis, pounded by light and heavy artillery batteries, struggled through to safety by swimming the swift-flowing, muddy Ebro River.

Less than a single company of the Lincoln Battalion survived those retreats. Yet in three months the battalion was back at full strength, and it fought as a shock-battalion in the Ebro offensive of July, 1938, which stopped the insurgent offensive against Valencia and kept the enemy troops tied up on a single front for four long months. The Lincoln Battalion fought at Fatarella, at Villalba de los Arcos, at Corbera and Gandesa, on the rocky crest of Sierra Pandols and on Sierra Caballs until the morning of September 24th. Then, following Premier Juan Negrin's speech at Geneva, they were withdrawn from the firing line to begin their long journey homeward.

2

In the course of the war in Spain men of fifty-four nationalities fought for the Republic against the Axis Powers' inspired and supported rebellion. They fought under a name which has become almost legendary throughout the world, synonymous not only with self-sacrifice and courage of the highest degree, but military strength and skill as well. They called themselves the International Brigades.

In the beginning the volunteers, most of them Italian and German exiles, fought singly or in small groups. Later they formed companies, groups of a hundred or a hundred and fifty men, working together with Spanish units. The first large force to play a vital role in the war was the International Column, almost two thousand strong, which reached Madrid in November, 1936, in time to stop the advancing Fascists at the very gates of the city. It was not until the summer of 1937 that the volunteers were finally divided into brigades, composed whenever possible of single-language units, or of men from adjoining groups of Central European countries.

There were five of these brigades in Spain: the Eleventh, composed mainly of German exiles and refugees; the Twelfth, made up Italian anti-Fascists who fought under the name of Garibaldi; the Thirteenth, which was predominantly Polish; the Fourteenth, composed of French and Belgian volunteers; and the Fifteenth—Americans, Canadians and British.

At no time in the history of the International Brigades were there more than 18,000 foreign volunteers in Spain. Even at this peak figure, a third of the men were in training camps and an additional thousand in the medical and other auxiliary services. It is accurate to state that never were there as many as 7,500 Internationals in battle at any given time.

It is important that this be recorded, because German and Italian propaganda for a long time exaggerated the figure to so fantastic a degree that the world outside was frequently given the impression that the entire Loyalist Army consisted of foreign volunteers. To the International Brigadiers in the trenches this was a tribute. Since all of Franco's setbacks were blamed on their presence, it testified to their courage and caliber. But it was a bitter tribute, because, partly on the basis of it, Britain and France were able to continue the slick and murderous lie of non-intervention,

THOSE WHO FOUGHT

to withhold arms from the friendly Republican Government, and thus do more to bring about its final defeat than the presence of Mussolini's regular army divisions, Hitler's Condor Legion, and the combined air fleets and artillery regiments of the two Fascist states.

I have said that 2,800 Americans went to Spain. Today, perhaps 1,800 are back in the United States. Most of those who returned still bear the wounds of the conflict; a fortunate few, like Milton Wolff, the last commander of the Lincoln Battalion, escaped without a scratch. Perhaps a hundred more are for one reason or another still in the concentration camps of Southern France, and an additional eighteen in Franco's prisons.

Who were these young Americans? What impelled them to leave the shores of a peaceful land to plunge into the horrors of modern war? To answer these questions fully, one would need the biography of each American volunteer. All I can do here is to indicate their origins, their background, their youth, in a cross-section of typical cases.

Robert Hale Merriman, the first commander of the Lincoln Battalion, was twenty-eight years old when he arrived in Spain—six feet, two and a half inches in height, his face with its broad, high forehead scholarly even in moments of most furious battle. Born of Scottish-American parents (his father was a lumberjack, his mother a writer), he worked his way through the University of Nevada, where he majored in economics, played end on his football team, joined the Reserve Officers Training Corps and the Sigma Mu fraternity. His scholastic achievements won for him the Newton Booth Traveling Fellowship in Economics and the post of head teaching assistant in economics at the University of California. He was in Europe in the winter of 1936–37, completing his studies of European agricultural problems, when the war in Spain entered its first critical period. Dropping his project, he sped to Spain, where, drawing upon his R.O.T.C. experience, he helped train the first American battalion. Later, as Major Merriman, Chief of Staff of the Fifteenth Brigade, the tall Westerner personally led hand-grenade squads in critical house-to-house fighting.

Paul Sigel, of New York, was twenty-one years old when, hurriedly taking his final examinations at New York University's School of Engineering, he boarded a steamer on his way to Spain. Always cheerful, smiling, he had but one worry on the trip across the Atlantic; and as the liner approached Land's End he sent a wireless to his sister: "Did I pass Thermodynamics?" He was killed in his first action, at Fuentes de Ebro on October 13, 1937, while laying telephone wire across a bullet-sprayed road.

Durward Clark, a twenty-five-year-old trailer-truck driver and mechanic of San Quentin, California, read about Americans in Spain for the first time when a warden of the near-by penitentiary withheld a radical periodical from one of the prisoners and turned it over to his father. Gathering all of his savings, he made his way first to New York, then to Paris, where he found ready assistance to Spain. He became chief of the American transport regiment, then took charge of transport for Colonel Modesto's Ebro Army headquarters.

John Murra, at twenty, had received his baccalaureate at the University of Chicago and was preparing for graduate work in archaeology when he left for Spain on February 20, 1937. His command of languages—he spoke five, in addition to English, fluently—made him invaluable to the American commissar at the Albaceté base, whose assistant he was for almost a year. Finally, tiring of the rear-guard work but finding that his linguistic abilities stood in the way of his ever being really released for front-line work, he "deserted," joined the American battalion in April, 1938, and remained with it until July 28th, when he received a bullet in his lung while leading his squad into an attack during the Ebro offensive.

Milton Herndon, a brother of the young American Negro Communist leader, Angelo Herndon, went to Spain in the summer of 1937. Tall, handsome, quick to learn, he was commander of a section in the machine-gun company of the Mackenzie-Papineau (Canadian) Battalion when he left his cover to go to the aid of a wounded soldier. He was killed while dragging the helpless man to safety.

George Boehm had worked in many parts of the United States. He was a slim, dark man with the gentlest of eyes, a tireless worker who was loved by the men with whom he fought. So quiet were his ways that few of the men outside of his section knew that it was he who taught the young

Spanish recruits most of what they knew about American folklore, American songs, while he trained them to know their light machine-guns so well that they could dismantle and reassemble them with ease in the dark. He died in action on the Ebro in July, 1939.

Alvah Bessie, a thirty-three-year-old novelist, left two young sons in the States when he embarked for Spain in the winter of 1938. He had hoped to pilot planes for the Republic, but when he found the air service closed to all except native young Spaniards he joined the Lincoln Battalion, fighting with it during the second half of the spring retreats and through the Ebro offensive.

Abe Smorodin and Jesse Wallach were products of the streets of New York and of the Williamsburg section of Brooklyn, across the river. Abe was about five feet three in height, Jesse about five four or five. Both went into action at Fuentes de Ebro with the Canadian Mackenzie-Papineau Battalion; both fought in every one of their battalion's actions in Spain. They were so consistently reliable in battle that when their names came up for citations for conspicuous bravery their commander laughed. "What?" he said. "Smorodin and Wallach? Good? I *know* they're good. I knew they'd be good before we went into this. Let's give the citations to some of the men who came through, men we thought would fold up."

I remember particularly two soldiers during the last day the Americans spent in action, September 23. They typify the completely reliable, if unspectacular, fighters who to the end performed their duties without a thought of reward or glory. A squad of ten men had been sent on ammunition detail by the MacPaps. I saw them approaching brigade headquarters on their way back to their battalion. First, eight tall Americans and Canadians walked by over the shell-pocked hill, each carrying two tin cases of rifle cartridges. Then followed two diminutive figures, staggering, stumbling, but managing to keep up with their companions. One limped along with cartridge cases under each arm and in both hands; the other was bent almost to the ground, a heavy box of hand-grenades on his shoulders. They were Wallach and Smorodin.

Roger Hargrave was born in Clay County, Iowa, on April 22, 1911. His mother's people "were among the million Pilgrims," he says, "who came over on the *Mayflower*." His grandmother's family on his father's side were traders and pioneers. The "old Chisholm Trail" is named after one of them. Others founded the town of Chisholm, Minnesota. His great grandfather, Alexander Chisholm, started for the United States in 1812, but the ship was picked up by a British man of war (during the War of 1812) and taken to a Canadian port, where he was forced to settle by necessity. His grandfather, J. J. Hargrave, left Quebec Province and settled in Clay County, Iowa, in 1869, "many years ahead of the railroad." The family homestead, where he was born and where he lived for the first seventeen years of his life, is located near where the town of Spencer, Iowa, now stands. In 1930 he enrolled at Iowa University, won the school's lightweight boxing championship while still a freshman, then turned professional, using the purse money to pay his school expenses. As a boxer he did fairly well, and at one time he had eight straight wins to his credit. "I was forced to drop out of school during 'Hoover prosperity,'" he said, "and for several years worked at all sorts of jobs to save enough money to return to the university." He re-entered school in 1935, and graduated with the class of 1936, a major in science and a minor in education. Then he accepted a position at the State University Hospital, resigning in March, 1937. The next day he left with his schoolmate, Milton Felsen, for New York. On March 31st they boarded the *President Harding* for France, and after a few days of the French "underground railway" arrived in Spain.

The rest of Hargrave's story, like that of others who have not as yet been mentioned, is elaborated in the pages of this book.

3

The list could be greatly amplified. These names were chosen at random, from among the 2,800 who went to Spain and the 1,500 whom, at one time or another, I got to know.

The Americans were younger, many years younger, than the men of any of the other nations who formed the five International Brigades. They came not from war-torn and Hitler-deranged Europe, but from the security of the

THOSE WHO FOUGHT

American continent. They were not exiles, nor political refugees, like so many of the Europeans. The French, German, Italian and Polish brigadiers were older men, men who had fought in the battles of the World War. Even the younger Europeans had served their military apprenticeships in the conscripted armies of their native lands. Among the Americans few had acquired any knowledge of military matters; those who had, like Merriman, were the exceptions. Many of them, before Spain's plight drew them magnet-like across the Atlantic, thought of themselves as pacifists, if they thought of war at all. Many others—the great majority, in fact—were young Communists.

Just what it was that sent each single one of these Americans across the Atlantic to fight for the independence of Spain will never be completely known. The bridge between the impulse and the act is a highly personal process, one that men rarely divulge to others, even when they themselves are conscious enough to trace its intricate path. There is a no-man's land between conviction and action into which the great majority of humankind never venture. Today, the final determining factor which set each single one of the Americans in motion on this democratic crusade has died with 1,000 of them. The others, who have returned, will probably guard some small part of the secret all their lives.

But it is just to declare that out of the amalgam of complex and complicated reasons which prompted each individual to embark for Spain one basic motive was clear:

their profound anti-Fascist convictions, so profound and so deep-going that they were ready to die to stop the advance of Hitler's and Mussolini's invaders. Long before they reached the embattled country they had shown this: the simple act of going to Spain was in many cases proof in itself.

Some men are blind to facts; others, like governments, ignore them. There are undoubtedly many who never fully believed that Hitler and Mussolini were waging an obvious war of invasion in Spain until the Nazi and Fascist governments themselves admitted, in June, 1939, that their intervention dated from the very first days of the rebellion of Francisco Franco and his fellow Benedict Arnolds. By that time the betrayal of the Spanish Republic by the democracies, and its mutilation by the Fascist dictatorships, was a tragic and accomplished fact.

But the young Americans who went to Spain to fight, and to die as so many did in their effort to preserve the Republic, were clearer sighted from the very beginning than most men are on the quiet deathbeds of old age. They saw through the self-imposed and cowardly censorship of the American press; they did not have to wait for Gallup polls to know that the American people were overwhelmingly on the side of the Spanish Republic. They anticipated their contemporaries and their elders. Their betrayal was too mocking and cynical, their deaths—for lack of arms, not courage—too bitter.

I have tried to tell the story of these Americans who

fought in the Abraham Lincoln Battalion, the George Washington Battalion, the John Brown Artillery Battery and a dozen other units, from beginning to end. Wherever possible I have used their own accounts, their own words.

The news from Spain is not too discouraging as I write these words. The Asturians are still fighting, the people of Galicia still hold out in their mountain caves, and in the steep Sierra Nevada of the south the *guerilleros* still keep the flag of the Republic and the spirit of democracy alive.

2

NEW YORK TO JARAMA

ON SATURDAY, DECEMBER 26, 1936, AT THREE IN THE AFTER-
noon of a crisp and sunny midwinter day, the *S.S. Normandie* churned away from its dock in New York Harbor, bound for its home port at Le Havre. Very few travelers had booked first-class passage. The tourist cabins were half filled. Only the third-class quarters were unusually crowded for the holiday sailing. The number of passengers in this section was swelled by the presence of ninety-six young men, few of whom had ever before crossed the Atlantic. Most of them were in their early twenties. All were bound for Spain.

Unfavorable tides held the ship in port for four hours beyond its scheduled sailing time. During these hours a youngster was discovered hiding under the canvas cover of a lifeboat and was promptly escorted back to land. Another stowaway, however, had hidden himself more skilfully. Aided by the food and water brought to him during the five nights at sea by some of his friends in third class, he made the entire journey without mishap.

For a week preceding departure, these young men had roved through the streets of crowded Lower Manhattan, in groups of four, five and six, buying whatever equipment they felt they would need. Each one purchased heavy army boots, breeches, puttees, khaki shirts, wind-breaker caps, army blankets, tarpaulins, ammunition belts, sheepskin-lined coats, mittens (always making sure the trigger-finger was detached) and an assortment of other odd articles. Army and Navy store owners were astonished at the sudden out-of-season demand for their wares. But they were too pleased to ask many questions. When they did venture to inquire, the answer was terse and simple: "Camping trip." And if they persisted, there was always a member of each group whose imagination could be counted on to invent an intricate and detailed trip through the Canadian Rockies while the others methodically went about their purchases, checking off the items on their lists.

A day after Christmas the ship sailed. Few of their fellow voyagers suspected the young men's destination. Most of them, since they came from a dozen-odd States in the Union, were unknown to one another. They mixed casually, in small groups. Their routine amusements were those of any passenger. They lolled around in the writing room, played cards in the saloon, occasionally took turns around the deck. A large number secluded themselves in their cabins, reading whatever books they could find. A few had ancient, flaking copies of obsolete American military manuals. These were passed from hand to trusting hand with the warning: better finish it while we're aboard—it's going through the porthole before we dock.

Two days out at sea, the ship's news bulletin published an item which caused much worry and speculation among the ninety-six Americans and added an additional headache to their list of sea-going illnesses:

> Chairman McReynolds of the House Foreign Affairs Committee [the report stated] declared he would urge the Department of Justice to apply the section of the criminal code providing $3000 fine or a year in prison for enlistment of Americans in a foreign war.

But there was nothing they could do about it, and so they resumed their usual shipboard activities.

On New Year's Eve the *Normandie* docked at Le Havre. The Americans disembarked, scattered through a dozen hotels, flocked to the exchange booths to trade their dollars in for the strange-looking francs, the value of which, since they remained in France for only four days, they never got to know or appreciate. With Spain and, as each one realized, possible death before them, money of any kind would have been valueless, something to spend quickly, to get rid of easily and most pleasurably.

After hotel reservations had been made, they again dispersed in small groups to look over the town, to order ham and eggs in the weird language which few of them, not even those who had studied it as it is painfully taught in American schools, could pronounce correctly enough to make the French waiters understand. One of them, finding his efforts at speech fruitless, began at the very beginning by hastily sketching a roosting hen before going on to indicate in a series of additional drawings his desire for the fruit thereof.

Their arrival was as secret as, almost twenty years before, had been the arrival of the first American Expeditionary Force. Their difficulties were far greater. To their joy, and to their momentary inconvenience as well, they discovered that Le Havre was a strongly pro-union, pro-labor city. The people were strangely suspicious of them, and none of them saw any reason for this until Douglas Seacord, a former teacher and engineer whose knowledge of French surpassed that of his companions, induced a dock worker to let him in on the supposed grievance.

"We know the *S.S. Washington* is on strike," the Frenchman told him.

Seacord didn't understand.

"And we know the whole crew is a scab crew," the Frenchman continued.

"What has that got to do with us?" Seacord asked.

"We won't have anything to do with scabs," the Frenchman said with finality.

"Look here," said Seacord, and he proceeded to explain. Whereupon, after a couple of vermouths, the dock worker went off to tell his friends that it was all a ludicrous mistake. The Americans weren't scabs! They were a group of students on an educational tour. Many of them planned to stay until the opening of the Paris Exposition in the summer. Scabs? No! Besides, they had all arrived aboard the *Normandie*, not on the *Washington* at all!

After that the Americans were welcomed warmly by the people of Le Havre, few of whom were fooled by the student-tourist story. But when they retold it, they winked and smiled and whispered, "*Ils sont volontaires pour l'espagne.*" Their smiles were as broad as those of the customs inspectors who, after opening the suitcases packed with khaki, had grinned happily for a moment before solemnly checking all the luggage through.

Rapidly they explored the city, were amazed to find that even the women they saw leaning out of windows along one mysterious street—"women of all dimensions in fish-net robes and nothing else on," one described them—carried union cards. Wandering casually into this red-light district, they were welcomed by the people, who sent an accordion player out into the street to ask them to sing American songs while he accompanied them. Through it all, however, the Americans remained painfully sober. Every one felt tense. The dignity of their pilgrimage weighed so heavily upon them that even the wine served at the tables with their meals remained untouched by all but a few of the most self-confident among them.

At 5 P.M. on January 2nd they boarded the train for Paris. But few of them saw the French capital. In the hour or so they spent before entraining again they dined and stayed out of sight. By noon of the following day, after an uncomfortable journey on the hard wooden seats of the third-class compartments, they were in Perpignan, the dismal city which was to grow fat during the war on the excessive profits of its food trade with the starving Catalans across the border. But they felt cheerful after the train ride. Almost every passenger was a volunteer. Twenty nationalities had been represented in the train, all, except the Americans, from Europe. They met a former Reichswehr officer who had just escaped across the border, and whose clothes, tattered and dirty, testified to the details he recounted of his escape. An American gave him his extra khaki shirt. They sat with a young Czech athlete, just out of school, who told them he "had to go to Spain to fight Hitler, so I will be able to fight him better when he tries to attack Czechoslovakia." This was long, long before Munich, but the Czech student had already read the signs. They met scores of Englishmen, scores of French and German and Italian volunteers, dozens of Yugoslavs, Poles, Austrians, Hungarians. There was even one Albanian among them.

In Perpignan their job was to remain inconspicuous until dusk, when again they set forth, this time on old buses, this time for Spain. The same night they crossed the Pyrenees border, while tough-looking French border guards in blue uniforms raised their fists in the Popular Front salute, and before midnight they were in Figueras, the ancient Catalan town through which every one of the 2,800 Americans who followed this first group into Spain was to pass.

At Figueras they slept in the deep cellars and underground vaults of the ancient fortress overlooking the town, hanging their clothes on the huge iron spikes which jutted downward from the massive stone ceilings.

The next day the Americans and the other volunteers crossed the great moat-bridge of the old fort and marched to the little town, where, dressed in their army-store uniforms, they paraded before the cheering Catalans, the descendants of the same people who had stopped Napoleon's invasion a hundred-odd years before. Then they returned to the castle, where again they slept in the huge underground halls on beds improvised of iron horses, three planks of wood and straw-filled bags which served as mattresses. Many, before they left Figueras Castle the next day, inscribed on the gray walls their names, their home towns and the dates on which they had arrived, for later volunteers to see and recognize.

There were still many long rides on decrepit slow trains awaiting this first contingent. At Barcelona they paraded again, lunched and went on. After a short stop at Valencia, where again they stopped only long enough to eat, they reboarded the tortoise-slow train on the final lap of their journey, which brought them to Albaceté, the headquarters town of the International Brigades, at ten o'clock in the morning of January 6th.

2

Albaceté is a small provincial capital. Apart from its manufacture of steel blades, which had made its name known throughout the world, and the small railroad terminal it boasted, its primary importance rested on the fact that it was a central clearing house for the wheat crops and other agricultural products which were sent to it preparatory to transportation to Madrid, Valencia and Barcelona. Albaceté Province is a relatively modern subdivision of New Castile. Within its boundaries lies the ancient and far better known region of La Mancha, which Cervantes made famous for all lands and for all time.

In the one large street of Albaceté and in the smaller, far more crowded business street which bisected it, the Americans spent two happy and exciting days. They did not as yet know that La Mancha is the granary of Spain, but they found evidence of it everywhere: in the well-stocked stores where they could buy almonds, dried fruits, marzipan, hazelnuts, bread, and trinkets to send home to their girls; in the small combination bakeries, candy shops and wineries, where for a few pesetas one could still purchase a breakfast of candied fruits, sweet rolls and salty white goat cheese, native marmalade, coffee, vermouth and malaga and cognac, sometimes even cigarettes. It was a town which many of them were to get to know well, but not on this first visit. At four o'clock of their second day in Albaceté, they crowded into Russian trucks for their journey to their first training headquarters. No one knew just where these quarters would be; all looked forward to their new home with tense excitement as they drove through the flat and rolling plains of La Mancha and looked out across fields which, to the two Wisconsinites in the group, looked and smelled like home. Finally they stopped at a little village called Villanueva de la Jara, a village which was to be their home until February 15th.

It was here that the first Americans were trained. It was here that they first learned the mechanisms of rifles and machine-guns, where they held almost futile rifle practice with a few ancient Canadian Ross rifles which jammed after every second shot. In the fields around the village they held their maneuvers, learning to advance in battle formations, to infiltrate, to take cover. At night they gathered in the few houses which were assigned to them as barracks to listen to lectures on the theory of fire, the strategy and tactics of warfare. There were a few Americans in the first groups who knew something of military science. These men—Robert Merriman of California, Douglas Seacord of Tennessee, Rodolfo de Armas of Cuba and John Scott, an Englishman who had spent almost a year in the United States—took over the professorships in this strange informal university. The same men, with Merriman at their head, were later to lead the Americans into their first action.

During their five weeks at Villanueva de la Jara, the original group was reinforced by some three hundred other Americans. Throughout the entire course of the war the flow of volunteers across the border was to continue, sometimes in groups numbering as many as a hundred, sometimes—especially during the periods when the French border was sealed while the Non-Intervention Committee procrastinated with the maximum effectiveness in Geneva and elsewhere—in driblets of one or two. The training was strenuous, but the siesta period was adhered to with the scrupulousness of the traditionally reared Spaniard. The Americans were unaccustomed to the sudden cessation of activity and to the midday slumber in which the Spaniards spent the siesta hours. And so they rambled through the square before the solitary stone church and through the few sleepy cafés, the interiors of which, well screened by dangling beaded ropes against the sun, were cool and musty as the numerous wine cellars which formed almost a second labyrinthine village under Villanueva de la Jara. In the evenings, after dinner at the mess hall, they were free to do as they pleased until nine. Before taps sounded, they gathered in the village cafés, spoke in stumbling pidgin-Spanish to the natives, studied, wrote letters home, or went off to optional lectures on the art of war. There were many such classes, on mapping, scouting, signaling. Each man considered himself a potential officer; and of those who received their training here and survived the first bloody battles in the Jarama Valley, few emerged without officers' or subalterns' stripes.

The villagers were suspicious and distant at first, but the Cubans, with the well-esteemed Rodolfo de Armas at their head, soon found a way into the hearts of the people. When the Americans mingled with the village folk, the Cubans, reining their rapid-fire machine-gun syllables, acted as interpreters. Soon the strangers were warmly welcomed, invited in groups to dine at village homes, to watch the preparation of meals in tripod pans over dried brushwood the smoke of which curled out through well-placed gaps in the ceilings. Often the men would rush from the mess hall to the homes of their village friends, sitting up beyond the appointed hour, sipping wine and cracking nuts, talking with gestures and simple words with the men and women. As they learned the new language, the Americans became teachers themselves. When they had first arrived, the few Anarchists, Socialists and Communists in the village were tiny and exclusive sects. But soon they combined all their forces to form a band which rendered welcoming tunes when subsequent groups of Americans arrived and outdid itself when the Irish company of the British Battalion voted to be transferred to the newly formed Lincoln Battalion.

On February 15th, a few minutes after midday, the men boarded trucks for Albacete again. Arriving at three o'clock in the small city, they waited around for further orders. Most of them vaguely assumed that they were being moved to a new training camp, but just as they were about to leave a motorcycle messenger drew up with word that they were to proceed to the town bull ring.

Few of the men knew that only two days before the battalion command had received instructions to provide full equipment for all departments of the unit. Al Tanz, the lawyer who was now serving as quartermaster, and his Japanese-American assistant, Jack Shirai, had been sent to Albacaeté for new, camouflaged kitchen apparatus. What none of them knew was that Dr. William Pike had received a new battalion medical kit, and that it was not the meager outfit provided for training battalions; it was the full trunkload supplied to army units entering into battle.

The order which sent them to the bull ring was their first intimation that they were bound for the front. They received further verification when Merriman and James Harris were seen emerging from Central HQ of the International Brigades, weighed down with compasses, field glasses, boxes of pistol cartridges. Then, when André Marty, the French Deputy who had helped to organize the Brigades, addressed the men in the bull ring for the first time since their arrival in Spain, he referred to Merriman and Harris as captains. The same series of commissions conferred lieutenants' stripes upon five others: Douglas Seacord, John Scott, Al Tanz, Rodolfo de Armas and Philip Cooperman.

In the bull ring, after the speeches of Marty and of Peter Kerrigan, British commissar of the International Brigades base, the men waited until darkness, when trucks rumbled into the large bowl. In the light of a single electric bulb which swung back and forth overhead in the wind, they saw huge cases being removed from the trucks. Out of them came rifles, still oily with packing-grease, a hundred and fifty rounds of ammunition for each man, cartridge belts, unwieldy bandoliers and steel helmets. Then the men crowded into the trucks. Just before they were ready to go, word went around that James Harris had been transferred from the Lincolns and that Bob Merriman was now in command. A few of them heard Lucien Vidal, French commander of the International Brigade base, when he approached Merriman in the darkness and whispered:

"Good. You know your orders. Go to."

3

Before dawn, the trucks stopped at the little village of Chinchon, less than ten kilometers from the front lines. The town overlooked the rich Jarama Valley, looked down on two rivers, the Tajuña and the Jarama. The Republican lines on this front had originally run north to south, to the right of and parallel with the road leading from Madrid to Pinto and Valdemoro. When the Fifteenth Brigade had first gone into action in these positions on February 12th— four days before the Lincoln Battalion reached the front— the enemy had broken through and crossed the Jarama River south of Vaciamadrid, as well as at San Martin de la Vega, a point twelve kilometers to the south. The brigade, still minus the Americans, had gone into battle on the road between San Martin and Morata, at a point north of Pingarron Hill.

When the convoy stopped at Chinchon, Captain Merriman proceeded with his staff officers and reported to General Gall, then in command of the Thirty-fifth Division, that the battalion was ready. The twenty-eight-year-old commander of the Lincolns explained that the rifles were still packed with grease, that the men had not yet fired a single shot. He obtained permission for the battalion to stop on the way and for each man to shoot five rounds into the hills.

Imagine the scene: A winding road among the hills overlooking the valley, the hills themselves strange and dark in the half-light of dawn, a convoy of forty-five trucks rolling slowly with lights out, stopping. And in the same weird semi-darkness, 428 men tumbling out of the camions, spreading across the fields on both sides of the road, hastily wiping the grease from guns which had never been used, shooting their few rounds against the flanks of the hills.

This was the only practice that fully half of the battalion had before entering battle.

Stephen Dadek, an American aviator who had reached Spain long before the first large group, was named adjutant to Merriman the next morning. At 3 P.M. the men again moved off in the same trucks, going northwest toward Morata de Tajuña. Before leaving they were told they might encounter the enemy, that they must be on the alert because the entire district, particularly the roads and bridges, was not only under artillery and aviation fire, but within rifle and machine-gun range as well. On the way to Morata the convoy moved at caterpillar's pace; the narrow road was lined with officers and men, and at various points they had to avoid stalled camions and cannon. The peasants, seemingly unmindful of death in the air about them, were stoically irrigating their fields. Much of the water overflowed the narrow dirt road, making it extremely difficult to make headway.

The expected soon happened. The enemy spotted the convoy. As soon as it arrived at the outskirts of Morata, and while food was being distributed to the men, the rebel aviation came over. Bombs fell, machine-gun bullets strafed the fields. It was the first time the Americans had come under direct fire. All of them stretched out full length, hugging the earth like experienced soldiers. The single lapse from perfect discipline occurred when one of the younger volunteers turned over on his back, nervously aimed his rifle skyward and took a single pot shot at the planes. The others remained silent.

An airplane machine-gun bullet is about three times the size of a rifle or infantry machine-gun cartridge. When you are in the fields, it sinks into the earth with a little hissing sound, but in town, or on the outskirts of a town, wherever there are roofs or pavement or stone of any kind, the sound is sharp and staccato, like hail. After this strafing the camions were separated. It was the first real lesson, the first clear indication of the necessity for rapid troop dispersal under fire. Before that the men had tended to crowd together, seeking safety in close companionship.

In the few minutes which remained before nightfall Republican aviators appeared and attacked the enemy planes, which immediately turned to flee. But they were not fast enough. Two of the rebel planes were shot down. Men of the British Battalion, who had been at the sector for almost two weeks, took advantage of the short sky duel to tell the Americans how good the Government's planes were. Their words, plus the visual evidence of the two rebel casualties, reassured the men, who cheered as the rebel and Government planes disappeared in the gathering darkness.

They would have been even more heartened had they known that the pilot of one of the Loyalist chasers, the pilot who had downed one of the rebel planes, was an American named Ben Leider.

The confusion of the moment was aggravated by the darkness. The raw troops asked innumerable questions. "Where's the front?" was the question most often asked. The only answer was a vague gesture which swept the entire horizon, and the words "Over there."

Again the men entered their trucks for a long uphill climb which brought them to the brigade field headquarters, a little crossroads hut. Merriman, speaking to one of the staff officers, recognized in the tattered, muddy, helmeted figure an Austrian named Captain Trauslitz whom he had last seen in a dandified uniform in Albaceté, seated at a piano, delicately playing Chopin. Trauslitz instructed Merriman to move the battalion across a near-by railroad track and up a hill which remained in the Americans' memories till the end of the war. No one knows its Spanish

THE LINCOLN BATTALION

name. The Americans, hearing the hiss and whistling of bullets all about them as they climbed its flank, dubbed it Suicide Hill.

To the man entering his first action there is no shape, no reason, no direction to battle. Almost everything is bewildering or frightening, or both. The sounds have no beginnings and no ends. One goes through one's first taste of fire almost automatically, if one is fortunate, or by an almost superhuman effort of will. But then, after the first hours or days have passed, and he has survived, a man analyzes his fears, charts and maps all threats to his life and to his effectiveness as a soldier. He begins to separate the sounds, categorize the dangers. He learns the different sounds that bullets make when they scream or crack past him. He memorizes, deep in him, the difference between a shell ripping toward him and a bomb tearing downward. The lead which punctures the leaves of trees over him holds few dangers, and if he thinks of it at all, he calculates the possibility of a bullet ricocheting earthward after striking a hard branch. He knows what is dangerous, and often to what degree. When one knows this, when one has, as the Spaniards say, *cojones*, he is master of himself, aware of his purpose, ready even for those flukes which kill men and can never be charted or predicted, ready even to say, "I am going to die," and feel not always unafraid but almost calm about it.

This is how a man alone feels. Multiply this strangeness and chaos by more than four hundred, the number of men in the Lincoln Battalion, and you get an idea of how this raw and untested unit felt on the evening of February 16th, going up the road below Suicide Hill. Republican tanks passed them, rolling back along the same road to their field base on the other side of Morata, on the road to Parales. Seeing them made the men feel good; the word "ours" passed from lip to lip. The tanks were manned by young Spaniards and by Russian boys, their heads sticking out of the open turrets. Even in the darkness they passed by at maddening speed—forty to fifty kilometers an hour. And the faces of the tankists, beaming, smiling, dirty faces with oil smeared over blond hair, did more to instill confidence in the Americans than anything that had yet occurred.

There was a general hush, no one was supposed to talk or even to whistle, and the lights-out order was still in force. Numerous other trucks and dispatch motorcycles, sweeping by, added to the confusion.

The enemy had already located the crossroads headquarters, and one rebel machine-gun had it perfectly spotted with indirect fire. Every five minutes the gunner played a tune; then, after another interval, he resumed firing. The men waited while the bullets went whistling and cracking over the crossroads; then, when the sound ceased, they made a dash for it. Even then, however, the danger was still present, still close. For the enemy gunner sent his bullets past HQ right up the hill. This was the spot where the Americans got their first real dose of infantry fire. Enemy observation planes had spied the men milling around the hut earlier in the day, and had correctly judged it to be either a division or brigade headquarters.

In the thick of this indirect fire the men took up their first positions, in the secondary lines on and around Suicide Hill. John Scott brought his Irish company to the west of the hill, while the Cuban Rodolfo de Armas placed his men in positions to the north. There the Americans remained until February 20th. Frequent aerial bombardments, averaging three or four a day, caused few casualties but angered the men because the enemy had the knack of beginning the bombardment whenever the food came up, either at lunch or dinner time.

"We'd see them coming from one direction," said Bernard Walsh, a young New York sculptor, "and dig ourselves in. Then we would stick our heads out to see our own planes coming from the opposite direction. After every bombardment, runners would arrive from brigade HQ to check on the damage. And it was always a miracle to them, as it was to us, that there were never more than a few wounded men."

"It did not take us long," Eli Beigelman wrote home, "to realize that we were in a war, a life very much different from that at the base. For five days and nights we held that hill. Every day we dug deeper, constructing a regular line of trenches. . . . The casualties on Suicide Hill were, under the circumstances, very low. The first man killed was Charles Edwards, who was making observations from an outpost trench. Edwards warned the men around him:

THE TOM MOONEY MACHINE-GUN COMPANY AT JARAMA

MAJOR ROBERT H. MERRIMAN, CHIEF OF STAFF

THE BEST SOLDIER IN THE BRIGADE, JOE BIANCA

A CAVE-DWELLER READS A LETTER FROM HOME

" 'You got to keep your head down. There's a sniper shooting at us here.'

"When he too was told to keep under cover, he replied:

" 'My case is different. I'm an observer.'

"The next moment a bullet went through his head."

4

When the Americans reached the lines, the Jarama fighting had been in progress for more than ten days. On the morning of February 6th the enemy had attacked with three columns, numbering three thousand men each, on the front at La Marañosa, San Martin de la Vega and Ciempozuélos. Supported by heavy artillery fire and by numerous tanks, they drove the Republican forces back to the edge of the Jarama River. While the Republicans massed to hold their positions at San Martin de la Vega, the rebels established themselves on the heights to the northwest of this position.

Up to February 10th battles were fought along the entire front from La Marañosa to Ciempozuélos, with the rebels attempting to cross the river. Five days of fighting, at the cost of heavy losses, enabled the insurgent troops to capture the Pintoca bridge after a surprise attack. Coming over with five battalions accompanied by tanks, the rebels advanced toward Arganda, the strategic town on the main Madrid-Valencia motor highway.

Concentrating ten thousand men and much artillery to the east of the Jarama River on the night of the 11th, they again advanced on San Martin de la Vega. The Loyalists, reinforced during the night, counter-attacked to the east and north. Throughout the entire day of February 12th continuous fighting raged in the Pintoca bridge zone and near an adjacent hill—Height 694—which the rebels had taken the day before. North of the bridge the rebels advanced three kilometers, taking the ford of San Martin de la Vega and approaching Pingarron Hill. But even the possession of these powerful positions did not help them when they attempted to attack in the direction of another strategic height, Hill 620 and Arganda. All attacks were repulsed with heavy casualties by the Republicans, among whom were four International Battalions—the British, the Dimitroff, the Thaelmann and the Franco-Belge.

On February 14th the enemy again began a series of almost incessant attacks, concentrating their efforts against Hill 694 in the direction of Arganda and Morata de Tajuña. During the next two days the battle reached its greatest intensity. On the 14th the fighting was savage. With a force of 25,000 men the enemy attempted to continue its advance, directing staggering fire against Hills 620 and 700, receiving support from more than thirty tanks, and a heavy artillery barrage on a front less than four miles in width. So fierce was this attack that the Government forces were obliged to retreat almost three kilometers to the east, while the rebels succeeded in penetrating in the direction of Morata. But again the Loyalists repulsed them in a tank-supported counter-attack. Here the lines became momen-

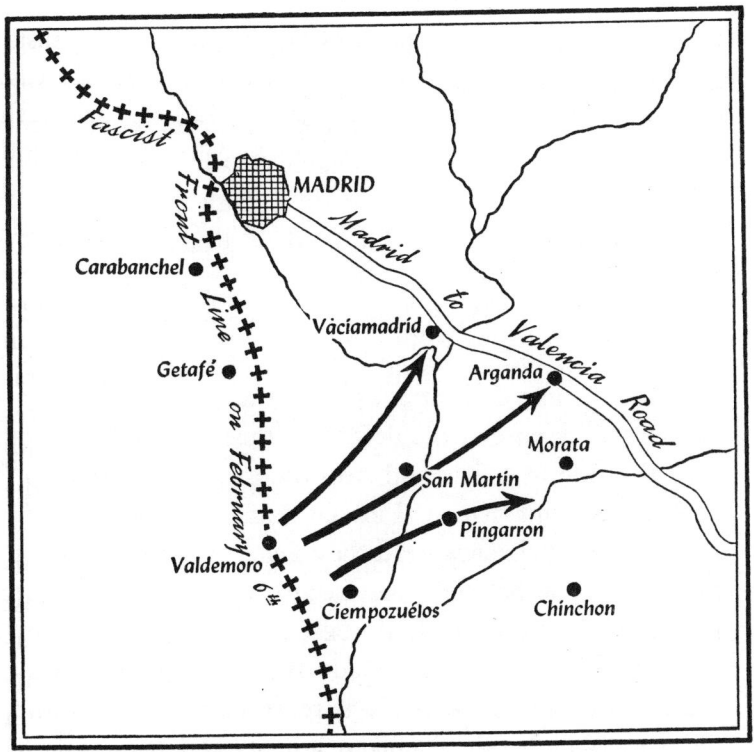

JARAMA

tarily stationary. The exhausted insurgents, whose Moroccan units had lost from 40 to 50 per cent of their strength, and whose air force had suffered the destruction of twenty planes, attempted on the 15th again to advance on Morata. Their aim was to secure their right flank by advancing as far as the Jarama River. But all their attacks were driven back.

At this stage of the fighting there were two possibilities: One was a period of rest and quiet which would enable the rebels to resume their attacks; the other so great a show of power on the part of the defenders that it would definitely turn the tide of battle and stop the insurgent offensive. It was at this point that the Lincoln Battalion entered the first lines, and on February 23rd they went over the top for the first time. The battalion had been ordered to move to the north side of the road, to take up the position of the Twenty-fourth Spanish Brigade and to prepare for an attack, the object of which was to force the enemy troops from their high-ridged entrenchments and thus make the road safe for Republican use. At 3 P.M. the men went over. They managed to advance down the slope of their own hill and up the ridge directly under the Fascist positions. But the attack failed because troops on the Americans' left flank held back, and it is axiomatic that without sufficient support from the flanks no single unit can fully achieve its objective. At sundown Captain Merriman, as well as the brigade command, realized that it would be impossible to seize the insurgent positions, and so the men returned to their original positions under cover of darkness.

Paul Burns, who took part in this attack, has described how "we made our advance, over a field dotted by occasional olive trees with only the scant shelter of vineyards. . . . Given a withered grapevine, a mound of earth, or the more pretentious shelter of an olive tree, and the boys dug in and opened fire on the Fascist lines.

"In one of those interludes beneath an olive tree I looked around—on my left was Charlie Donnelly. Beyond him the Cuban section stretched between the road on the extreme left and the Irish section. To the right of the Irish section the Americans dug in and fired.

"A few yards away in a little hollow of earth was Captain John Scott and with him Frank Flaherty, one of the three Flaherty brothers of Boston, who distinguished themselves by their heroic service and leadership under fire.

"Donnelly joined me under the olive tree. We fired until our rifles burned our hands, with scarcely a word beyond the 'Hi, Charlie, how's it goin'?' and the reply, 'Pretty good, how's the rest of the boys?'

"The infantry continued the advance. Explosive bullets split the air and the machine-gun bursts raked the field. From behind a row of trees the Fascists increased their fire.

"Captain Scott, rising, had only time to shout, 'Continue the advance,' when he fell with three bullets in his body.

"MacDonald and Bill Wheeler, company runners, had both been wounded. Eddie Flaherty, the other runner, crossed the field to call Bill Henry, leader of the Irish section. Bill took over command. . . ."

Compared to succeeding actions this attack was merely a light skirmish. Even so, it was costly to the young American battalion. John Scott, commander of the battalion's shock First Company, as well as Rodolfo de Armas, were killed. Severely wounded was Eugene Morse, Scott's second-in-command. The death of Scott has been described in one of the most vivid first-hand documents which has emerged from the war in Spain. It is the account of Joe Gordon, who left the security of the trenches no fewer than three times in his attempt to bring in the bullet-riddled, bleeding—but still living—body of the commander:

"It was already dark, the First and Second Companies had already advanced quite a distance, the firing was still heavy. One of our tanks had been hit, it was burning like all hell; it lit up a big area. Everything and everybody moved out of that area; the Fascists had expert snipers and besides we expected artillery bombardment. I was in a machine-gun group, but our gun had broken down. It was impossible to fix it. We were then told to move up with the infantry because there were no more machine-guns available.

"No sooner had we reached the rear of the Second Company than a cry for volunteers came through, to bring shovels to the First Company. Four in our group volunteered; we were given two shovels apiece, told to find the First Company. No specific direction was given because nobody knew where they were exactly. They had advanced so far that they had lost all contact with everybody. Rumors were flying thick and heavy that the First Company was wiped out, that so-and-so was killed, etc. It was our first attack. Sweat was dripping from everyone even though it was cold.

"The four of us started out together. We had to spread out, take all possible shelter we could find, and so in about three minutes we lost each other. I called their names, low as I could, but got no answer. Walking, running, flopping, the fire was hard. At last I saw somebody digging in. Running up to him, I flopped. 'Say, where's the First Company?' 'Don't know,' he answered and kept on digging feverishly with his hands. I got up, kept on running, called out, passing other comrades on my way. Some answered, some didn't. The bullets were coming very close, and besides I didn't know where the Fascist lines were. At last I bumped into somebody. I knew he was in the First Company. He told me where the main body of men was. Advancing farther, I finally bumped into Bill Wheeler whom I gave the shovels to. He in turn gave the shovels to two Cubans and told them to start digging a trench.

"I was pretty well out of breath by that time, so I took time out for a rest. Bill Wheeler then mentioned to me that Scott was wounded and where he was lying. I crawled about twenty yards farther and there I came upon Scott and Bill Henry who was now acting commander of the First Company. Scott was lying flat on his stomach with his right arm under him, his head twisted sideways. Bill Henry was pushing dirt in front of Scott's head to give him some protection. At every move he made, he drew fire. The fire coming from the Fascist guns was very visible. When I asked Henry how far the Fascists' lines were, he told me about sixty meters, and that all told we had advanced about 500 to 600 meters.

"I moved over to Scott. 'How do you feel?' I asked him. With his left hand he took hold of one of mine. No pressure. I could feel his strength slowly ebbing away. 'I'm all right,' he answered. He continued to hold my hand. I then told him I would go back and bring aid; he squeezed my hand hard for a few minutes and said, 'Don't do it, it's a waste of time.' 'What the hell do you mean, waste of time?' I answered. 'You're a human being, ain't you, and besides you're Captain Scott, see, and besides Joe Strysand will never talk to you again if you died.' With all the suffering that he was going through, a smile came over his face; he loved Joe Strysand, his runner. I then told Henry that I was going to bring aid. I hated to break hands with Scott. It seemed as though I was giving him strength through my hand.

"Instead of going back the way I came, I crawled to my left about 150 yards. There was a road, but there was a high bank to get down. No sooner had I crawled down the bank than the Fascists opened up a burst of fire on me. Hugging the side of the embankment, I waited till the firing had ceased, then continued crawling on, passing a dead soldier in a very queer position. Knowing the ground a little, I knew the first-aid station was near.

"I got up and sprinted a little, got down then, sprinted again until I finally burst right into the first-aid station. 'Captain Scott's wounded, he's dying,' I yelled at the first-aid men. 'Where's a stretcher? Hurry up!' Nobody paid attention to me. I then realized that they were French and Hollanders. I tried the sign language and my twelve words of Spanish. They thought I had gone crazy. Finally a Hollander who could talk English came up to the station. I pounced on him, told him about Scott. 'Look, comrade,' he said, 'I don't know what you're talking about. Sit down and collect yourself.' So I cooled down and told him about Scott once more. He then called together two stretcher-bearers and we proceeded to go for Scott, with a white canvas stretcher, the only thing we could get.

"The four of us went up the road about 300 yards. I then suggested that we get off the road and start crawling on the dirt. This we did. We had crawled quite a bit and all the while it seemed they were firing right at us. Why not? A white stretcher in the black of night! One stretcher-bearer refused to go farther, whereupon the Hollander who spoke English drew a gun and threatened to shoot him. I guess he didn't like the idea of himself lying out there wounded, so he came. After what seemed hours we finally got to Scott. We then grabbed Scott, none too gently—we couldn't help it—put him on the stretcher or put the stretcher under him, I don't remember. He was groaning slightly; he couldn't groan any harder if he wanted to, he was so weak. We then called for some volunteers to help us. Paul Burns, Shapiro and one other helped along. What a target! But luckily no bull's-eye.

"Now, the question of how to get back to the first-aid station: were we to crawl along the dirt and mud or go along the road? We decided to go by way of the road even though it was more dangerous. Four men then grabbed the handles, lying flat on their backs, counting three, then up and backward, then digging your feet in the dirt, pushing your way back to position. Poor Scott, what a target! It's a good thing he didn't know what was going on. After what seemed ages, 150 yards all told, we finally reached close to the road. We pushed up to the embankment. I immediately hopped off the embankment, grabbed the two handles of the stretcher and gave a hard pull just as the Fascists opened up terrific fire right on us. Everyone was wounded except myself. Paul Burns, Shapiro, the first-aid men, everyone got close to the embankment. Scott also was placed close to the embankment. Being the only one who was not wounded, the first-aid man who spoke English told me to go back and bring help. This I started to do right away.

"What a hell of a situation! You go after one wounded man and now look at the mess!

"I started crawling on the side of the road. About three minutes later a terrific barrage of fire opened up, from left, right, the back and front of me. Not moving, lying flat on my face, I was hoping the fire would subside a little so as I could move on, but it seemed to get heavier. Artillery and tanks started to bang away. The bullets were spattering close. I decided to push on, knowing that if I stood in the same spot, sooner or later I'd get it. Pushing myself with my feet and using my hands, not daring to raise my body, I moved forward slowly. I got a cramp in my left leg, also started to vomit. Resting a few minutes, then continuing onward, I finally came in sight of the dead soldier. Crawling up to him, I fixed his body so as to give me as much protection as possible. Soaked with his blood, which continued running, I don't know how long I lay. I'm sure he saved my life. I was almost afraid to breathe lest I sniff in a bullet.

"The firing started to quiet down. I left the dead soldier all to himself, and began crawling on, hoping that one of our own men would not shoot at me. Finally I came into the first-aid station. I saw Cooperman, battalion secretary, told him what had happened. He told me to see Merriman. I went to Merriman and told him what had happened. He couldn't leave his post, but told me to do and use everything I could to bring back the wounded. Going down to the first-aid station I saw Cooperman again. There was an ambulance and one of our food trucks near by. I asked Cooperman whether or not we could drive down the road with the ambulance. He said yes. Both of us climbed into it. Just as we were about to start off, somebody came running up and told us to get the hell out of the ambulance, that it was pure suicide, that we didn't have one chance in a million. We got out, got together Toplianos, our first-aid man, Ralph Greenleaf, and another man from the food truck, Tanz and myself. We took a stretcher with us, and started to go out again. Two of the first-aid men came in. Both were wounded in the legs; I don't know how they managed it. The firing was almost nil. We started walking up the road almost to the halfway mark, when we bumped into Paul Burns and Gomez, carrying in Scott. Telling the others to wait for us, Toplianos and I took the stretcher and carried Scott into the first-aid station. Scott was still alive. I felt very glad all our efforts had not been in vain.

"Toplianos and I went up the road again and caught up with the others. We got off the road and started crawling, but not too far from the road because I knew if there was anybody left he would still be on the road. The Fascists opened up bursts of fire. Whenever they opened up, we would be still, and then continue. After a hard burst of fire at us had ended, I pushed the comrade next to me and said, 'Let's go!' He didn't move. I looked at him, and found that Ralph Greenleaf had been shot right through the helmet. He died instantly, without a sign, a pool of blood forming quickly.

"We continued pushing up. Hearing groans, we stopped, called softly, 'Where are you?' No answer except the monotonous groans. We could tell by the sound that he was near by. Toplianos finally spied him. We climbed down the bank. When we got there Shapiro was lying in the middle of the road, groaning very loudly. He was in terrible pain. A bullet had struck his ankle. He had been bleeding hard, now it was already dried up. We grabbed hold of Shapiro, he was very heavy; we got him to the embankment where he was grabbed by the two comrades above. All together we lifted him off the road onto the dirt, where we got him on the stretcher.

"Again we started back in the same manner we had taken with Scott. After each yard we had to rest, he was very heavy, dead weight. His ankle or his foot kept turning around and around. All the while we were taking him in, he kept groaning terribly, drawing fire. After what seemed a lifetime, we finally got him into the first-aid station.

"What a night! Killing can be a pleasure compared with the saving of life.

"Cooperman told me to go to battalion HQ and take a rest. I was thoroughly soaked, as if I had jumped into a pool of water. At this moment Joe Strysand came dashing up to me, throwing his arms around me and kissing me, tears streaming down his eyes. We were sure Scott would live.

"I walked up to the lines again, trying to find the members of my group. Food had already been brought up. All fire had stopped; all quiet. I took two pails of food, walked out into the fields, met Landetta, commissar of the Cubans, gave him the food. Just then word had come through to come back. We were amazed, stunned. After all the advance, and all the fighting, to get ordered back! Everybody, First and Second Company in one body, they all arose, stood up straight and dashed back to our trenches!

"When it was all over, I walked back behind our lines, feeling punch-drunk, too tired even to see. My foot bumped into something soft, lying on the ground. It moved. I looked down, and it was X——, lying on the ground with a blanket over his head. His face was white. He asked, 'What's up?' I didn't answer him, I just kept walking. I felt disgusted. He had been lying there, with the blanket over his head, all the night."

5

The rebel snipers resumed their activity early in the morning of the next day. One of their first victims, ironically enough, was Joe Gordon. Less than five hours after he had brought in the last of the wounded men, a sniper's bullet caught the twenty-two-year-old machine-gunner in the forehead, above the left eye, emerging near the ear. Nine times out of ten such a wound is fatal, but the sturdy young volunteer, although he lost the sight of his left eye, recovered and took part in two more long campaigns of the war.

Not so fortunate was Robert Norwood, another twenty-two-year-old American who participated in the first attack. John Tisa, a young cannery worker from Camden, N. J., who later became assistant and then editor of *The Volunteer for Liberty*, the official Brigade publication, has described Norwood's death.

"Because the Lincolns moved so much," wrote Tisa, "and the kitchen staff was just beginning to get properly organized, they received hardly any rations for three days. On February 24th a huge bowl of coffee was sent through the trenches. Each man took his share and passed the bowl to others. When it got to Bob Norwood and a group of his companions who happened to be chatting together, he got his cup and dipped it into the bowl with great eagerness. As he raised himself from a bent position with cup in hand, he said, 'Come on, boys, dig in, I've got mine.' At that very moment an explosive bullet struck him in the head. He fell face down into the coffee . . . His brains seeped into it."

In the hours following the attack the Spaniards re-entered their old positions north of the road, and the Lincoln Battalion returned to the reserve lines on the second ridge south of the same road. Throughout the night and early morning the men kept coming back, shouting, "Don't shoot!" The stragglers, caught in the no-man's land between the two first lines of trenches, were exposed both to enemy and Republican fire. Two of them, George Jacobs and Jack Lenoris, not knowing the battalion had been withdrawn, sheltered themselves behind a tree less than thirty yards from the rebel positions. All night they remained there, huddled together for warmth, digging frantically in the earth to get out of sight of snipers who, seeing the dirt fly, kept the spot covered. It was only at dawn that they discovered where they were and realized that they were alone. At once they began the long retreat back to their trenches, crawling, making short zigzag jumps of three and five yards. They had covered more than half the distance, and were making another desperate leap forward, when Lenoris was riddled in the back by a deadly accurate machine-gun burst. His dead body was recovered that night. Jacobs succeeded in crawling, twisting and running to within fifty yards of the Lincoln trenches before he collapsed. He was brought in later that night, and it was discovered that his shoes had literally been ripped from his feet by bullets, and that his trousers,tunic and sleeves were dotted with bullet holes. After a short rest he regained his normal strength. Not one of the bullets had done more than scratch the surface of his skin.

The men knew why the attack had failed. Not only had the action begun too close to darkness, giving the men only three or four hours to dig in before nightfall, but there had been little flank support. These and a dozen other questions raised by the day's fighting were mulled over by commanders and commissars and men during the twenty-four hours that followed. There would have been even more discussion, but on the following night the Lincolns were again shifted, this time to a new position from which, three days later, the attack of February 27th was to be launched. By this time the British Battalion had been moved up to a former Franco-Belge outpost trench, which by dint of incessant digging had now become the first line. The French and Belgians had been relieved and sent to Morata for a rest. The plan of the division command at that time was to

A FRONT-LINE MONUMENT
AT JARAMA

AN INTERVIEW WITH
COL. FUQUA,
U. S. MILITARY ATTACHÉ

MAJOR MERRIMAN, J. B. S. HALDANE AND LT. COL. COPIC

ROBERT STECK, TRANSPORT COMMISSAR, SPEAKS

LIEUT. BILL WHEELER AND
SGT. JOE TAYLOR

JOSÉ MARÍA SASTRÉ,
35TH DIVISION COMMISSAR

send one battalion after another out for rest, using the Lincoln as the reserve battalion.

By the time the Americans moved up, a communication trench had been dug from the Franco-Belge outpost to a stone hut which had been used as a machine-gun outpost by Douglas Seacord and a group of his men. The hut itself was surrounded by freshly dug trenches. The Americans found themselves placed in shallow new trenches to the right of the English all the way up to the macadam road. There was also a sunken dirt road between two rises in the ground, with sandbags piled high but not higher than the battlements, so that for two days the enemy snipers in the large olive trees behind the insurgent positions were able to hit a dozen men. Most of them, fortunately, were slight head and shoulder wounds. The Americans could easily have crawled behind the sandbags across this dip in the terrain, but they were too inexperienced to know that caution is not synonymous with cowardice. Not only did they not know how to keep low, but many of them disdained to duck. It was in this manner that the first American Negro, Alonzo Watson, a painter, was killed.

On the morning of the 27th the officers and commissars of the different companies were called together and informed that the object of the impending attack was to take the rebel trenches, move the enemy back in the direction of the Jarama River, three kilometers away, and ultimately to drive them back across the river itself. Zero hour was set for 7 A.M. The men were told that there would be artillery preparation for the attack and that they would be supported by Republican tanks and planes. When Merriman relayed the information and instructions to the entire battalion, he told them to stress the fact that the sky appeared to be too cloudy for aviation. (When the planes finally did appear, no one could tell, and few know even to this day whether they were insurgent or Republican.) Aviation signals were to be placed on the macadam road —crosses and T's of whatever white cloth was available. It was while placing these signals that Joe Strysand and Robert Pick, the latter a twenty-one-year-old German-American seaman, were killed. The macadam road constantly drew the most hellish fire.

The plans were for the Lincolns to go over only after the Twenty-fourth Brigade, occupying adjacent positions farther back, had come up to a line as advanced as that of the Americans. And if the Spanish brigade was stopped, the Americans were to go over nonetheless, thus showing the way to, and setting an example for the others.

Promptly at 7 o'clock the Americans began to fire. Soon the rifles and machine-guns of the Twenty-fourth Brigade were heard. The Americans waited an hour before the Spaniards moved, but they came out of their trenches for only a short distance, never advanced very far. When brigade HQ saw that the attack was not developing according to plan, the order came for the Lincolns to go over alone. This was between 9:30 and 10 o'clock. Captain Merriman telephoned brigade HQ; there was a long debate, in the course of which Merriman maintained firmly that if the Lincoln Battalion were to go over it would draw ferocious and impassable fire, since the Twenty-fourth Brigade was in no position either to provide covering fire or to draw enemy fire away from the attackers. The argument veered back and forth. Finally Merriman was overruled. The order remained: Attack. It was then almost noon.

"The sun was hot," wrote a young rifleman who took part in the action. "Group after group hopped the trenches, charging the Fascists who were only 250 meters away. A few groups got over with scarcely any casualties. But then the enemy machine-guns began their ugly work. They pitted the sandbags all along the line in a constant staccato. Heavy firing came from both sides. Bullets sprayed in our direction . . . cross-fire from many machine-guns created an impenetrable steel wall against advance. More groups and sections went over. Soon the calls for first aid came, first singly, then louder and insistently. Many were wounded just as they climbed the parapet to go over. Some of the newcomers (sixty-six Americans, all new arrivals, had come up to the lines the night before), raw and inexperienced, went over the top with full packs on their backs and charged toward the enemy. Many wounded men crawled back to the trenches safely, but many others were killed in the attempt."

Captain Merriman was among the first casualties; a bullet drilled through his left shoulder as the first waves of men leaped over the ramparts. As the Lincolns spurted forward

THE LINCOLN BATTALION

the British Battalion left its trenches, the men entering a field sparsely dotted with fire-scarred olive trees and bare grapevines. Without the covering fire from its flank, however, the Americans were caught in a ghastly cross-fire coming at them from the rebel positions ahead and sweeping diagonally across the field, parallel with their advancing bodies, from a fortified hill to the right.

Douglas Seacord, second-in-command of the battalion, was among the first to be killed. Bill Henry, successor to Scott (whose wounds had been fatal), was shot dead shortly afterward. Paul Niepold, the Katonah, N. Y., teacher who had been made a section leader in the Second Company, was hauling a wounded man back to the safety of the trench when an explosive bullet entered his chest. Rudolph Tieger, returning to the lines with a shoulder wound, stopped to aid another wounded man; a sniper's bullet killed him. Among the others who did not survive the assault was John Lenthier, the lanky Bostonian who had been an actor in New York, and who had reached the front only a day before. For the few hours that he spent with the men in the trenches he had brought with him the melody and the words of Earl Robinson's Abraham Lincoln song. "There are only three things I care about in the world," he confided to a friend just before the attack, "the theater, the labor movement and my wife."

John McCrotty, the Irish-Catholic minister who had become Henry's adjutant in Company One, was dead too. The list was long: Sidney Arnold, Louis Barale, Robert Wolk,

Joseph Seligman, Clyde Lenway, Clare Leige, George Laskowski, William Hathaway, Dan Haskell, Maurice Jelin, Fred Lackey, Arthur Carlson, Milton Burdick, Joseph Campbell—and scores of others, men from every part of the United States, most of them boys a few years out of their teens—all were dead. Of almost 500 who went over the top, 127 were killed and almost 200 wounded.

The survivors, lying exhausted and inconsolable in their trenches at the end of the day, with the rain coming down, soaking the trenches and freezing into their skin, knew the attack had failed. But it had not failed; it was a complete success, in a way which none of the Americans who took part in it could then foresee. For the attack of February 27th succeeded completely in impressing the insurgents with one inescapable fact: that the Jarama front was too heavily, too perfectly defended. From that day until the very end of the war, the rebels never succeeded in advancing another meter along the line which, they had hoped, would cut the Madrid-Valencia highway, effect the encirclement and the capture of Madrid.

3

TRENCH VIGIL

THE RAINY SEASON BEGAN WITH A CHILLING DOWNPOUR while the men, still out in the fields before the rebel trenches, waited for darkness and a chance to crawl back to their own lines. It poured almost incessantly during the weeks that followed. "In between the deluges," wrote Paul Wendorf, "the trenches had to be drained and deepened. Always it rained. The mud clogged the rifles. The icy wind from the Guadarrama froze us in our trenches, on the heights above the Tajuña Valley.

"We awoke in the mornings to find mud in our dugouts, blankets soaked, tunics damp. The coffee was carried in urns (we had no hot containers those days) up more than a mile of mountain path, on foot. We often crawled back to our dug-outs without drinking the cold, muddy coffee. On guard in the trench we tried to keep warm by taking a turn with pick and shovel. When we got tired, we sat down in a niche. As the damp from the mud soaked in, up and at the pick-work again.

TRENCH VIGIL

"Most meals were as cold as the morning coffee.... The wind whirled and eddied, and mud joined the food on its way to our mouths.

"Those were the early days. Gradually things were better organized. A road was built where there had been only a mule-path before. The food truck came up to within a few hundred yards of the trenches. Hot food warmed damp bodies.

"In April, the sun peeped out occasionally. Slowly the dampness left our bones. The vines in no-man's land sprouted green. We wondered if we would be in possession of that territory by the time the grapes ripened. The days became longer and warmer. Suddenly, we realized we were sweeping the dust out of our trenches instead of bailing out water. Spring had come to Jarama."

The Americans suffered no losses until March 14th, when a surprise rebel attack, supported by tanks, succeeded in making a breach in the trenches to the left of the Fifteenth Brigade. Two Lincoln men, Philip Cooperman and Robert Raven, a former University of Pittsburgh student, went out past the Spanish positions to summon aid from the Loyalist tanks corps.

Cooperman left Raven near the trenches as he went off to summon the tanks. When he returned to the agreed meeting place Raven was no longer there. Back in the American trenches, he listened to a terse account of what had happened. But it was not until some weeks later that he received Raven's own account of his serious and tragic wounds. The letter was written in the American base hospital at Villa Paz, where Dr. Barsky and a number of other American medical men and nurses were speeding the blinded and shrapnel-torn boy toward recovery:

"Dear Coop [Raven wrote], just writing to let you know what happened to me after you left. I rushed up about 350 meters of empty trenches, bringing up all the Spaniards I could rally around. Then I met a Canadian. The trenches had been filling up gradually at our exhortations of *No pasaran!* Suddenly we ran into four soldiers who we thought were our own at first; but their helmets and clothes proved them to be Fascists. They advanced toward us. But we tore away from them, ran back thirty meters and grabbed some grenades. The Canadian opened the lever of his grenade and handed it to me, which he should not have done. However, I crawled up toward the Fascists under cover of the fire of the Spaniards who had just come up, and was about to toss the grenade when there was a terrific concussion in front of me and I felt my face torn off. Naturally, I just dropped the grenade, my hand having been knocked out. My own grenade exploded at my feet, filling my legs with shrapnel.

"My comrades must have retreated again, and I kept crawling blindly, dragging my body through those trenches over all kinds of obstacles, calling 'Comrade, comrade!' Words cannot describe the agony, the exhaustion, with which I dragged myself through those narrow trenches. Finally I felt somebody near me, and he touched me, and

TRENCH VIGIL

an hour or so later somebody was carrying me, and I landed at the hospital here. Most of the shrapnel in my legs has been removed, also both my eyes. They were too bad for repair. Tell the boys I said '*No pasaran*' and I hope we didn't lose those trenches."

The attack which cost Raven his sight was only a momentary setback. Early in April the Garibaldi (Italian) and Dombrowski (Polish) Battalions, fresh from their triumphs over Mussolini's motorized divisions at Guadalajara and Brihuega, counter-attacked and regained the section of trench lost that day.

After the 27th, the Fifteenth Brigade spread out to the right and left. It was no longer necessary to concentrate the International Brigades powerfully at one point. The thinning and spreading of the lines, coinciding with the complete stalling of the insurgents' plans in the Jarama, ushered in a period when new and young Spanish recruits were mobilized by the thousands for service in the Spanish army. All of the battalions on the front were getting numerous replacements, and it was the veterans' task to transform these *quintas* into an adequately trained fighting force.

It should be remembered that this was a period in the war when the largest effective unit in the army was still the battalion. The organization of brigades and divisions was still, with a few notable exceptions, on paper. There were, of course, several loose brigades and divisions, and some trade-union and political party units, the most distinguished of which was the famous Communist Fifth Regiment, which included among its young captains, lieutenants and commissars such still unknown men as Carlos, Enrique Lister, Valentin Gonzales (El Campesino), Juan Modesto and Paco Galan.

But the largest militarily organized mass which functioned smoothly and properly up to this time was the battalion. It was a period in the organization of the Spanish army which Ralph Bates was fond of calling "the romantic period"—a period when, having achieved the utmost through the spontaneous enthusiasm brought to the fight by scattered volunteers, the army was beginning to recognize its own formal inadequacy and to plan a centralized command for all the armed units in Republican Spain. This, then, was the beginning of the period of transition from scattered militia units, loose brigades and battalions to a regular army.

The Lincoln Battalion itself was no longer the same battalion which had moved up to the front on February 16th. Fewer than 150 men of the original 500 were left. The wounding of Captain Merriman had made necessary a rapid shift in command. Before he was removed to the hospital, Merriman transferred the formal command of the battalion to Philip Cooperman, who, knowing his own military limitations, insisted that he be relieved. A Belgian, Captain Van den Berghe, replaced him. Not wounds, but an old illness aggravated by the incessant rain, forced Van den Berghe to leave for the hospital. His departure on March 20th restored the battalion command to an American, Captain Martin Hourihan, a native of Towanda, Pennsylvania.

It was Hourihan who commanded the battalion when, on April 5th, it attacked, together with the Garibaldi and Dombrowski Battalions, to recapture the section of trenches lost on March 14th. The Lincolns supplied covering fire this time while the other battalions went over; then the Americans themselves left their entrenchments under British covering fire. When the attack was launched there was some hope of pushing on beyond the first objective, but the English, facing open and suicidal terrain, did not move; and again the attack was launched too late in the day. Heavy fire met the attackers, but relatively few were wounded or killed.

The entire sector, comprising the five battalions which then composed the Fifteenth Brigade—the Franco-Belge, the Lincoln, the British, the Dimitroff and the Twenty-fourth (Spanish)—was under the guidance of Captain Allan Johnson, another American, who had arrived in Spain only a month before. The Americans suffered twenty casualties that day.

Two of the Lincoln boys performed unique, although militarily useless, feats. One, who had advanced a great distance beyond the trenches, was called back by mistake. He ate a hearty meal, went over the top again and crawled with difficulty to the position which he had left, only to be recalled at nightfall. He was informed while he was eating that the order to retire would be given; but, feeling lonesome in the half-empty trench, he preferred to risk the bullets in the open fields to rejoin his comrades in his own section.

Another, returning to the trench at nightfall, found that he had left one of his prized possessions out in no-man's land. Neither his officers nor fellow-soldiers could dissuade him. He went out again in the darkness, under the heavy nervous fire which almost invariably follows a day of attack. A short time later he dropped back into the trench. "I've got it," he announced. Digging into his breast pocket he pulled out the object for which he had risked his life. "My girl's picture," he said. "Isn't she a honey?"

2

The attack of the 5th of April made but a passing, momentary impression on the Americans and, although it straightened the lines, had slight effect on the front. Ten days later the Americans were to celebrate the completion of two full months of trench warfare, and it was not until the end of June that they were finally to be relieved. The period of quiet in the Jarama trenches became known as "the long vigil." When the rainy season ended, the men took advantage of a sharp dip in the ridge behind their trenches to set up a ping-pong table and to make use of odd bits of scattered baseball equipment near the lines. The ever-present bullets sped by overhead, but they felt reasonably secure; they knew that a bullet could not deviate from its normal trajectory to so great a degree that it would endanger their daily sports.

TRENCH VIGIL

With the front inactive, the men asserted their American right to grumble and to gripe about almost every conceivable subject under the sun. Any reason was sufficient: tardy and irregular deliveries of mail from home, the discovery of a pebble in a plate of chick-peas, the fact that few of them had as yet been given furloughs.

It is a curious fact, but altogether in keeping with the American character, that the boys and young men of the Lincoln Battalion were more voluble and militant in their complaints about more grievances (imagined and actual) than most of the other nationalities which made up the International Brigades. The reason for this was evident to everyone, to commander and commissar as well as to the most vociferous griper. The Americans did, after all, come from a country whose standard of living so completely surpassed that of any European nation that the break from peace-time pursuits, with the abundance which filtered through even to the most poorly paid worker, to the scarcity of war-time life was more of a shock to them than to any of the other volunteers. The European's luxury was the American's commonplace. The Frenchman was easily satisfied, for example, with his *Gauloises,* with its dark, tongue-biting tobacco; the Spaniard had never known any other smoke except the small, black-leafed, strong cigarette which Juan March had foisted on him through his profitable tobacco monopoly. To them, and to the other nationalities in the International Brigades, the insistence on *tabaco rubio,* such as was contained in any of the popular-priced American brands, was at first mystifying. They suffered from other things, too. Their palates could not become accustomed to the olive-oil-soaked Spanish food, particularly since most of the oil now used was raw, crude, unrefined, frequently rancid. They missed their baths as only a people which boasted more bathtubs per capita than any other nation could miss them. All soldiers, in all wars, experience this terrible let-down. But the American volunteers seemed at first to be a particularly pampered lot.

In the long run, of course, they grew accustomed to the dirt and the lice of the trenches, as all soldiers must. They learned not only to tolerate the olive oil but to like it so well that one of their special delicacies, particularly at morning, was bread toasted a dark brown in sizzling oil. When cigarettes from the States were scarce—as they were almost at all times since the shipments from friends at home were lost or waylaid in a hundred ways, they smoked the Spanish "pillow-slips" and that other abomination which they dubbed "anti-tanks." And when even this supply gave out, they soaked the leaves of hazelnut trees in the vile war-cognac of the country, dried the leaves in the sun and rolled them. It was not a satisfying smoke, but then, you get used to everything.

The Jarama trenches and the life in and around them improved despite the incessant griping. On the initiative of William Pike, the battalion doctor who soon attended to th e medical and hygienic needs of almost the entire brigade, a road was built all the way up to a point only a few hundred meters from the lines. It was good enough to be used by ambulances and by small trucks which henceforth brought food directly to the secondary trenches, thus doing away with the long uphill climb which the daily food details had previously had to make to and from the halfway cookhouse, a long stretch away. Spurred on by Davy Jones, this very same cookhouse recruited men from the tranquil lines whose sole job on different days was to prepare barrelfuls of coffee, tea, cognac and even cold lemonade.

During the months of May and June the men received additions and replacements for their well-worn sports equipment. Baseballs, bats, ping-pong sets, checker and chess sets and even a few horseshoe-pitching outfits made their appearance. The crack communications man of the Lincolns, a former wireless operator named Hendrickson, rigged up a radio right in the trenches. Every few days impromptu entertainments would be organized, to which the British, and frequently the other battalions, would be invited.

Visitors also livened the long, tedious vigil. Herbert L. Matthews, the dour-faced, lanky correspondent of the New York *Times*, was among the first to break through the strict prohibitory orders of General Gall, the divisional chief who had previously refused to let him and other correspondents out to the lines to see the Americans. "It was not, as he dryly explained," Matthews afterwards wrote,

THE LINCOLN BATTALION

"that he cared what happened to us, but since we could not go there without being spotted and drawing rebel fire some soldiers might well be lost unnecessarily." Matthews later described * a visit he paid to the Jarama front in the latter part of May. He found "the Americans playing ping-pong, baseball and soccer just to pass the time away. They had dug in strongly on the crest of a hill in what had been an olive grove, and some of the dugouts were gems of comfort. Every now and then someone would get hit by the incessant dropping of stray shots, among which were a fair sprinkling of explosive bullets, not to mention a trench mortar shell now and then. But on the whole it was a quiet time, and I found them all healthy and reasonably happy, with plenty of zest left for fighting.

"I went up to the lines with Vladimir Copic, the Yugoslav commander of the Fifteenth Brigade. The ping-pong tables were going strong. They had been set about fifty yards behind the front line, which itself was only a hundred yards or so from the rebel lines, but the spot was completely hidden by a slope in the ground. As usual they all jumped on me for news of the States, of what Americans thought about Spain, of how the strikes were getting along, and what about the baseball season. The old complaint about not receiving any American cigarettes was made a few dozen times. That always was an unsolved mystery. Cigarettes were sent from New York often enough, but

* *Two Wars and More to Come,* by Herbert L. Matthews. New York, 1938. Carrick and Evans, Inc.

TRENCH VIGIL

somehow they rarely could get past Barcelona and Valencia. . . .

"The trenches were very well built—even deep enough for my height. As I walked along, one young chap impulsively offered me his rifle and asked if I would not like to take a shot. When I refused, he said, 'Of course, that would jeopardize your non-combatant standing.' It never occurred to him that anyone would not really care to take a shot at Fascists.

"The trench dugouts were particularly snug. An Irishman from New York grinned slyly when I complimented him on his home. 'Sure,' he said, 'we aren't going to pay rent after this war. We'll just build dugouts in Battery Park.'

"The trenches were constructed through what had been a vineyard, and spring weather had brought many of the vines to flower right along the parapets. Some ex-farmer had evidently been touched by that natural miracle and had lovingly placed little signs at twenty-yard intervals. 'Care for the grapes!' one of them read. 'They suffer when you hit them.'"

During these days the Americans were visited by a dozen other people who brought them tidings of home and who in many different ways brightened their humdrum day-to-day routine. J. B. S. Haldane, the eminent British scientist, three of whose sons were fighting in the ranks with the English battalion, remained with them for four days, spending most of the time in the trenches with the men. Ralph

THE LINCOLN BATTALION

Bates, the English novelist who at that time headed the Anglo-American commissariat in Madrid and edited the English newspaper of the brigades, *The Volunteer for Liberty*, was a frequent visitor. To this day the Americans attribute much of their knowledge of the early history and background of the Spanish war to his long, vividly detailed and fascinating talks.

Among the American visitors, the outstanding one, and the one best loved by the Lincoln boys was, with Matthews, Ernest Hemingway. The presence of this huge, bull-shouldered man with the questioning eyes and the full-hearted interest in everything that Spain was fighting for instilled in the tired Americans some of his own strength and quiet unostentatious courage. They knew he was himself a veteran of one war, that he still carried in his own body the steel fragments of an old wound; and the fact that such a man, with so pre-eminent a position in the world, was devoting all of his time and effort to the Loyalist cause did much to inspirit those other Americans who were holding the first-line trenches.

Hemingway was not the only writer who came to the trenches. There was Josephine Herbst, the novelist. She survived an encounter with a Spanish *soldado* who greeted her with the four-letter English word which was the only one the Americans had so far taught him. She spent an exciting although uneventful day with the Americans, accompanied on her inspection by Captains Johnson and Hourihan. There was Martha Gellhorn, who arrived in the midst

TRENCH VIGIL

of the April 5th attack, and was forced to spend the day at the brigade's first-aid post, watching the bodies of the wounded and the dead being brought in on stretchers. She afterward memorialized the day in a magazine article, a few copies of which reached Spain and were carefully and gratefully read by the American volunteers. Mr. and Mrs. George Seldes came on assignment for the New York *Post*, corroborating for themselves and for their readers the vivid truth of Matthews' early dispatches. Robert Minor, representing the *Daily Worker*, and James Hawthorne, of the *New Masses*, came on numerous occasions, once with the American Negro Communist leader, James W. Ford. Together with Douglas Roach, the Negro machine-gunner from Provincetown, Lieutenant-Colonel Copic and a number of other officers and men, they spent a typical visitors' day in and near the lines, their activities only slightly ruffled by the occasional singing of stray bullets.

3

The men found an outlet for the endless and wearying days in a quiet and self-deprecatory cynicism which was revealed most accurately in the songs they sang. One was the "Jarama Valley," sung to the tune of "Red River Valley":

> *There's a valley in Spain called Jarama;*
> *It's a place that we all know too well,*
> *For 'tis there that we wasted our manhood*
> *And most of our old age as well.*

THE LINCOLN BATTALION

*From this valley they tell us we're going,
But don't hasten to bid us adieu;
Even though we'll soon make our departure
We'll be back in an hour or two.*

*Oh we're proud of our Lincoln Battalion
And the marathon record it's made.
Now please do us this last little favor
And take our last words to brigade:*

*"You will never be happy with strangers,
They would not understand you as we,
So remember the old Jarama Valley
And the old men who wait patiently."*

The "old men" ranged in age from nineteen to thirty.

The Americans were proudest of a composition which referred to their own institution, the halfway cookhouse—a plaintive and complaining but stoically resigned ballad which told the following sad tale:

*There is an old cookhouse,
Far, far away,
Where we get sweet . . . . all
Three times a day.*

*Ham and eggs we never see,
. . . . all sugar in our tea,
And we are grad-u-ally
Fading away . . .*

*Old soldiers never die,
Never die, never die,
Old soldiers never die,
Merely fade away.*

TRENCH VIGIL

Not until later did the unofficial "theme song" of the battalion become popular among the men. No one knows who was the author of the ribald and carefree chant of a dozen varying verses, only the first of which I shall quote here:

> *Oh, the Lincoln Battalion, by cracky,*
> *Were a bunch of brave bastards but whacky,*
> *They held down the line for months at a time*
> *And they . . . Franco, Il Duce's lackey.*

With the long, inactive spring days, the men turned to other pursuits. They established "wall newspapers"—*periodicos murals*, the Spaniards called them—in which the survivors wrote stories, poems and impressions of the three nightmarish attacks. Sam Levinger, the Ohio University student who lugged a rifle until his death in the Aragon during the fighting for Belchité, contributed many of the stories, some of them revealing a talent which would surely have been recognized in the United States had he lived. The most original talent in the entire battalion had died in the February 27th attack: Charles Donnelly, the twenty-six-year-old member of the Irish section. Among his papers were two poems, prophetically written before the action which cost him his life, both of which were pasted up on the board, outlined in black. One was called "The Tolerance of Crows":

> *Death comes in quantity from solved*
> *Problems on maps, well-ordered dispositions,*
> *Angles of elevation and direction;*

THE LINCOLN BATTALION

> *Comes innocent from tools children might*
> *Love, retaining under pillows,*
> *Innocently impaled on any flesh.*
>
> *And with flesh falls apart the mind*
> *That trails thought from the mind that cuts*
> *Thought clearly for a waiting purpose.*
>
> *Progress of poison in the nerves and*
> *Discipline's collapse is halted.*
> *Body awaits the tolerance of crows.*

The other, entitled simply "Poem" is too long to reprint in its entirety. These are the opening lines:

Between rebellion as a private study and the public
Defiance, is simple action only which will flicker
Catlike, for spring. Whether at nerve-roots is secret
Iron, there's no diviner can tell, only the moment can show.
Simple and unclear moment, on a morning utterly different
And under circumstances different from what you'd ex-
    pected.

Your flag is public over granite. Gulls fly above it.
Whatever the issue of the battle is, your memory
Is public, for them to pull awry with crooked hands,
Moist eyes. And villages' reputations will be built on
Inaccurate accounts of your campaigns. . . .

On the same Lincoln wall newspaper were pasted the cartoons and the haunting wash-drawings of Deyo Jacobs, the artist of the battalion, and numerous letters from home. One letter particularly moved the survivors deeply:

"My dear comrades of the Abraham Lincoln Battalion:

"I have been a long time in writing to you, but I have not been well. Please forgive me. I am the mother of Inver Marlow—your dear friend John Scott. I just send you a message of great love and my deepest wishes for the great cause that he and you give your lives for. I most sincerely trust that all is well, especially with those who so splendidly helped my son and so kindly have written to my other son, Denis. He is abroad in Poland, but I know he will write himself.

"There is nothing to say. My son is gone but I am very proud of him and so grateful to him and to all the other splendid men—the living and the dead—in this horrible struggle for Right and Freedom.

". . . all your kind and tender messages to me have touched and helped me so much.

"From your sincere and affectionate friend,
"Sylvia Marlow."

Late in May the battalion sent John Tisa, who had preserved many of the original documents of the first days of the Americans in action, into Madrid to work on a history of the brigade. With him went Deyo Jacobs to do the art work. The book finally appeared, in French, as *Nos Combats Contre le Fascisme: Le Livre de la 15ème Brigade Internationale.*

4

While the battalion continued to hold the trenches, the center of American activity shifted to the tiny village of Madrigueras, in Albaceté Province. During the months of

THE LINCOLN BATTALION

March, April and May, enough new volunteers arrived from the United States to form a new American battalion —the George Washington Battalion—under the command of a Yugoslav-American named Mirko Markovicz and a Chicagoan, Dave Mates, as his commissar. Among the company commanders was a lanky mining engineer and prospector, Hans Amlie, a native of Wisconsin. Other, lesser posts were held by Philip Detro, a twenty-six-year-old Texan, and two students, Harold Smith of New York and Owen P. Smith of Iowa. An obscure but competent machine-gunner was Milton Wolff, a twenty-one-year-old Brooklynite, "six feet two with my shoes off." Another bright young man, fresh from the officers' training school in Pozo Rubio, where his instructors were two wounded battalion commanders, T. H. Wintringham of the British and Robert Merriman, was Leonard Lamb. He was twenty-six.

As the volunteers continued to arrive by the hundreds, the Washington Battalion found it necessary to move to larger quarters, which it found in a near-by village, Tarazona de la Mancha. But here too the men were soon crowded out by the steady influx of volunteers from the United States and Canada, and in the third week of June the Washington Battalion moved to reserve positions at Jarama. Less than a week later the men who had been left behind, together with the new arrivals, had formed a third American battalion, with Bob Merriman, his left shoulder still in a cast, in command. Many names were suggested, but they finally simmered down to two. Fifty per cent of the men wanted to call it the Patrick Henry Battalion, the other half just as firmly insisted that they wanted to be known as the Thomas Paine Battalion. While the controversy raged, the Canadians put in their bid—and won. Although fewer than a third of the men in Tarazona were Canadians, there had been many men from Canada in the Lincoln and the Washington Battalions. Many more were on their way. The Patrick Henry-Thomas Paine partisans were deadlocked. So, after the Canadians' claim to a name of their own had been fully presented to, and aired by, the men, the new unit became the Mackenzie-Papineau Battalion, in memory of two early nineteenth-century fighters for Canadian independence from Britain, one of them the grandfather of Prime Minister Mackenzie-King.

Most of the new American volunteers who reached Spain during these months came on the crest of the enthusiasm created throughout the world by the miraculous defense of Madrid. Some set out after the victory over the Italians at Guadalajara. All of them, however, whether they embarked after a victory or a defeat, knew that they were entering an unequal battle, that the odds were against them. Very few had an inkling of the overwhelming superiority in ammunition, airplanes and artillery which the Berlin-Rome Axis was even then beginning to send in huge quantities against the meagerly armed defenders. That Italy and Germany were on the side of Franco, and that no international agreement or promise would stop their military participation, was clear to all of them—clearer even from the very outbreak of the war than it was ever to become to the French and British experts who cradled the Non-Intervention Committee. They came into the battle despite it.

These Americans traveled in groups of varying size, ranging from a dozen to a hundred men, filling the third-class sections of the liners crossing the Atlantic. Usually they landed in France, occasionally in Belgium. The ocean voyage was the most uneventful part of their odyssey, which did not properly begin until they reached the legendary and fabulous capital of France. There they separated into groups of six or seven and registered at small hotels where they waited while their group leaders established contact with the Paris committee which arranged their southward journey to the Pyrenees.

Here is the itinerary of a typical group:

Fifty-eight Americans and Canadians boarded the slow Cunard liner *S.S. Lancastria* on the morning of June 5, 1937. After a short call at Boston the steamer proceeded to its first port, Dover. Then it continued on toward Helsingfors. Halfway up the Channel a smaller steamer met the *Lancastria* and landed the fifty-eight volunteers at Ostend, Belgium, on June 15th. From Ostend they continued on to Paris, which they reached at midnight. Contrary to their expectations, they spent less than a day in the French capital. Another train ride brought them to Béziers, where they spent two days before continuing their southward journey to Perpignan. There they boarded buses which dropped them, just at dusk, on a road leading downward into a ravine where, stopping only long enough to stock up on hard rations—bread, cheese, chocolates—for the ensuing day, they set forth on their long climb over the Pyrenees, a climb which kept them moving swiftly, in a snakelike coil the length of which increased as the more exhausted began to straggle and fall back, over successive ridges of the great mountain range. For fourteen hours the men marched. The pace, set by two Catalan guides who were as familiar with the steep tortuous mountain paths as they were with the stairs of their own stone huts, was swift and exhausting. But the guides rarely paused. For an hour or more the long single file advanced, over an exposed crest which had to be surmounted quickly, past a crag in whose crevices still gleamed the white of last winter's snow, even in mid-June; then down into a valley, where for periods ranging from ten minutes to a half hour the guides permitted the men to rest. Whenever grumbling was heard, they explained to the tired ones that the group had to be out of the mountains and in Spain by daybreak; that otherwise they risked detention and arrest.

As dawn approached the men began another long ascent. The hill began to rise more gently toward the peak as they climbed; once they passed an ancient, sleeping farmhouse. A few hundred yards beyond, they heard the strange and gentle tinkling of bells, musical but strangely disquieting there, remote from everything in their past experience, in the wilderness of the Pyrenees. It was a small herd of cows grazing.

Finally the crest was reached, and the tired mountain-climbers closed the ranks in their file, wondering why the guides did not hurry them, as they had over every other crest. One of the men had been carried, by relays, for the past three hours; they placed him under a tree, almost unconscious, telling him to wait, that the guides would return later to get him. The others were too tired and too dispirited to ask "Spain?" They had done that at the peaks of every ridge they had climbed, only to get the answer, "*No, no, paciencia, paciencia.*"

But now the older of the two guides, an old lean man with a face gnarled and browned by wind and sun, stopped and looked down over the rolling hills and fields spread before him; they seemed small from the crest on which he stood. He surveyed the endless country, bathed in the awakening glow of a full, sunny dawn, flung his right arm outward in a long, sweeping operatic gesture, smiled, and shouted,

"*España!*"

The journey over the Pyrenees in midwinter by an earlier group, which arrived just after non-intervention had gone into effect, has been described by Harry Hakam, a plumber's helper who left New York a few weeks before his apprenticeship was to be completed.

"When we arrived in France," wrote Hakam, "we were informed by the American consul that the border to Spain was closed and that we might as well go home. We would be allowed to return by the same boat and the steamship company would bear the expense. He threatened us with jail and deportation.

"We realized that there were many Fascists in France; therefore we dared not expose ourselves. We separated into small groups of no more than ten each. In all there were two hundred and fifty of us. We traveled, acting and dressing like tourists, refraining from singing union songs, appearing as inconspicuous as possible. We did not know how we would eventually get into Spain, but we had confidence in those who had taken the responsibility of directing us. After a week, because our presence in Paris was becoming noticeable, we traveled south to the Spanish border.

"We drove into the Pyrenees Mountains. We were a group of city workers, students, farmers, mechanics.

"Then the time came for us to start walking.

"Once we came across an irrigation ditch seven feet wide. In the darkness we jumped across it. I took a running leap into the dark and landed with both my shins against the hard, rocky bank. Luckily two of my companions grabbed my arms and prevented me from falling into the stream.

"No lights or cigarettes were to be used, so as not to attract the attention of the border guards. We traveled up a steep mountain into the night. For every hour we climbed, we rested a few minutes. The pace was rapid, but we had to go on if we wanted to cross the border before daybreak.

"Tired and panting, we struggled upward. The strain proved too much for one of our group, who collapsed. Some of the stronger fellows took turns carrying him through the winding mountain paths. We thought that he would recuperate in time for the most difficult part of the climb. He didn't. When we got to a point where it was impossible and foolhardy to attempt to scale the mountain with a sick man, without ropes, lights or anything, we found a place where he could rest and remain concealed until he recovered completely.

"The night grew colder and the peak did not seem to have gotten any closer. Though slipping, cursing, bruised and footsore, we continued. All around us was blackness. A strong wind had begun to blow. Thousands of feet above the sea level we followed the guide. We walked through deep snowdrifts. It was more than physical stamina that carried us on. It was the determination to fight to the utmost for the democratic people's government of Spain.

"We had walked for many hours when suddenly the peak loomed before us. The wind had reached the proportions of a gale and the clothes were almost torn from our bodies. At one time the wind had grown so strong that we had to hug the ground for fifteen minutes until it had abated and our guide considered it safe enough to continue. We tramped across the peak, and about a kilometer away was another smaller peak which we had to cross before getting into Spain. With renewed hope and vigor we struggled on to our destination.

"We arrived at daybreak. Everything seemed beautiful. We could see for many miles ahead the land that lay before us. The sun rose slowly. A wonderful purple haze covered everything. We approached a huge white house from which the Catalonian border patrol rushed out to meet us. Walking to the house, we began to sing. The sun rose in all its glory!"

Not all groups were as fortunate. These came through mostly with blistered and swollen feet which they had to soak in bucketfuls of purple potassium permanganate and water when they reached the citadel at Figueras, and some had to wait many days before they could get their feet down to their own shoe size again. But that was all. Another group, headed by Joe Dallet, was stopped in Southern France and jailed for forty days. After their long and chafing imprisonment, in the course of which they studied Spanish and French, and won a strike for better food, they too set out across the arduous trails into Spain.

Several scores of men made the crossing by sea, in the holds of small fishing vessels which left the southern coast of France in the dead of night and attempted to run the dual blockade of the Italian non-intervention cruisers and the Spanish insurgent warships in order to land safely on Spain's Mediterranean shore. One group attempted the Mediterranean crossing twice, only to be forced back both times. The men who were thus frustrated then traveled inland, where they too tramped across the snowy crests of the Pyrenees.

The most spectacular, and at the same time the most tragic crossing of all was that of the *Ciudad de Barcelona,* a small steamship in which more than fifty men, twelve of them Americans, perished when it was sunk by an Italian torpedo off the coast of Malgrat, north of Barcelona, on May 30, 1937.

"We were on the deck near the rail, talking about the beautiful color of the Mediterranean, when the torpedo struck the ship," recalled Harry Rubin, one of the survivors. "In less than ten minutes the ship was gone. Almost the entire crew died when the engine room exploded."

Sidney Shosteck, another American who survived the disaster only to meet his death by a sniper's bullet in Belchité four months later, described the resulting scene:

"I was in the last boat to be lowered. What I'll never forget is the absolute lack of hysteria. There was no jostling, no pushing, no mad scramble for life preservers and boats. The men died helping each other. In the brief seven minutes before the ship sank I saw more bravery, more self-sacrifice than I ever expect to see in all my life. . . .

"While we were being lowered, the sinking ship lurched and our lifeboat tipped over. We swam around, those of us who knew how, helping the ones who couldn't swim. The men were swearing and shouting words of encouragement to one another."

Fishing boats quickly put out from shore, a mile and a

half away, and soon all of the survivors were on land, drinking the coffee hastily prepared by the shocked population of Malgrat. Among the Americans who went down with the *Ciudad de Barcelona* were Caspar Anderson, Joe Klimowski, Herbert Solomon, John Ingot, William Schultz, William G. Hadley and Michael Hondorf, who had been one of the members of the original Malraux air squadron.

5

A group of forty Americans which reached Madrigueras on the eve of the last intense Jarama action was combined with 50 Englishmen and 300 French, Austrian, German, Czech and Polish volunteers to form a special international battalion. On April 1st, after five weeks of training, this battalion left for the Cordoba front, on the extreme south of Republican Spain, under the command of an Italian exile, Captain Morandi. John Gates, a twenty-three-year-old steel workers' organizer, became commissar of the Anglo-American company, which fought with the Eighty-sixth Mixed Brigade on the Southern front until late in June. The Internationals were sent north after fighting on the Cordoba front for more than three months, but Gates remained until October, rising to the rank of Adjutant Brigade Commissar.

On the eve of the Cordoba journey a number of Americans, among them Leonard Lamb, were ordered to stay behind. They were sent to the newly established officers'

THE LINCOLN BATTALION

training school at Pozo Rubio, together with other promising Americans who had just arrived in Spain and a number of men who had been through the Jarama battles. Among the newcomers were Al Robbins, two of the three Stone brothers, Roy McQuarrie, Saul Wellman and Wallace Burton. Recalled from Jarama for further training as officers were Walter Garland, Owen P. Smith, Bernard Walsh (later transferred to the John Brown Battery, an American artillery unit which served for almost a year on the Toledo and Levante fronts) and a number of others.

By the time the George Washington Battalion left for the front, many of these youngsters held important posts. Amlie's commissar in the first infantry company was Morris Wickman, a Philadelphia Negro. Edward Cecil-Smith, a Canadian, commanded the second company, with Bernard Addes, a Washington, D. C., lawyer as commissar. The third company, led by a Yugoslav named Yardis, boasted the commissarship of Harry Hynes, a West Coast seaman who in the few months before he was killed in action was recognized as the most courageous and popular of the Americans in Spain. Commissar Carl Geiser, an Ohio student, helped Walter Garland direct the machine-gun company.

Other outstanding Americans in the Washington Battalion were Rico Rusciano, an Italian-American from Queens, who led a platoon; Philip Detro, adjutant to the commander of the First Company; Leonard Lamb, chief of the headquarters staff, and Rubin Schechter, battalion clerk.

TRENCH VIGIL

Among the privates were first-aid man Roger Hargrave of Iowa, Harold Smith of New York, Lawrence O'Toole, the two Hutner brothers (Daniel and Herbert), Jack Hoshooley of Canada, Leo Grachow, Sol Rose, David Smith, Sidney Graham, Ernest Arion, Donald Thayer and Milton Wolff.

In a field beyond Fuencarral, not far from Madrid, another group of Americans served in the First Transport Regiment of the Fifth Army Corps. Headed by Lieutenant Durward Clark of San Quentin, California, its other officers were Robert English, a Kentuckian, Mike Raddock, a deep-voiced Chicago trade-unionist, and Dave Thompson, a nephew of the novelist Kathleen Norris. The commissar was Jack Freidman, of Accord, N. Y., and among the men were Leslie Hutchins (whose sister, Evelyn, a small blonde girl, drove giant trucks and ambulances over the antiquated Spanish roads for more than a year and a half); Bunny Rucker, a light-skinned Cleveland Negro whose quiet efficiency won him the respect of the entire regiment; Kibby Goodman of Boston and Sol Neuman of New York; Jack Quinn and a youngster named Tchaikowski; Lou Ornitz, who left the transport group to fight at Bruneté, was captured and remained in a Franco prison camp for almost eighteen months before he was released; Max Hendler, who was killed while hauling a huge load of wood for fortifications over the hazardous winding roads of Aragon; James Benét, who had left a job on the *New Republic* to drive ammunition and supplies in Spain, and Robert Steck, of

THE LINCOLN BATTALION

Davenport, Iowa, who had worked on a theater magazine in New York before leaving for Spain.

In Albaceté, three Americans correlated the activities of all their countrymen in Spain. Their chief was Bill Lawrence, a young New Yorker with prematurely gray hair, who was American Commissar of the International Brigade Base. Edward Bender was in charge of the American personnel, and it was he who kept the records of the men in the different units and on the different fronts. John Murra, whose phenomenal memory compensated for the rudimentary state of his files, was Lawrence's assistant. Later others came to work in Albaceté. John Gates succeeded Lawrence in October, with Sol Rose, who had been wounded at Bruneté, and Eric Parker taking Bender's place. The International Brigade Base, with commissars for each nationality, continued to function until the winter of 1937–38, when the rapid absorption of the Americans into the regular Spanish Army made the posts unnecessary and obsolete.

This, then, was the set-up. While the Lincoln Battalion sunned itself in and behind its trenches and the Washington Battalion held down reserve positions in the Jarama, training and preparation for future battles were in progress in other parts of Spain. The forty Americans on the Cordoba front, the transport regiment outside Madrid, the John Brown artillery battery, the Mackenzie-Papineau Battalion at Tarazona—all were preparing for the day when the Americans would take part in their second major campaign under fire.

4

BRUNETÉ: WHEN THE RIVERS WENT DRY

THE BEGINNING OF JULY FOUND THE SPANISH REPUBLIC AT a critical point in its fight against the rebellion. Although the Italians had been defeated decisively at Guadalajara, Largo Caballero had dissipated the full effect of this victory by his stubborn and unreasoned order for a frontal attack against the enemy at Madrid—an attack which was disastrously attempted, with the staggering and needless loss of five thousand lives. Not an inch of ground had been gained.

In the southeast, treachery and incompetence had cost the Republic the strategic and important port of Málaga. In Barcelona, the May uprising had been ample testimony to the fact that the Fifth Column had found easy reception among the weak-minded and the traitors within the Government's ranks. And along the Biscayan coast, in the north, Mussolini's totalitarian warfare—most graphically and cruelly epitomized in the aerial bombardment which on

THE LINCOLN BATTALION

April 26th had leveled to splinters and ashes the Basques' Holy City of Guernica—was making slow but unceasing progress. Despite the tranquillity in the Center Zone, and the war communiqués which daily repeated the words "*Sin novedad*," it was common knowledge that something would happen, must happen, soon.

The Lincoln and Washington Battalions were in fine spirits. Not only were they enjoying a well-earned rest away from the lines, but it was the day of days for all Americans—the Fourth of July. Every man had been issued double rations of American chocolate and cigarettes, American packets of twenty. An unusually good meal was being served. While the men ate, they looked forward to the celebrations which were to be held all through the day and evening. But the celebrations never came off. Just as the meal drew to its close and the men sat back comfortably, exhaling the smoke of the rare *tabaco rubio*, the orders arrived:

"Battalions, stand to, ready to move."

A few hours later the entire brigade was on the march.

For two days they marched, starting at the villages of Torreladones and Valdemorillo, up along the Madrid-Escorial road to get in line with the other brigades and divisions, for the offensive southward toward Bruneté and Navalcarnero which was to relieve the siege of Madrid and, if possible, divert many of the insurgent troops from the far northern front. The attack southward from the Madrid-Escorial road was to be only one half of a pincer attack

BRUNETÉ: WHEN THE RIVERS WENT DRY

designed to crush and cut off the enemy's rear; the other point in the pincer was to dig in westward from a starting point north of Toledo. The two advancing columns, it was hoped, would meet after they had crushed all enemy resistance. By thus establishing contact, they would bottle up the Moors across the Manzanares River and the German batteries on Monte Garabitas which since the beginning of the siege had made life a nightmare for the civilian population of Madrid.

After a few ineffectual skirmishes the southern half of the pincer was stopped in its tracks, leaving the northern half, to which the Fifteenth Brigade was attached, to carry on the entire campagin. After two days of marching the Americans stopped to rest at a large estate on the roadway, a broad, cool expanse of pine forest through which ran a number of small streams. Because the entrance to the grounds was marked by two large whitewashed posts, they called the spot "the pearly gates."

The Government troops swept into action on the morning of July 6th, and by nightfall they had driven a wedge of more than 150 square kilometers into rebel territory. Within two days the towns of Bruneté, Villanueva de la Cañada, Quijorña and Villanueva del Pardillo were in Loyalist hands, and Villafranca del Castillo was threatened.

Both the Washington and Dimitroff Battalions were instructed to infiltrate and push past Villanueva de la Cañada, while the Lincolns and British surrounded and took it. The snag occurred when, seeing the steady exodus of people fleeing from the town, the latter battalions assumed that the entire town was being evacuated and proceeded to advance toward it in a frontal attack. Unfortunately for them, the departing figures had been those of civilians only, as the two battalions discovered when machine-gun fire burst out from the church tower within the town, killing a number of Lincoln men and making further advance impossible. Faced with this resistance the Washington Battalion was hurriedly thrown into the attack. By the end of the day Villanueva de la Cañada was captured.

With the Cañada garrison subdued, the Americans continued their advance, over a plain which made the operation seem like a cinema spectacle to all observers, crossed the Guadarrama River and marched on toward the Heights of Romanillos. Before approaching the heights they drove the enemy in the direction of Boadilla de Monte; and Franco's troops did not stop running till they reached the highest crest in the hills, Mesquite Ridge.

The delay caused by the mistake at Villanueva de la Cañada had by this time given the rebels sufficient time to bring up reinforcements. When the Americans attempted to storm the heights of Mesquite Ridge, they found they were facing not only the scattered Fascist forces they had driven before them, but a strong, consolidated enemy line, composed of fresh troops holding an almost impregnable position. Five times within the next day the Republican troops attempted to storm the heights, and five times they were repulsed by the fire which swept through their ranks

BRUNETÉ

from the dominating insurgent positions. The mid-July heat was unbearable. All the rivers were dry, and the only water the men could find had to be dug for in the dried riverbeds. It came up muddy and bitter to the taste, but the Americans drank it; it was the only water available.

Food, too, was scarce. "Down from our positions into the valley," said one of the men who lay beneath the crest of Mesquite Ridge, "and up the hillside behind us, ran the line of communications. It was raked night and day by snipers and machine-guns, artillery and aviation. Yet the ration parties ran the gauntlet, using mules when they could be used, and when these were killed, running, ducking, stumbling down the hillside, laden with sacks of grub. The boys in the trenches could see them coming down the hillside, like flies on a wall, and laid bets on whether they would get through.

"The wounded simply couldn't be got out until nightfall. Yet a dozen times, with desperately wounded men bleeding to death, the ambulance men loaded them on to a mule and flogged the wretched animal up the hillside to give the man a chance. One man lay for hours in the grilling sun, twice wounded, bullets whipping inches over his head, three men hit before his very eyes, while he patiently murmured, 'I'm O.K. He's bleeding badly. Get him away and give him a chance.'"

Lying in the hollow below Mesquite Crest, the artillery raked the valley behind the Americans. But the shells did little damage. The men hugged the ground and argued about Al Capone—was he really a tough guy?—a Chicagoan said yes, plenty tough—but in the end everybody agreed he was only "a big stiff who got his break with prohibition—just a yellow rat who'd have turned tail here in the first half hour."

The aviation was different. A solitary enemy observation plane spotted the men, circled for a minute, and flew off. Thirty minutes passed. Then:

"We first heard a low hum. It was low but very strong and it was coming from the Fascist side. It was getting stronger by the second and we knew we were in for it. It was a roar that filled the air you were breathing. It was a roar that almost lifted you up, shaking. It was getting stronger and stronger and, Christ! it was coming straight at you. . . ."

Morris Mickenberg, of the Lincoln Battalion, told how he pressed into the earth "with my hands, with my feet, with my face. But the roar set the whole ground shaking and the ground was pushing you up, higher and higher. . . .

"Then they let loose. That awful whistle, scream and rush of the bombs, then the explosion. The whole earth was blasted into pieces. It heaved and rocked and swayed and roared and smoked, and the bombs kept coming down, and every time you heard that whistle and scream you knew there was a shaft pointing to the small of your back and the bomb would hit you right there and blow you to a million pieces. . . . Waiting for that next explosion everything in you would be wound up tighter and tighter

THE LINCOLN BATTALION

till you felt like screaming, 'Come on, you bastards, drop it, drop it!'

"Then the bombing stopped and they began strafing.... Suddenly you didn't hear the roar at all. The planes were going, they were going away. You sat up, you looked around to find everybody dead and you saw others sitting up and looking around—your whole group, your whole section, the whole company...."

The bombings caused few casualties, but artillery took its heavy toll and machine-gun fire and snipers' bullets were deadly. Martin Hourihan, adjutant commander of the regiment composed of three battalions, the Lincoln, Washington and British, was seriously wounded in the knee and thigh, an explosive bullet shattering the thigh-bone. Oliver Law was killed in the attack on Villanueva de la Cañada, his place being taken by Steve Nelson, his commissar. Paul Burns and Hans Amlie were wounded. Brigade Commander Copic, wounded during an aerial bombardment, had to return to a hospital in Madrid.

Moe Fishman and Al Robbins received grave leg wounds, and Maury Dash's thigh-bone was splintered as he was carrying a loaded stretcher back to safety. Leo Grachow, ambushed by a group of Fascists while on patrol, was killed. Ernest Arion, the young composer from New York, was killed in one of the attacks against Mesquite Crest. Jack Weiss, a middle-aged Socialist, died in his sleep when a bullet penetrated his helmet. Norman Dorland, a writer and sailor from the West Coast, almost had his arm torn off by a shell splinter. Sam and Joe Stone died while their brother, Hy, fought on. Later, crazed by grief when he heard the news, he attempted to leap the rampart and attack the Fascists single-handed. His companions held him back only after they overpowered him. Walter Garland was wounded going to the aid of Leo Kaufman, who had been wounded in the chest. Hundreds of others were dead, wounded, sick.

In a brief moment of rest the battalions counted heads. Fifty per cent of the Washington Battalion was still unhurt. Similar casualties had reduced the Lincoln Battalion to half its original strength. Altogether, not quite enough men remained to form a single battalion. These were hastily merged, between battles, into one battalion, and the name of the new unit was hyphenated. The Lincoln and the Washington Battalions became the Lincoln-Washington Battalion.

2

The new battalion found itself in a dangerous spot, in reserve positions less than two kilometers from the front lines. After July 18th the force of the Loyalist offensive was spent, and the insurgents, strengthened by fresh reinforcements, began their counter-attack. Spanish brigades had relieved the Internationals along the whole front; at Quijorña, which had been captured by El Campesino's Forty-sixth Division, the same men who had fought during the first days were still in the front lines. But the Americans had advanced far beyond any other troops; they had fought as part of the shock-brigade of the entire campaign.

And now, decimated by losses, and in momentary reserve, they found themselves in the direct path of a counter-attack so powerful that the battalions between them and the enemy were giving way under its impact. To make matters worse, there was no reserve ammunition, and the entire machine-gun company was unarmed—when the battalion had been withdrawn from its first-line positions, all of the guns and ammunition had been loaded into camions to safeguard the arms and to speed the retirement. Now the machine-guns were safe but useless at the armory, several miles away.

Knowing that haste was essential, Sergeant Lamb commandeered a truck in which he sped to the armory, retrieved the guns and hurried back to the battalion. When he arrived, he found the path of the truck blocked with dozens of other camions, ambulances and swarms of retreating troops. The lines had broken under incessant pounding only fifteen minutes before, and the enemy had already advanced almost to the position where the Americans were in reserve.

But there was no panic among them. When Lamb arrived he found them spread out in perfect military formation, prepared—despite the lack of machine-guns—to swing into a counter-attack.

Only the riflemen were armed; each man was loaded with his usual, regular maximum of 150 rounds of ammuni-

BRUNETE: WHEN THE RIVERS WENT DRY

tion. But there were few grenades among them, and the grenade is invaluable both in defense and attack. Even they, however, would not have been able to hold out long without the power of the machine-gun company's fire and without the reserve supply of ammunition which any unit must have to carry on a protracted battle. The camion arrived just in time to get the heavy guns to the machine-gunners, who were thus able to take up dominating positions behind the infantry. For two days, with Lt. Garland back in command of his company again, they held up the attacking insurgents; and during these days their loss in territory never exceeded the small strip gained by the enemy before the Lincoln-Washington had gone into action.

The Americans retreated from this position only after the marines and other forces on both flanks gave way, leaving the Lincoln-Washington Battalion in a dangerous bottleneck, surrounded, and under enemy enfilading fire, on three sides. When they withdrew, they did so under orders to straighten the line. "On one occasion," says the official *Book of the Fifteenth Brigade* in describing this action, "the Lincoln-Washington Battalion, in support near Villanueva del Pardillo, were for a long time shelled, bombed and strafed in turn. When the onslaught ceased they were just in time to reinforce the line and repel a Fascist attack. Subsequently, on another section, they and the Franco-Belge Battalion were instrumental in repelling a break-through by the Fascists."

THE LINCOLN BATTALION

The Americans held their new positions, farther back, in the face of almost incessant counter-attacks until they were again ordered to withdraw, this time back to the foothills from which the entire operation had begun twenty-one days before. A Spanish brigade replaced them in the lines. Out of action at last, it was found that the battalion was the last of all the units which had taken part in the offensive to withdraw from the lines.

They found themselves again in the small pine-forested Castilian Eden, "the pearly gates."

Machine-gunner Milton Wolff, in recalling the Bruneté campaign, said, "Every one agreed with us that we in the machine-gun company were performing a herculean task. We were loaded down with pre-World War Maxims, the shields of which were Colt, vintage 1914. The men not engaged in carrying the guns carried 500 rounds of ammunition for the guns, in addition to their rifles and 150 rounds of rifle ammo. I was grateful for the ten months I had spent in a CCC camp, for I had developed the strength, if nothing else, to make me almost equal to the task. I couldn't help marveling at the sight of men like David McKelvy White, a college professor who had probably never performed a day's manual labor in his life, struggling gamely and silently under their loads. . . . During the fighting the hills stank of burning sage and scrub oak, of dead men and animals cooking in the fierce July heat. . . .

"In the twenty days of Bruneté the Americans covered every sector of that front, with the exception of Bruneté, the town itself, where the Listers (the Eleventh Division) were holding down well enough without us. There had been few nights when we hadn't moved some eight or ten kilometers to new positions. At Pardillo we were caught in a terrific bombing and shelling when the Fascists spotted us coming up. For three solid hours they had relays of Junkers overhead, flying low, for they were meeting with no opposition. They let go with the big bombs and then swung around to throw out basketfuls of .51 trench mortars—all this while their artillery never ceased to lope over 75's and 5.15's. And when it was all over we had lost three men.

"Once, when we were caught in a ravine by a lone German flyer who dropped three bombs on us, eight of the men had their lives crushed out of them when the concussion caught them against the wall of the gully. . . .

"Bruneté was the toughest thing I ever went through. The nightly forced marches, the fighting in the burning July heat, the absolute scarcity of water, and the bombings and the shellings. Though I was to go through worse bombings and shellings, none seemed as terrifying as those first ones at Bruneté. At Bruneté I realized that, given half a chance, we had the stuff to make of Spain the tomb of Fascism."

When the battalion finally left the field of battle it added dozens of names to the already swollen list of dead and wounded. Two physicians, Dr. Randall Sollenberger of Baltimore and Dr. Robbins of New York, were among the dead. So was Harry Hynes, the machine-gun company commissar, and Ray Steele, "the best machine-gunner of us all," his comrades said. Harry Sachs, of the First Transport Regiment, was killed by an aerial bomb while transporting the wounded. Rubin Schechter was dead, and Max Krauthamer, the studious New York attorney, and Jack Shirai, the little Japanese-American machine-gunner, "the man with the laughing heart." Jean Bronstein, who had said, "I know I'm going to get killed," was dead, and so were David Walba and Roy Peters. Among the wounded and seriously sick were Joe Drill of Philadelphia, Edward Lending, Lester Gittelson and John Hunter of New York, nineteen-year-old Stephen Revere of Chicago, Lawrence Maynard and Morris Taubman, who was later captured in the Aragon, the oft-wounded but indestructible Larry O'Toole. Tauno Sundsten, a giant Scandinavian from the Middle West, walked around Madrid with an open and running head wound for a month afterward, and a little five-footer, Joe Rosenstein, took advantage of an afternoon's leave from his hospital in the shelled capital to uncover a Fascist spy ring which put Government police on the trail of associated groups in Valencia and Barcelona.

Most seriously wounded of all was Roger Hargrave, the machine-gun company's first-aid man who had dragged the wounded Hans Amlie off the field under intense machine-gun fire, and who had been with Ray Steele when he died. On the very last day of battle, after he had made a number of trips out into the field of fire to bring back the last of

BRUNETÉ: WHEN THE RIVERS WENT DRY

the wounded men, he lay down under a tree to rest. A moment later he felt himself lifted from the ground as an artillery shell landed ten feet away. Shrapnel tore into his body in six different places—both feet, both knees, hip and forearm. The strip of hot steel which hit his arm gouged a chunk of muscle and bone out of his forearm. Gas-gangrene was setting in as they placed him in an ambulance bound for Madrid.

The most popular man among the Americans to emerge from the Bruneté offensive was Steve Nelson, the commissar. The Pennsylvanian with the broad smile and furrowed face had a way of meeting a new soldier and saying "Hy'a, old timer!" in a manner which immediately convinced the recruit that he *was* an old timer, that he and Nelson were intimate friends, and that so likeable and sincere a man could do no wrong—which was an achievement in a democratic army where the commissars particularly, since they were the ones whose job (among other things) it was to give the pep-talks, came in for more criticism than any other officer. But Nelson was more than a likeable man; he was an organizer of proved ability, he was an indefatigable worker, and he possessed the kind of courage which was quiet at most times, but which could become spectacular when he felt the men needed such an example to spur them over the last stretch of a difficult advance. Nelson kept the food supplies going in a steady stream during the hottest fighting; reserve ammunition was almost always on hand; and when any of the services broke

THE LINCOLN BATTALION

down, the Americans knew it wasn't Nelson's fault, and they knew more—that with Nelson around, the stuff would soon be rolling in again. No wonder they tried always to keep him from harm, no wonder that their watchword during the most difficult days of Bruneté became "Don't let them get Steve!"

One incident, least important but most significant, can illustrate the quality and temper of the man:

During the final withdrawal, the almost thirst-crazed Americans came upon several small kegs of wine hidden in the cool earth of a hut. All of them drank eagerly but temperately. One of them, however, deceived by the mild-tasting liquid, drank steadily for more than a minute, swallowing the liquid in great gulps. It was Harry Fisher, a small youngster who, as one of Nelson's runners, had worked tirelessly during the three searing weeks of the campaign. As he finished drinking, Nelson came in with a written message. "Here, Harry," he said, "be a good guy and get this over to the British. Step on it!" Fisher took the note, whirled around, staggered and pirouetted on his feet, then wobbled off—in the enemy's direction. Nelson, who had turned to another man, spotted him through the corner of his eye. "Whoa, there, Harry," he said. He walked over to him, took the message and handed it to Jerry Weinberg, his other runner, clasped Harry by the hand, laughed and said, "You better stay with me, old timer." Holding him by the hand, he led Fisher a half mile back. Then, when his attention was called to another matter, he entrusted the little runner to another soldier, warning him before he left:

"Hold on to his hand. Stick with him. I want to see him when we get out of this."

Harry Fisher got back safely. And after the offensive Steve Nelson became brigade commissar.

The most trying moment for the Americans occurred after they had reached the Pearly Gates. Resting among the small pines, word reached them that the *marineros*, who had relieved them, were cracking. Quickly they were called together, and the situation was explained: three weeks of battle, with all of its gains, would go for nothing unless the line was strengthened. Then the question—not an order—was put to them: Will you volunteer to go back into the lines?

The men hesitated; all were tired, knocked out after their long ordeal. There was not one among them who had not lost a friend, a close companion, in the fighting. More than half of the Americans had been killed or wounded, and to those who stayed to fight on, a casualty, no matter how slight, was a disappearance of someone they knew; it might not mean death, but in the heat of battle they assumed the missing soldier was dead. Aching in every bone and muscle, tired to death, longing for sleep and rest, shocked after the long battle, they hesitated—and all volunteered to return to action!

Fortunately, while the men voted, a contingent of fresh Spanish troops arrived to strengthen the line. A few minutes later the news came that the *marineros* had rallied, and were fighting back the assault. There was no need to return again to immediate battle.

For the Americans, that was the last of Bruneté.

5

THE ARAGON OFFENSIVE

DURING THE STEAMING SUMMER DAYS WHICH FOLLOWED, the Government reviewed the lessons of the Brunete campaign. Even though not all of the original gains had been held nor the key town on the rebel communications route, Navalcarnero, taken, the military command considered the operation a success. For the first time in the war, a Loyalist army under unified command had taken the initiative in battle, forcing Franco to fight at a time and on ground of its own choosing. In the course of the fighting a number of weaknesses had become glaringly prominent, but these were considered incidental and secondary to the fact that, after a year of heroic but constantly disorganized and planless fighting, the Republic had finally centralized its fighting forces on one great and important front. Even the military and tactical mistakes committed during the operation could, and would be, overcome. But two ominous shadows haunted and dulled the efforts of the Loyalists to the bitter end: the presence of the Fifth Column, the saboteurs and traitors, within the ranks of the army itself, and the scarcity of effective mechanical heavy military arms—cannon, planes, artillery shells.

The Fifteenth Brigade retired for rest to Ambité, east of Madrid, and the Lincoln-Washington Battalion found barracks at the near-by village of Albarez. Here the men rested and, with the arrival of a group of fresh Americans from the training base at Tarazona, began to reorganize their ranks.

Wounded Americans were scattered through the Madrid hospitals. The overflow from Madrid was sent to the American hospitals at Tarancon, Castillejo and Villa Paz. The latter were two vast landed estates, formerly the summer stamping grounds of members of the royal Bourbon family. Here, under the direction of Dr. Irving Busch, who had succeeded Dr. Barsky as chief of the American hospitals in Spain, the wounded men of all nationalities were returned to life. Here Robert Raven, whose sight was irrevocably lost, still underwent the many operations which removed from his tortured body the chunks and slivers of shrapnel imbedded in his flesh on March 14th. Here Captain Hourihan lay motionless in his surgical cot, his bullet-shattered leg gripped tightly in the painful traction apparatus for long and agonized but stoical months.

In the Palace Hotel in Madrid, which had been converted into a military hospital, were Court Bevensee, Maury Dash and Norman Duncan, all of them suffering from iden-

THE ARAGON OFFENSIVE

tical wounds, the dreaded broken femur. In another hospital, sunnier, less crowded, a few blocks away from the headquarters of the International Brigades at 63 Calle de Velasquez, was Roger Hargrave, the lone American among five hundred Spaniards. In the early days of August his closest friend came to see him—Milton Felsen, who had been his classmate at the University of Iowa, who had traveled to Spain with him, and who had been wounded at Bruneté while fighting with the machine-gun company.

"It was horrible, almost broke your heart to see him. You remember his red cheeks? They're sunken, white. His blond hair? Shaved off. He's on a small cot. Can't move. The sheets are stained with the pus that seeps through his bandages. He can't smile. Looks as if he weighs about eighty pounds—no flesh on his arms or legs, just bones with the knobs big at his elbows and wrists and knees. And the stink of the gangrene. . . . I don't think he wants to live any more. I held his hand for an hour. I cried for the first time. . . ."

Ralph Bates wrote to an English surgeon about him, but he was busy with hundreds of cases in his own hospital, and couldn't come. Fortunately Dr. Busch came to Madrid, stopped in to see him, spoke to him and to the Spanish medical staff of the hospital. Dr. Busch spent a half hour with him, examining his wounds, speaking to him in his own language. No one knows exactly what occurred in that half hour. But the next time I saw Hargrave he smiled and said, "I'm going to pull through."

THE LINCOLN BATTALION

For a full year Hargrave remained in the hospitals of Spain—in Madrid, Villa Paz, Barcelona, Sagaro. His citation for bravery in action, which appeared in *La Voz de la Sanidad*, the medical service publication, cheered him toward recovery. On July 10, 1938, he left Spain, back again at his normal weight of 160 pounds. His leg still remained rigid and unbending at the knee, his arm still useless, his life ambition—to be a surgeon—a thing of the past. But he looked forward to work at home and "maybe the specialists will be able to do something more."

Those weeks in Madrid were quiet only in contrast with Bruneté. The city hummed with activity, crackled with the war at its gates. Four or five times a week—many times even more frequently—the batteries on Monte Garabitas opened up, and shells burst in the streets and houses. Once they landed on the Palace Hotel hospital, but no one was hurt. On the outskirts of the city, in the Casa del Campo and the University City, the Loyalist and Fascist trenches were close, and the clatter of machine-guns became almost an unnoticed part of Madrid's life. The Americans arrived in droves from Albarez, on two-day furlough. They mingled with the crowds in the hotels, the cafés, the cinemas. They went to see James Cagney in a four-year-old picture. Over at the Capitol Theatre, opposite the Hotel Florida, Los Hermanos Marx in *Un Noche en la Opera* were bowling the Madrileños over, rolling them in the aisles, and the visiting Americans joined the throngs and roared with laughter as the Spanish syllables rolled off

THE ARAGON OFFENSIVE

Groucho Marx's tongue, playing havoc with the familiar patter of American wisecracks. The artillerymen on Monte Garabitas knew when the theaters on the Gran Via closed, late in the afternoon, and they timed their bombardments and set their range accordingly. Hundreds were killed in this way. Fred Keller and three companions, in Madrid on leave, spent their rest period in the front lines at the Casa del Campo. The shellings continued, the hospitals slowly were drained as the wounded returned to health, the Americans went in and out of Hemingway's rooms at the Hotel Florida, talking, using his always-flowing bathtub and his bottomless flask, trying not to disturb him in the hours when he wrote; the peddlers hawked cigarette-papers and *matcheros* and raisins and a thousand other odd articles (but not *tabaco*) in the streets, and the shells never kept anyone away from the variety shows and the movies. Madrid was still the livest city in the world, the best to wake up in.

2

Pablo, one of the International Brigade House's night guards, woke me at four o'clock in the morning of August 19th. An American who had crossed the Atlantic with me was at his side, with a message from Robert Merriman, now a major and Chief of Staff of the Fifteenth Brigade.

"Paul is responsible," the note read, "for bringing all the men possible from our brigade who remain in Madrid on leave. All nationalities. You must help him. Get him dry rations for the men to eat on the way. Also a *Salvo Conducto* for all ten trucks. The food is important. Help him —he must get close to 200 men and do it fast.

"Merriman."

We got into a truck, sped down the quiet and dark Calle de Velasquez, turning right at the Retiro onto the wide Alcala. We went from hotel to hotel, waking the concierges to get the lists of all Americans from them. Armed with these we banged on door after door, waking men still in deepest sleep. Then we chased around for gasoline, two hundred loaves of bread and tins of meat and sardines.

At 10 o'clock the caravan of trucks, crowded with 192 men—we had managed to get all but five of them—pulled away on its long journey to meet the main column of the brigade, already on its way from Ambité.

This was the first hint that the long-awaited "activization" of the Aragon front was about to begin. We had all known it was going to happen. All of Aragon had remained an open front since the beginning of the war; there were powerful, fortified points, but these were scattered. Unlike Madrid, there was no long, consecutive line of fortifications. The Anarchists, involved in impractical though courageous schemes in Barcelona, had refused to initiate an attack on this front, claiming that Quinto was an impregnable fortress. Since the Fascists were advancing in the extreme north and had their hands full in the center fronts, they were only too content to make no move to disturb the inactivity in Aragon.

Only a few weeks before, the Civil Governor of Aragon had been removed. A dangerous situation existed among the peasants of the entire province, due largely to the activities of the "uncontrollables." These were bands composed of the worst elements among the Anarchists who lacked all sense of the reality of the situation. With them, and leading them in the destructive work which gave them the name "the uncontrollables," were the members of the POUM, the Trotskyist sect in Spain which had fomented the May uprising against the Government in Barcelona, whose few battalions, as Herbert Matthews had reported, had played football with the Fascists on the front lines near Huesca instead of attacking the city. Its activities had attracted to its ranks every type of Fascist and Fifth Columnist in Republican territory, a fact which was shortly to bring about its suppression by the Government of Spain. But its work had been cleverly done in Aragon. Without regard for the feelings of the peasants of the backward province, these bands had attempted to force what they euphemistically called "collectivization" upon them. The process soon turned into open expropriation of lands, theft of cattle and all live stock, seizure of crops. The resentment of the peasants smoldered, then flamed into open antagonism.

It was necessary, therefore, to start things moving in Aragon for two reasons: for the sake of internal unity, to counteract the misdeeds of the uncontrollables, and for the sake of closing the front, gaining invaluable territory, and strengthening the Loyalist defenses against the day when Franco's main attacks would shift to Aragon. On this basis the Loyalist command deemed this the most logical place to initiate a wide-scale offensive.

The main body of the Fifteenth Brigade left Ambité and Albarez and surrounding towns on August 19th, in trucks which carried them past Parales into Valencia. There, after camping for two days in the bull ring, they boarded trains on the roofs of which machine-guns had been mounted, and proceeded on to Hijar, where they received a welcome shipment of new Russian light machine-guns. The entire brigade was at this time composed of four battalions: the Twenty-fourth (Spanish), the Lincoln-Washington, the British and the Dimitroffs (Yugoslav). Steve Nelson was commissar and Major Merriman Chief of Staff. T. H. Wintringham, the British poet and military historian, was Chief of Operations, assisted by the same Belgian who had commanded the Americans for brief periods at Jarama and Bruneté, now Major Van den Berghe.

During the last week of August the Lincoln-Washington Battalion encamped on the high plateau around Purburell Hill. Hans Amlie, now recovered from his wound, was in command, Leonard Lamb was adjutant and John Quigley Robinson, a little seaman from New York, was commissar. Five kilometers to the south of the Americans were several stretches of powerful fortifications which extended in broken bits along the road from Azaila northward into

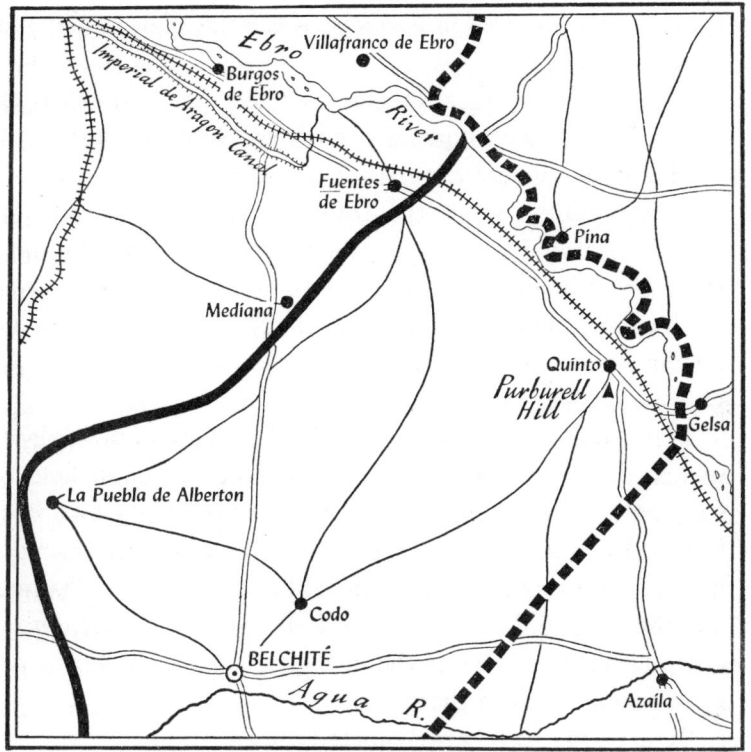

THE ARAGON OFFENSIVE

THE LINCOLN BATTALION

Quinto. All the land in between was a flat plain, as level as a football field.

Moving into attack in the morning, the Lincolns advanced about two kilometers north and slightly west of the fortifications, where they lay low in a thin olive grove as a reserve battalion while the Dimitroffs moved ahead to attack Purburell Hill. From their positions among the olive trees the Lincolns could see a battalion of Lister's men skirmishing with the enemy, attacking and destroying machine-gun posts whose presence might have held up the entire advance.

While the Listers stormed and broke up the gun-emplacements, the Lincolns moved forward over an open field to support the Dimitroffs, who were attempting to storm Purburell Hill from the south. Heavy machine-gun fire from the hilltop positions made it impossible for them to advance, and the Lincolns themselves were stopped by machine-guns on the southern crest of the hill, guns whose fire raked the open ground before them.

By 9:30 the Listers had quieted the enemy machine-guns. Then began the battle for Quinto and the strategic Purburell Hill which commanded not only the town but every approach to it as well. On the first day the Americans moved eastward to get into position behind the Dimitroffs, but after covering half the distance they found further advance impossible, and moved north past two small hills to a position outside the cemetery on the western fringe of the town itself. At three in the afternoon, after a fifteen-

THE ARAGON OFFENSIVE

minute Loyalist artillery barrage against the hill and against the rebel positions outside of the cemetery, the battalion attacked. Again, as at Bruneté almost two months before, it was like a moving-picture attack—with the infantry advancing in sections, each section flanked by tanks which moved parallel with the riflemen. "The tanks came on," an American said, "blasting the Fascist fortifications, and over the top we went, following the tanks. The Fascists ran back to the town and we followed closely on their heels, capturing the trenches outside the town. The tanks pursued the fleeing foe right into Quinto, firing at fortified houses and destroying machine-gun nests. Most of the enemy took refuge in the church, situated on a hill which dominated the landscape. By the time our battalion reached the cemetery, night was fast approaching. One of our tanks made a direct hit on a Fascist ammunition dump, and the shells and grenades kept on exploding like firecrackers all night. That evening one of our artillery pieces was brought up to cover the hill while we set our machine-guns, placing them at strategic points. The machine-gun company was commanded by Emanuel Lanser. Mike Pappas was adjutant and Ruby Ryant company commissar. The company stood guard in case the Fascists should try to counter-attack under cover of night." One infantry section of the Lincolns had already entered the town, moving in a wide arc, but finding resistance was still strong it retired to the cemetery to await daybreak and the second day of battle.

On the morning of the second day the entire battalion

entered the town, penetrating deep into the streets, fighting with hand-grenades, dynamite bombs and nitroglycerin bottles. Going from house to house, one of the Americans made the mistake of entering an open door before throwing a grenade through it. In a few seconds he staggered out, blood flowing from a deep bayonet wound. This was the battalion's first lesson in street fighting. Thereafter the men were careful to throw grenades through open doors and windows, first calling for all occupants to leave, before they themselves ventured inside. Slowly, going from house to house, they fought their way into Quinto. The town was filled with snipers who, aided by machine-guns in the church and other key buildings, kept up a deadly fire against the advancing parties.

The Americans advanced halfway into the town before it was discovered that the Fascists, retreating to the southeast, were themselves beginning to encircle the attackers by weaving backward along the outlying buildings behind the Americans' advance. Again they retired from the town and spent the night and all of the following day on the heights overlooking the cemetery.

The third night the Lincolns moved southward to the heights overlooking Purburell Hill. All night and all day the Loyalist artillery pounded the town, the hill and a smaller height on the southern outskirts of Quinto on which the enemy maintained a revolving artillery emplacement. Moving farther south, the first and second companies of the Lincoln occupied the crests of two small hills west

THE ARAGON OFFENSIVE

of Purburell while the third company advanced to the base of Purburell Hill itself, where it established contact with the English battalion which two days before had replaced the Dimitroffs. Meanwhile a group of ten Americans, all of whom had volunteered for the job, re-entered Quinto, led by Carl Bradley, an American longshoreman.

"We went armed with glycerin bottles, took a position twenty-five feet from the wall of a large building, biggest in town, commanding the entire positions," said Bradley. "The Fascists held it. Walls three feet thick, a real fortress. The windows had machine-guns poked through them, and it would be next to impossible to take Quinto if this place wasn't taken.

"We hid outside the building and waited till after twenty-five shells, well directed, hit the place. The walls were so thick they did not demolish the building. The main purpose of the shelling was to force the Fascists into their holes, away from the windows with their machine-guns and snipers.

"Out of our ten men two were wounded as we snaked our way to the building. Three of the gang had to carry them back. That left five of us to carry on. We took our bottles, filled with this deadly explosive glycerin, picked windows, and threw them in with well-directed pitches that came from good baseball arms. Tremendous flames exploded inside the building. We came back twice with the bottles and then rolled a big drum of gasoline into the structure with a fuse attached to it. It exploded inside."

THE LINCOLN BATTALION

While Bradley and his men were demolishing the last Fascist stronghold within the town, the Loyalist batteries opened up with the most intense artillery barrage of the battle. The insurgent positions on Purburell Hill were so effectively pounded that soon the insurgent soldiers, exhausted and parched after days of shelling and lack of water, appeared above their battlements, waving white flags. The Thirty-second Spanish Brigade immediately advanced into Quinto from the south, and with the capture of this strategic height, the battle for Quinto was over.

3

With Quinto taken, there was hardly a moment of rest for the troops. Despite the fact that the capture of the town had disclosed German artillery of the most modern type and fortifications which only a highly industrialized nation could have devised, the Government was out for bigger game. It had in mind a daring and swift plan of operations which, if it succeeded, would be the greatest victory yet recorded for the Republican side in the thirteen-month-old struggle.

Northwest of Quinto, along the western shore of the Ebro River, was the town of Fuentes de Ebro—the last strongly fortified position on the path to Saragossa. Even in pre-war days Saragossa had been a trade-union stronghold; and during the month which had preceded the opening of the Aragon offensive there had occurred a series of scattered rebellions against the Fascist garrison in the city

THE ARAGON OFFENSIVE

which had finally flamed into open revolt. The Fascists had hastily and brutally suppressed it; the dissidents—those who had not been killed—had been driven underground, into hiding. But resentment was still smoldering, still strong. The people were ready to fight in the streets if the Republican troops approached the city.

With this situation prevailing, the Fifteenth Brigade was given no rest after the capture of Quinto. The battalions were immediately sent up to positions about three kilometers southeast of Fuentes de Ebro. There the Americans remained hidden in gullies, waiting for another brigade ahead of it—a unit which had thus far seen no action in the Aragon offensive—to take the town. Once the town had been taken, the plans were for the Fifteenth Brigade to move past in solid convoy, with armored cars and tanks, machine-guns mounted on camions, guns posted in firing positions at the hood of each troop-truck, anti-tank guns and brigade staff—all ready to sweep through in a flying column to lay siege to Saragossa from the south. Completely equipped and ready for action, the brigade waited in the gully for three days for the order that would set the flying column into motion.

But the fresh troops ahead failed to take Fuentes, and the plans for the flying column were abandoned. Again it was evident that the Government had not enough heavy artillery, nor enough planes, to pound the strong positions of Fuentes heavily enough to enable its infantry to follow through. Later on, General Kleber's division was to approach within artillery range of Saragossa from the north, and Lister's incomparable Spanish troops were to advance on foot to a point within a mile of the city. But the strategic moment for the conquest of Saragossa had passed, and it was never to return during the entire course of the war.

Meanwhile the political situation in Barcelona had become worse; disgruntled elements—disguised Fifth Columnists among them—were attacking the International Brigades, and the Anarchists had published a report in their own papers that Anarchist troops had already taken Belchité. In order that the falsity of the report might remain hidden—discovery of the truth might have further demoralized sections of Catalonia—the Fifteenth and the Thirty-second Brigades were ordered to advance on the town. In the original campaign plans Belchité was to have been taken by the Thirty-second Brigade alone, sweeping on from Codo, which had just been captured after a bitter battle with crack Moorish troops. However, in the approach to Belchité proper the Thirty-second Brigade had lost a good deal of its forces. The Spaniards had attacked over terrain against magnificently constructed fortifications—pillboxes and trenches prepared, as at Quinto, by German engineers; iron stakes and sharp steel prongs built into the ground to hold up infantry and cavalry attacks. There were two lines of these prongs, set about 200 meters from the pillboxes from which enemy machine-guns commanded all avenues of approach.

In attacking over such well-fortified terrain, it was re-

THE ARAGON OFFENSIVE

membered that Belchité was probably one of the richest towns in Aragon, the summer residence of the wealthy industrialists of Saragossa. It was famous in history as the town which even Napoleon had been unable to conquer. Strategically, Belchité was of incalculable importance because it commanded the crossroads which would make possible the further penetration of Aragon; and it straddled a road which would give the Government forces a direct highway for communication with Madrid from the north.

It took six days to capture Belchité. Only the Lincolns moved against it on the very first day, attacking against heavily fortified positions from the point to which the Thirty-second Brigade had moved up. By nightfall the men were entrenched in shallow ditches less than a hundred meters from the church, on the Belchité-Azaila road. Most of the first night was used sending bombing parties out in attempts to dislodge the defenders from the church which, solidly constructed of heavy rock, was one of the most powerful fortresses in the town. As dawn approached the battalion moved 200 meters back, behind a ledge which promised protection from snipers. Yet morning found the ledge under fire from the battalion's left. Snipers opened fire from another church within the town, and by the end of the day every company commander and a number of adjutants had been hit. Wallace Burton, a veteran of the World War, was dead, and Howard Goddard, a young Californian, was so badly wounded in the chest that he was given up for dead. Fortunately a Spanish veteran of many battles who had formed a deep attachment for the young officer pulled his body from the field, and Goddard, after a long stay in a hospital, recovered to take part as Chief of Operations in the last campaign the Americans fought in Spain. Another American company commander, Owen Smith, had received a dangerous chest wound during the initial attack.

Dave Engels, one of the men who was cited after the taking of Belchité, described the day in the shallow, exposed trenches of the ledge: "They were very shallow, just deep enough to give us cover if we lay flat. Once in, we had to lie there all day without food or water. The position was . . . completely exposed; it was impossible to bring up supplies. The Fascists in the outlying houses raked us with enfilading fire; everybody who as much as sat up in the trench was certain to draw fire immediately. It was very hard on the men to lie there like that all day in the hot sun, hour after hour, without being able to do anything about it. The work of Paul Block, acting commander of Company Three, who had taken Smith's place after he had been wounded, was inspiring. Block kept the company together in that position and set the necessary example of steadiness and coolness which the men carried on after he himself was later fatally wounded in the assault on the church."

It became apparent, as the Americans lay in wait outside the town, that the church was the key to Belchité. Behind it was a large plaza—or square—from which the streets ran like spokes of a wheel. The church was the hub; once taken, it would enable the Lincolns to cover the central areas of the town with their fire.

Several frontal attacks on the church failed; the rebels were too secure behind the thick walls and small doors and windows. The Americans' casualties, already high, mounted with each assault. Henry Eaton, one of the company commissars, was killed. Sam Levinger, who had left Ohio State University to go to Spain, died as he directed machine-gun fire against the enemy positions.

Casualties included two of the top-ranking Americans in the brigade. One was Steve Nelson, brigade commissar, who was painfully and dangerously wounded in the face and in the groin by enemy bullets. Dave Doran, a twenty-eight-year-old organizer who was witnessing his first fighting in the Aragon, took his place. Hans Amlie, commanding officer of the Lincolns, was wounded in the head, and his adjutant, Leonard Lamb, took over the command.

By this time there were perhaps a hundred men left in the entire battalion. The town had to be taken rapidly, or never. Artillery was useless against the church, because the open approach did not permit an immediate infantry follow-up. The only way was to send small squads of riflemen, loaded down with grenades, against it. The final assault began.

Off at one flank, Carl Bradley led twenty-nine men toward the town. "We charged uphill some 350 meters under enemy machine-gun fire," he said. "We could see the fasces of the Fascists stencilled on the buildings. Three of our men were killed, seven wounded. The Americans had to put up their machine-gun stand. The bullets flew so thick that we had to take our ponchos, fill them with sand, and under that bit of protection, set up our guns.

"We took a street to a point where Charlie Regan was killed. Charlie was one of the bravest men in Spain, a World War vet, an Irishman with pleasant blue eyes. . . . We called the spot where he was killed Dead Man's Point. . . . At Dead Man's Point, where the bullets were ricocheting, we built a barricade of bags of grain taken from cellars of abandoned houses, and gave the Fascists hell from behind it with bombs and rifles. Then we decided to move the barricades forward, a few feet at a time. Two volunteers were needed for this, and two stepped forward immediately. One of them was Ephraim Bartlett, of Colorado, a man with some Indian blood, a miner who had been a soldier in the United States Cavalry and who had seen a lot of duty on the Mexican front. . . . Back to the sides of the building, he took sack after sack from the barricade, and holding them in front of him in direct fire of the enemy he piled them in the new position.

"Then we began to advance through the buildings by digging holes in those thick Spanish walls. We got a commanding position from two houses on the right and began to harass the enemy by sniping."

Meanwhile the small squads of five were advancing. Daniel Hutner, a former New York University track

THE ARAGON OFFENSIVE

champion, left the medical group to advance with the scouts, rifle in hand. He was killed by a sniper. Others fell as the assault on the church succeeded in driving the rebels from the windows, back through the church itself, out into the plaza and down the open streets.

The Americans were now within the town, but a large group of rebels still held out in the central buildings. At this point a deserter appeared. Taken to Doran, he was told to return to the town and convince his former fellow fighters that resistance was useless. A few hours later, just before daybreak, he reappeared, leading three hundred men, all of whom laid their arms down before the Americans and surrendered.

As the prisoners came forward, another strange thing occurred. For several nights the enemy planes had flown over the town just before dawn, blinked their lights, received an answering signal from the besieged Belchité garrison, then dropped huge bags containing ham, bread, and notes of instruction into the officers' quarters. There was no need for the food, as the Lincolns discovered after they entered Belchité; the town was well supplied. This was merely a gesture to keep the rebels' spirits up, to keep them from surrendering, to tell them to hold out till help, already on the way, showed up.

That night, however, seeing the blinking plane lights in the sky, one of the Americans held up his flashlight, which he turned on and off several times, "just to see what would happen." Suddenly there was the heavy whir of something dropping, close at hand; and the men around one machine-gun scattered for cover as a heavy weight hit the ground with a great thud. When the expected explosion failed to materialize, heads popped up and soon all the men gathered around the projectile, which turned out to be a great burlap sack. The letters were turned over to Commander Copic and Commissar Doran, the ham was carefully cached, and as the machine-gunners turned their attention to the town again, they made plans to go searching for eggs as soon as the battle ended.

Only one last incident remains: as Bradley's group and the hand-grenade squads penetrated deeper and deeper into the town, the strains of the "Hymno de Riego," the Republic's anthem, boomed voluminously through the air. It was a record being played in the brigade's loud-speaker propaganda truck, amplified so greatly that the sound of the cracking of rifles and the explosions of hand-grenades were dimmed by it. Then, as the strains of the anthem ended, a voice spoke, in Spanish, the words which Doran had written a short time before.

"It was a simple little speech," said one of the Americans who heard it, "but its effect was deadly. It told the Fascists how futile their position was. It told them what the Republic stood for. It told of Mussolini and Hitler and the Moorish invaders. Then the national anthem sounded again.

"Two minutes elapsed. Silence. Then a few scattered shots. We afterward learned these were some Fascist officers being killed by their own soldiers. Suddenly we heard

THE ARAGON OFFENSIVE

the soldiers, the rebel soldiers, start shouting '*Viva la Republica! Viva la Republica!*' and we knew victory was ours.

"Then all their soldiers came over. They surrendered, and Belchité, the stronghold that Napoleon couldn't take, was in the hands of the International Brigades."

As the men swarmed openly into the town, they came across one building which was the town garrison's hospital. As the Americans entered, seven nuns, working around the beds in which the wounded were lying, drew back, expecting death or torture. They had been filled with horror stories about the International Brigades, and they looked as if they were resigned to worse than death.

"Then," said one American, "we came forward and gave them milk, eggs, bread. Our battalion doctor asked them which were the most seriously wounded cases; he wanted to give them immediate attention. The nurses gladly showed them. Their faces relaxed, and timid smiles appeared for the first time as we helped the sick and wounded—and they repeated, over and over again, '*Muy bien, muy bien.*'

"Then we helped the nuns over the barricade and took them to safety."

4

Belchité fell on September 3rd, and while other parts of the army occupied the captured fortresses and the new front lines, the Fifteenth Brigade moved back into rest at

THE LINCOLN BATTALION

Azaila. In the two weeks of fighting the Loyalists had taken more than nine hundred square kilometers of territory; the Americans had led the fighting which had won for the Republic the two prizes of the campaign, the towns of Quinto and Belchité.

Still the fighting was not over. The Americans resting at Azaila knew the ultimate possible goal of the campaign was Saragossa; General Walter, the commander of the Thirty-fifth Division, had announced this at a meeting of officers and commissars a day before the attack on Quinto had begun, and the officers had relayed the information to the men. So they rested with the curious kind of concentration on their leisure hours which men have when they know there will be fighting soon.

Ernest Hemingway, visiting the front in mid-September, described them in a cabled newspaper story:

"When we got up with the Americans, they were lying under some olive trees along a little stream. The yellow dust of Aragon was blowing over them, over their blanketed machine-guns, over their automatic rifles and their anti-aircraft guns. It grew in blending clouds raised by the hoofs of pack animals and the wheels of motor transports, and in the gale of clouds of dust rolling over the bare hills Aragon looked like a blizzard in Montana.

"But in the lee of the stream bank the men were slouching, fearful and grinning, their teeth flashing white slits in their yellow powdered station. Since I saw them last spring, they have become soldiers. . . ."

THE ARAGON OFFENSIVE

For more than a month the brigade rested, moving from spot to spot in preparation for further attacks toward Saragossa. From Azaila the men moved thirty kilometers south; shortly afterwards they reached Azuara, going into positions near Grañen. From these positions they could see the spires of Saragossa rising above the hills and the haze of dust in the air. A new attack was planned, and the men speculated about it, but before it could be put into operation the rains came, and the plans were automatically shelved.

While the Americans waited for the next action, the Mackenzie-Papineau Battalion, which had been in training at Tarazona since June, moved up to the Aragon and was incorporated into the brigade. Since the day in June when the new battalion had been christened, many of the Americans who had trained, and been trained in it, had moved up to the lines. Groups of fifty and more had been sent to the Lincolns to replace the men wounded and killed at Bruneté; leading officers had been sent to fill important posts in the brigade. Merriman, the MacPaps' first commander in training, was Chief of Staff of the brigade; his secretary, Sidney Shosteck, who was later killed by a sniper's bullet in the streets of Belchité, had been the MacPaps' first battalion secretary. Captain Rollin Dart, who had been in command for a short time after leaving the Cordoba front, had subsequently held important posts during Bruneté, and was now on his way back to the United States. Despite the many transfers, however, the MacPaps were still predominantly American, both in leadership and personnel. Bob Thompson, a twenty-three-year-old Californian who had been seriously wounded at Jarama in February, was in command. Joe Dallet, of Youngstown, Ohio, was commissar. Only one of the three rifle companies was Canadian; the other two were American.

The rains brought cold with them, and the men spent miserable nights in the raw Aragon country. But spirits were high among the Americans; there was fortification work to keep them occupied, and a traveling motion-picture apparatus, mounted on a truck, visited their headquarters. Besides, the casualties at Quinto and Belchité had been fewer than the Americans had experienced in any previous campaign. Of the five hundred-odd Americans who had taken part in the two operations, twenty-three had been killed and sixty wounded.

Now that the MacPaps were part of the brigade, it was ready to go into action for the first time as an all English-speaking unit. Only one battalion, the Twenty-fourth, was Spanish, and this was in keeping with the policy of the International Brigades and the Spanish Government to mix the native and foreign soldiers whenever and wherever possible, a policy which was not to reach its full maturity until the spring and summer of the following year.

When the entire brigade was ordered to move on to Fuentes de Ebro, the picture became clear again; the men knew they were going to attempt again to sweep past the only remaining Fascist line of fortifications which stood

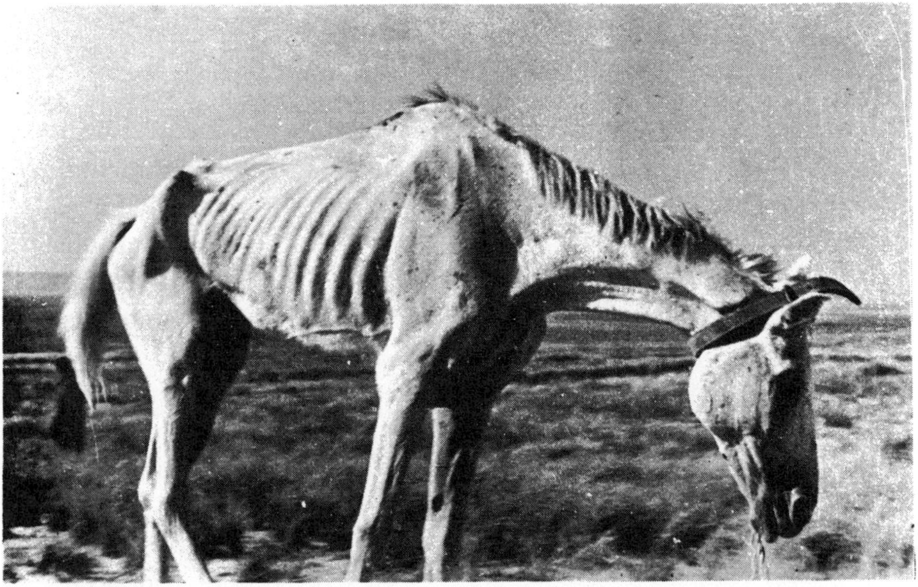

A WAR CASUALTY NEAR QUINTO

BELCHITÉ AFTER ITS CAPTURE BY THE AMERICANS

FRANK ROGERS, COMMISSAR   ROBERT THOMPSON, COMMANDER

SAUL WELLMAN, COMMISSAR, AND
EDWARD CECIL-SMITH, COMMANDER

OFFICERS OF THE MACKENZIE-PAPINEAU BATTALION

THE ARAGON OFFENSIVE

between them and Saragossa on the southern bank of the Ebro, the same Fuentes de Ebro at which, more than a month before, they had waited vainly for three days to launch the flying, mechanized column which never was put into motion.

The attack was made on October 13th. Over open fields which sloped gently upward toward the rebel trenches outside the town, the men advanced, spreading out as they ran, rifle in hand. While they charged, they looked for the planes which the Government orders had promised; the Republican planes were supposed to be bombing the town's defenses. But there was nothing to be seen in the sky. Signals had either been garbled again or, more probably, there hadn't been enough planes to spare for even so important an operation as this. A preparatory artillery barrage had also been promised, but had failed to come off. When the shelling of the insurgent positions finally did begin, it was in a desultory fashion, the shots, few and irregular, falling wide of their marks. No barrage materialized, and instead of the enemy dispersing and enabling the attackers to rush their fortifications, the advancing men found themselves caught in a field alive with bullets, fired in almost incessant bursts from the slight eminence behind which were placed the rebel machine-guns.

Despite the failure of the artillery and planes, the battalions advanced steadily and swiftly. Casualties were heavy from the moment, at 1:40 P.M., when the attack began, but three of the battalions quickly spread out fanwise, in a series of arcs, across the open fields. The fourth battalion created military history when its men mounted the tops and turrets of dozens of tanks, firing rifles and machine-guns at the enemy and suffering heavy losses at the same time, as the whippet tanks thundered across the field at a speed of fifty kilometers an hour. It was the first time in modern warfare that men had ridden into action on tanks.

The entire field of attack covered a front width of less than two miles, with the MacPaps infiltrating across the central area directly below the main line of Fascist fortifications, the Lincolns on their right flank across the road, with the English on the Lincolns' flank up to the river itself. North of the river another brigade was attacking, but it too was held up and its efforts nullified by the tardiness and ineffectiveness of the Government artillery. (Planes finally did appear, but the attackers were already spread out below the enemy fortifications, and it was therefore impossible for them to attempt direct bombing and strafing of the rebel lines without endangering the lives of the attackers. Later, when the operation was over, it was discovered that the failure of artillery and airplane preparation had been caused by the sabotage of the tank corps commander.)

Greatest casualties were suffered by the Mackenzie-Papineau Battalion. "We received our first taste of fire at dawn," wrote the machine-gun company commander, "while we were entering a shallow communication trench leading us to our position. The enemy machine-gunners spotted our movements and in the fire one man was killed and a few wounded, including Douglas Hitchcock, battalion secretary. He was hit in the leg while cutting a strand of barbed wire at the mouth of the communication trench.

"The fire took us by surprise, but it did not in the least affect the high spirit and discipline which characterized all our actions.

"Positions were assigned for each of the three rifle companies as points of departure for the attack. Two sections of my machine-gun company were placed on the heights to cover the advance of the infantry, while the third section was held in reserve.

"The attack started at 1:40 P.M. When our tanks went over and the order was given to advance, the battalion, including its staff, went over the top as one man. Joe Dallet, battalion commissar, went over with the First Company on the left flank, where the fire was heaviest. He was leading the advance when he fell, mortally wounded. He behaved heroically until the very end, refusing to permit the first-aid men to approach him at his exposed position."

Taking advantage of the cover offered by a small white stone house in the center of the field and of a sharp dip in the earth several hundred meters from the insurgent trenches, the Americans and Canadians advanced 900 meters to a point directly below the fortifications. Then, sapping forward, an observation post was established under the very eyes of the Tercio—Franco's Foreign Legion—

who were manning the defenses. A small periscope was raised above trench level, and Douglas Taylor and Leonard Levinson, looking through it, relayed information steadily back to headquarters. Both men—one a New York artist and the other a young lawyer who had given up a government post in Washington to go to Spain—described the heavy fire they drew, the bullets whizzing by inches above their heads as they watched, speculating every few minutes about the rebel marksmanship and how soon their periscope would be hit.

Farther to their left, twenty-three-year-old John Field, of Mena, Arkansas, a tall youth with the smooth and tireless gait of an Indian, kept his section under cover, waiting for orders. In the trenches, almost a kilometer behind, was his father, fifty-three-year-old Ralph Field, who had tried to pass himself off as John's older brother when the two had reached Spain in June. The deception had been discovered, and despite the old man's indignant protests he was not permitted to go forward with the attacking men. Later he was assigned to the commissary department.

By late afternoon the men reconciled themselves to the knowledge that their attack had failed, and they waited for nightfall to return to their lines. The battalions in which the Americans predominated—the Lincoln and the MacPap—had again suffered serious and heavy losses. Captain Phil Detro, the lanky Texan who had replaced Lamb as commander of the Lincolns when the latter had been wounded a week before, was untouched, but most of the

THE ARAGON OFFENSIVE

other commanding officers of both battalions had been hit. Bob Thompson, the twenty-one-year-old Californian who commanded the MacPaps, was deathly sick, suffering from fever and from an old leg wound received at Jarama, but he refused to leave his post. Joe Dallet's death left the commissarship vacant, and Saul Wellman, a twenty-three-year-old truck driver, took over the post in the heat of battle. Carl Geiser, the Ohio student who was commissar of the Lincolns, was wounded, and Fred Keller, the young Irish-American who had led young elevator servicemen in New York, replaced him. Company commanders Bill Neure and Isidor Schrenzel were mortally wounded, and Milton Herndon, who had led his machine-gun section in the unusual task of infiltrating across open terrain with their heavy guns, was dead. Owen Appleton, Lincoln Battalion secretary, was killed while bringing water out into no-man's land. Ruby Kaufman, who had fought at Jarama, was so terribly wounded that he lay among a row of corpses for almost a day before someone discovered he was still alive and rushed him to a hospital. Joe Dougher, MacPap company commander and Pennsylvania miner, had suffered a foot wound which ended his active participation in the war, and Saul Cohen, the fragile-looking Chicagoan who had led a section of men into the action, was similarly hurt. Victor Franco, who had changed his name in training camp to avoid the kidding of his comrades, was dead. The list again was long.

The death of Sam Kaplan, a New York boy who went

into action as a member of the British Battalion, has been described by John Patterson, a young Englishman whose life he saved:

"I was badly wounded," wrote Patterson, "and Kaplan and another American, and two English comrades, decided to get me out of the line of fire and to safety by running relays with me in the stretcher. They had to make the long dash for the ambulance, which was located in a sunken road some four hundred meters away.

"We started for the ambulance, but we had barely begun to move when suddenly we were met by a burst of machine-gun fire from the Fascist lines. The only thing that could be done then was for the stretcher-bearers to take me to a patch of ground where I would be comparatively safe from their fire. This they did.

"But almost immediately the two Americans fell, one killed outright, and the other, Sam Kaplan, mortally wounded.

"Turning off the stretcher on to the ground, I received another bullet wound, this time in the arm; but it was slight, just grazed through the fleshy part. It was the bullet in my chest that pained, so much that I hardly felt the new wound at all. . . .

"As I crawled along the ground, attempting to make the trench again, I reached Sam Kaplan, who by this time was bleeding profusely from the nose and mouth. With what may have been his last breath, he told me in a forced whisper to get my head close down near his chest, as another

THE ARAGON OFFENSIVE

bullet wouldn't make any difference to him any more but might kill me. With his own body he gave me cover, shielded me from all harm. . . ."

Although Fuentes de Ebro still remained in the rebels' hands, the men of the Fifteenth Brigade stayed in their newly won positions, a kilometer closer to the town, for twelve days, digging trenches, setting up machine-gun and listening posts, clearing lines of communication. Then, on October 24th, when the new lines were completely consolidated, the Americans were relieved by a Spanish brigade.

6

BREATHING SPELL

FOR A WEEK AFTER IT LEFT THE TRENCHES, THE ENTIRE BRIgade rested in Quinto; the battalions barracked in whatever shelter the surrounding countryside offered. Usually the shelter consisted of no more than an open field or hillside, a shallow trench dug into the earth and the branches of trees above it. Here, for the only time during the entire war, an American official visited the Lincoln Battalion. Colonel Stephen Fuqua, the American military attaché in Republican Spain, stopped for a few hours in the captured city and spoke a few carefully chosen, noncommittal words to the men when the battalions lined up in review. It was little enough, but the American volunteers—veterans now of three grueling campaigns—were cheered by his mere presence.

It should be remembered that this was an army of articulate, thinking, reasoning human beings—young men who fought not as automatons, but as highly conscious anti-

Fascists. There was no officer-caste among them, and therefore none of the blind obedience exacted of soldiers during the World War. There was discipline, of course; no army unit can function without it. But the discipline was of a rare kind, far deeper than the usual surface discipline of military machines, with its outer formalities and trappings. The surface forms were, indeed, almost entirely disregarded by the Americans until many months later, when they adopted the salute to officers largely as an example to the young Spanish recruits at a time when Spain's last great available man power was being mobilized to stave off the Italo-German juggernaut of limitless planes and artillery. The officers were not professional military men. No West Point had produced them, then placed them in charge of companies and battalions of strange soldiers whom they regarded merely as impersonal cogs in a fighting instrument. The officers and men were friends from the very beginning. Those who rose to command did so only after they had proved their abilities in battle. The battalion commander and the third ammunition carrier were men who not long before had slept under the same blanket or huddled sweating and powder-grimed behind the shield of the same gun. It was difficult for Bill Wheeler, who had fought side by side with Bob Thompson at Jarama, and who had been wounded at almost the same time, to call him Captain Thompson. So at most times he didn't even try. The battalion commander remained "Bob" to most of the men.

Although their knowledge of practical soldiery con-

THE LINCOLN BATTALION

sisted only of their current experiences in Spain, even the youngest of the American volunteers knew one basic fact which few men besides professional military theorists ever considered. They knew von Clausewitz's words, "War is the continuation of politics by other means"; and they realized deeply the significance of the words. Although they cursed in anger and bitterness after they were halted at the outskirts of Fuentes, they knew that more than the sabotage of a single man was responsible. They understood that nothing could have kept them from victory had the Republic possessed sufficient planes and heavy arms to spread them liberally over every front, every sector—sufficient to balance the planes and cannon of the enemy. And they could trace the reasons for the lack, and were conscious of these reasons, even during the moments of heaviest fighting—in the simple, appalling moment when the 1898 rifle grew so hot that the hands blistered against the barrels, when the hand fumbling in the last pocket of the cartridge belt disclosed the last few precious rounds, or when the single ancient Maxim holding up the enemy on the flank suddenly and tragically jammed. They cursed the guns and the shortage of ammo, but they were really cursing the international political set-up of the countries which posed as the friends of Spain: perfidious (they used the American synonym, "double-crossing") Albion, and France, which contrived and concocted non-intervention and kept the border closed to the arms which might have saved them and ended the bloodfest in its first months; and even their own country, which, by its embargo and its refusal to sell arms to Spain, had crippled the democracy for which they were dying.

That is why Colonel Fuqua's brief visit cheered them. That is why they stood erect and proud before him, their eyes saying: Here, we've fought for almost a year and we're still fighting. We've won battles, but we have yet to win the war. And we'll do that if we're only given arms. You know that for yourself. Tell it to the people back in Washington; get them to lift the embargo. If America does the decent thing, maybe England and France will follow. And if that happens, we can't lose!

2

November found the Americans back at Ambité and the surrounding villages, back on the Madrid front and again part of the Fifth, regular, Army Corps. Reinforcements—Americans, Canadians and Spaniards—came up from the training base in Tarazona, now under the command of Major Johnson, the same man who as Captain Johnson had been sector-commander and Chief of Operations of the brigade at Jarama. Johnson had returned to Spain after a brief foreign leave, taking over the post of twice-wounded Walter Garland, the machine-gun company commander, who left for the United States.

The Americans again returned to the routine of rest, reorganization and training, but this time with an intensity which would have startled some of the earliest of the volunteers. The International Brigades, like the entire Spanish Army, had gone through its romantic period—the period of lax, catch-as-catch-can organization, the period when individual heroism—often reckless and unnecessary and foolhardy—had taken the place of discipline and effective organization, the period, too, when the Americans considered themselves as a separate entity, organizationally linked with the Spanish Army only through the fact that they fought against a common enemy and for a common cause. In this they merely reflected the decentralized stage of the Spanish militias of the early days.

Now, however, as the Americans settled down in Ambité and the fortunate veterans left for short furloughs in Madrid, they discovered that the entire brigade was going through an entirely new experience; the transition from the early romantic organization to what was to become the volunteers' complete and integrated incorporation into the regular army was definitely under way.

The Spanish Government decree which formally announced the new status of the International Brigades was first published in the November 1st number of *The Volunteer for Liberty*. Its text, significant in itself, also illumined the right of the Spanish Republic to make use of the volunteer services of foreigners, a right which was later to be sacrificed in a last-minute hope that it might help to awaken international morality to the point where the officially blessed German and Italian invaders would be withdrawn from Spain. This is the full text of the decree:

The units constituted by Spanish and foreign volunteers were organized by the decree of August 31, 1920 (*Diario Oficial*, Number 195) developed in the circular order of September 4th of the same year. Neither of these orders is, however, fully applicable to the forces similarly recruited which are at present fighting heroically as part of the Republican Army.

Even though the units now existing under the name of International Brigades are legally those which the Spanish State, using its sovereign rights, has constituted to take the place of the units which revolted in July, 1936, and are analogous to those which under different names exist in the armies of almost all countries, it is necessary to lay down fresh norms which should regulate their recruitment, organization, administration, etc. To meet with this necessity I have determined:

1. To take the place of the *Tercio de Extranjeros* (Foreign Legion), formed under the decree of August 31, 1920 (*Diario Oficial*, Number 195) the International Brigades are formed as units in the Spanish Army. At the present time five of the above-mentioned brigades should be constituted on the basis of those formed spontaneously in the course of the present war, adapting their constitution to the norms indicated in the present order.

2. Tactically the International Brigades will be used as front-line troops and in all the services of peace and war, with no restriction other than that of their military utility.

3. Their organization will follow the model assigned to the mixed brigades in the Spanish Army. The troops forming these brigades will be subject to the Code of Military Justice and to the Army Statutes, in the same way as Spanish soldiers.

4. The training of the International Brigades will be adjusted to the same regulations and instructions as those which are in force in the other units of the army.

5. The uniforms and equipment will be the same as those of the other forces in the Spanish Army with no difference other than that of wearing on the right side of the shirt or jacket, two centimeters above the pocket, the emblem which will be published in the *Diario Oficial* and which only those incorporated in these units, whatever their military rank, will be entitled to use.

6. In Albaceté the International Brigades will have their base, the fundamental mission of which will be to receive the volunteers, both Spanish subjects and foreigners who present themselves to swell the ranks of the brigades, to train them and send them to the brigades as circumstances demand. Once the recruits are incorporated in the brigade they will cease to be subordinate to the base whenever the brigades are tactically subordinate to the corresponding military commands, and will constitute administrative units in an analogous manner to the other mixed brigades of the army.

Nevertheless the International Brigades will depend on their base for the following:

a) In addition to their reports to their own military commanders, the brigades will report to the base all their movements from one place to another, their losses, leaves granted for the interior of Spain and in general all that supposes a change of any importance in the life of the brigades.

b) Petitions for leave abroad will be noted by the brigade commanders and forwarded to the base. In no case will the applicant be authorized to absent himself from the ranks of his unit before the leave has been granted.

c) All proposals for promotion to whatever rank, beginning with promotion from corporal to sergeant, will be forwarded to the base by the brigade commanders.

d) When any brigade has a soldier who, after previous medical examination in the unit, is declared to be presumed unfit, the brigade, without removing him from its list of effectives, will send him to the base, where his case will receive final medical examination. When his unfitness is confirmed this will be communicated to the brigade so that the latter can remove him from the list of effectives. In cases where unfitness is not confirmed the person concerned will return to his unit.

e) The brigades should send to the base all particulars, statements and reports for which they are asked.

7. In addition to the organs necessary to execute the above functions, the base of the International Brigades will have the organs corresponding to the following:

a) To collect and distribute among the brigades all the gifts which international solidarity may send expressly to the brigades.

b) To take the first steps in matters of pensions for death or incapacity, collecting the documents and antecedents demanded by the legislation in force and then forwarding them to this Ministry for decision.

c) To forward to this Ministry, after investigating them, the petitions for permission to leave Spanish territory made by members of the International Brigades of whatever rank.

d) To report to the Ministry on the incorporation of recruits and their departure for the brigades.

e) To keep a file which will contain all the relevant particulars concerning the members of the brigades.

f) To propose the formation and when necessary to undertake the direction of centers for re-education necessary for members of the brigades who stand in need of this as a result of injuries received in war service.

g) To propose the formation and when necessary to undertake the direction of rest homes in which those combatants who have their families abroad, and who have no residence here, can spend their leave in Spain.

8. In no case will the base intervene in the functioning of the Supply and Medical Services relating to the International Brigades. The brigades will make use of the general services of the Army in the same way as the other mixed brigades. Nevertheless, on the basis of a proposition which the base will make to this Ministry, the General Medical Inspectorate will be able to organize, under the Inspectorate's control, the installation of special hospitals with the qualified staff and assistants necessary for the wounded and convalescent members of the International Brigades who are in need of lengthy hospital treatment. Entrance to the said hospitals will be regulated at all times by the General Medical Inspectorate.

9. The relation between this Ministry and the base of the International Brigades will be effected through the Foreigners' Bureau, attached to the Section of Services of the Undersecretariat of the Army.

10. The International Brigades will be formed of Spanish and foreign volunteers. Nevertheless, this Ministry reserves the right to send directly to the brigades the soldiers, non-commissioned and commissioned officers, and commanders whom it deems desirable. The personnel at the base will consist preferably of members of the brigades who are unfit for service at the front, and in any case it will be indispensable for the members of the personnel to have

MILTON WOLFF

LEONARD LAMB

PHILIP DETRO

HANS AMLIE

FOUR COMMANDERS OF THE LINCOLN BATTALION

COMMISSAR JOHN GATES, LT. MELVIN OFFSINK AND CAPT. WOLFF

LINCOLN SNIPER AT TERUEL

been at the front for the minimum period of three months, which is laid down in the decree of June 19th of this year (*Diario Oficial*, Number 148). The personnel of the Foreigners' Bureau will be appointed by the Ministry.

11. The foreign personnel of the brigades will consist of those who of their own accord present themselves at the Foreigners' Bureau or before its delegates and who, after admission, will be sent to the base for registration. The Spanish personnel will consist of those who apply for admission to the brigades to this Ministry, either directly if they are not subject to military service, or through the regulation channels if they are in the Army. The petitions will be dealt with as a matter of urgency, and in the event of their being answered in the affirmative by this Ministry, the order will be given for the person concerned to be removed from the list of the effectives of the unit from which he proceeds, his entry at the base of the International Brigades and his immediate enrollment in the brigades.

12. The Spanish or foreign soldiers of the International Brigades will fill by promotion 50 per cent of the vacancies in the brigades for sergeants, officers and commanders. With this object the brigades, when reporting to the base that such posts are vacant, will propose those members in the brigades whom they regard as deserving of promotion. To pass from one post to another it will be necessary to have held the lower post for a minimum period of two months. If the brigade does not possess sufficient personnel to fill the vacancies, they will be filled by the nominees of other International Brigades, and in the event of there being none they will be filled by the Ministry by direct nominations of military personnel. A vacancy will not be considered to have been created except in cases of death or when

the base communicates that the post is vacant through unfitness, a change in post, or removal from the Army. Absences due to wounds, illness or leave will not be considered as vacancies, and when necessary the posts concerned will be filled temporarily by men from lower posts, without this supposing any promotion. Those who are promoted will receive the corresponding rank of sergeant, officer or commander of the International Brigades, and when the present campaign is ended they will constitute the permanent commanding cadres in the said units. The sergeants, officers and commanders of the International Brigades cannot be sent outside these units. They can be isolated, expelled or reduced in rank for obvious incompetence or impropriety in the execution of their duty, after a report has been made by the commander of the corresponding brigade and by the commander of the base.

13. The other 50 per cent of the vacancies of sergeants, officers and commanders will be filled with men sent directly by the Ministry of Defense, from among those who are already recognized in those posts in the Army. These men will remain subject, as far as promotions are concerned, to the general existing norms in the matter of recompense.

The commanders, officers and sergeants who desire to be sent into the International Brigades should send in the appropriate application to the Personnel Section of the Undersecretariat of the Army.

14. Soldiers, non-commissioned and commissioned officers and commanders, both Spanish and foreign, belonging to the International Brigades will in cases of incapacity or death have the same rights as those in the rest of the Army.

15. All members of the brigades will have the right to

thirteen days' leave for every six months at the front, always providing that the necessities of service permit it and providing that the conduct of the soldiers concerned makes them deserving of this in the commander's opinion. For this purpose the corresponding turns, two a month, will be fixed in each brigade, so that each month leaves can be begun once they have been passed in review by the commissar. Those who wish to spend their leave outside Spain should apply in advance, abiding by the decision which is taken. The commander of the base of the International Brigades will communicate to each of the brigades the number of places at their disposal in the rest homes which may be installed by virtue of the provisions of Section g of the Seventh Article of this order.

16. The measures laid down in this order will be put rapidly into operation by the soldiers and officers now constituting the International Brigades and their base as they receive the appropriate instructions from the Foreigners' Bureau of the Undersecretariat of the Army.

17. The Commanders of the International Brigades will send to the base of the brigades with all possible speed a statement of the leading forces, specifying their nationality, date of birth, date of entry into the International Brigades and date at which they were given their present posts, so that the Ministry can proceed to confirm them in those posts when it considers this fitting.

18. The necessarily variable condition of the organization of the personnel constituting the base of the International Brigades makes it impossible, at least for the moment, to assign to it a fixed organization. For the purpose of the review by the commissar the numerical account will be sent monthly to the Foreigners' Bureau and in relation to this the review should be made.

THE LINCOLN BATTALION

19. To those foreigners who have served for more than a year in the Army with a clear record and very deserving conduct a certificate will be forwarded which will serve as the basis for according them Spanish nationality should they so desire.

20. All those who voluntarily enter the International Brigades undertake to remain in them until the end of the present campaign. When this campaign is finished the norms will be laid down in accordance with which these units should be organized in the future.

I communicate this to your Excellency for your information and for application.

PRIETO

Valencia, September 23rd, 1937.

It was in the spirit of this decree that Dave Doran, the brigade commissar, undertook the retraining of the men. There had been Spaniards in the brigade and in the Lincoln Battalion since their formation, but now, for the first time, they were introduced in greater numbers. Whenever possible, a Spanish company would become part of a battalion; if there were not enough Spanish soldiers for a company, a section would suffice. The commingling of Americans and Spaniards, which until then had been a casual process, was consciously pushed by the twenty-nine-year-old commissar, who realized that the war would be a long one, that difficult times lay ahead of the men, and that their haphazard knowledge of Spanish would not suffice in times when casualties would have depleted their ranks. The Americans had much that they could teach the Spaniards—

their efficiency at all sorts of mechanical tasks, their ability for rapid organization, their understanding of the worldwide issues at stake in the war. But he felt that the Americans had not yet learned the lessons that the Spanish soldiers could teach them. Not only the language was important, but the fortitude, the self-abnegation, the austere and tragic sense of human dignity which clothed the most illiterate Spanish peasant. To set an example for the rest of the men in the brigade, Doran "adopted" a young Spaniard, twenty-two-year-old José María Sastré, as his assistant commissar. They studied together, bunked together, outlined together the educational projects, both military and political, of the brigade. And in the battalions the commissars began slowly to follow suit.

The Americans took to the new discipline slowly, feeling their way. Some, at first, refused to salute at all. Others, better aware of its purpose, did so cautiously, raising the right arm with the hand clenched loosely, not taut in a fist, barely higher than their shoulders. It took the gracious explanation of one of the Spanish soldiers to convince the Americans. "*Hombre*," he said, "it isn't a sign of deference, nor has it got anything to do with superiority or inferiority. It's just courtesy, *hombre*, like when you meet a friend in the street. You kiss him on both cheeks, no? Or you clasp his hand. Well, in the army your hands are dirty, or you haven't shaved for a week, no? So you salute. Understand?" The ingenious explanation pleased many of the men. Slowly the salute was adopted.

THE LINCOLN BATTALION

While they rested and trained under the direction of their battalion officers, the men thought often of the commissars who had shared the leading positions with the battalion commanders. They remembered one who had been so useless and so obstructive that he became known as the "comic star," an epithet which was to be used loosely and good-humoredly by them for the duration of the war. That one had gone home, and the epithet had taken on the underlying tones of affection and respect when Steve Nelson had become commissar of the Lincoln Battalion. When Nelson left the battalion to become brigade commissar his place was filled by a little seaman from New York, John Quigley Robinson, known to the men simply as Robbie. It was Robbie who had been with the Lincoln men through the Aragon offensive, tough, wiry, red-faced Robbie, until Carl Geiser, a quiet Ohioan had succeeded him at Fuentes, only to be wounded in the thick of the attack. Then Fred Keller, who like Robbie and the rest of the seamen had bantered most loudly about the comic stars, himself became the Lincoln Battalion commissar. And the men realized that the job was a big one, one of the biggest in the army; and they realized too that the value of the post, like that of any other in the army, lay in the character and abilities of the men who filled it.

They thought of these men as the figure of Dave Doran made itself felt among them, down to the squads and all the services of the battalion. His actions were new, and often strange and disturbing to them. He was willful, strong, and when a policy had been decided upon he let nothing and no one interfere with its execution.

The first commissar of the MacPaps, Joe Dallet, had been somewhat like Doran. He had been in a group of seventeen Americans and eight Canadians who were halted in mid-Mediterranean while attempting to reach Spain in a small French fishing boat. That had happened in March. After a short prison term in France, Dallet and his group had reached Spain, where he had become, first, commissar of the Officers' Training School and then commissar of the newly formed Mackenzie-Papineau Battalion. He was something of an enigma to the men for all the time that he led them. Tall, sharp of face and movement, his words when he addressed the battalion were tough in sound and meaning, inflexible in purpose. The syllables were those of a man who had been a longshoreman, a steel worker, an organizer of working men in the mills of Youngstown. Yet he could be gentle and completely understanding when he spoke to a man alone. In the five weeks I spent in training with the MacPaps I saw much of Dallet, yet he remained a remote and complex character to me as he did probably to all but Steve Nelson, his closest friend. Of the many Americans who went to Spain the most numerous single group was composed of students. Making up a much smaller but still considerable group were the seamen. Yet neither students nor seamen in the MacPaps could fathom Dallet's personality. To the former he was a tough guy, but he astonished them when he quoted Eliot and Yeats and Rilke at them out of the corner of his mouth. The seamen detected something softer in him than his surface hardness, but they knew he had worked in jobs as heavy—or almost as heavy—as theirs. The figure of the commissar became more puzzling and stranger as the men discovered Dallet's odd bits of knowledge in a hundred out-of-the-way fields, as they found, by an accidental encounter as astonishing to them as it was embarrassing to Dallet, that he was a far better than average pianist. Later they found that his knowledge of European languages exceeded that of all but a few of the men in the battalion.

It was only after he died, pistol in hand, at Fuentes, struck by a bullet as he led his men out of the trenches into the attack, that they learned what had caused the endless arguments and discussions about him. He had been born into a family of wealth, had attended Woodmere Academy and Dartmouth College, which he left, dissatisfied with what formal education had to offer, in his third year. He became first a longshoreman, then a steel worker and organizer in Pennsylvania, Indiana and Ohio. In his attempt to bridge the gap between wealth and self-imposed poverty, leisure and the roughest of manual labor, he tried to make himself over completely. He throttled the evidences of his earlier, sheltered life; he hardened himself consciously, every part of him, even the sound and inflection of his speech. He tried in every way he could to kill the vestiges of a background which might in any way separate him from his newly found friends and co-workers. The puzzle that his character had presented to the men in Spain was proof that he had not completely succeeded. The whole process had been too courageous and foolhardy—the attempt to change himself overnight had created a powerful but still-divided, still-unintegrated man. And his fellow Americans in the brigade paid him the final tribute when, after his death, they said: "That's one thing he always had, guts."

Many other commissars, as well as company and battalion commanders, were to lead the Americans in their battles on Spanish soil. It was one of the strange things that happened in the Spanish war: to be an officer, a high-ranking commander, even a general—as Lukacs, the eminent Hungarian critic and writer proved by his death—did not mean that one was safe from enemy bullets. It is a tribute—a tragic tribute—to the youth and spirit and sincerity of the volunteers who fought for Spain that their officers not only directed their men, but led them personally in battle; that the proportion of officers and commissars killed and wounded among the Americans was greater even than that among the men in the ranks.

7
TERUEL: SPAIN'S VALLEY FORGE

MY NOTEBOOK CONTAINS THE FOLLOWING ENTRY UNDER THE date of Saturday, November 6, 1937:

"Period of quiet in Madrid, quieter than I've ever seen it before. Very few—and scattered—shellings; few sounds even on outskirts of city as we approach the first anniversary of the defense of Madrid (November 7–14, 1936). The stillness is not even offset by the gay flags and posters and decorations in celebration of the event and of the twentieth anniversary of the U.S.S.R., which all Madrid—all of Republican Spain—is commemorating with the warmth and spontaneity so characteristic of the people. Spanish flags wave from the electric poles of all street cars, huge signs and posters are plastered over all central buildings, even on the great arch in the Calle de Alcala. Numerous huge pictures of the founder of Spanish Socialism, Pablo Iglesias, and of the well-loved and richly bearded (in the most fantastic colors) Carlos Marx.

"But the people who walk in the streets of the city are

TERUEL: SPAIN'S VALLEY FORGE

sober, grave, thoughtful. The quiet is too complete, the lull too unusual. Most of us feel that, with only three weeks of halfway decent weather left this year, there will be no real fighting till next spring. Some of the best of the American correspondents agree. But there are many who hold that, since time works in our favor, and since the Fascists know this, they will undertake a large-scale offensive against (a) Madrid, or (b) Teruel toward Valencia in an attempt to cut Madrid off from Catalonia, regardless of weather. It's too early to know, but the air is too quiet; the war communiqués report all quiet, day after day; and almost any night you can hear Franco or Quiepo de Llano on the radio, telling us they're going to deliver the final blow soon.

"Some of the people here argue that even the cessation of the artillery bombardments of Madrid is meant to lull us into a state wherein a surprise attack will really take us by surprise. Despite the theatrical and moral advantages for Fascism in going after Madrid exactly a year after its first unsuccessful attempt, I doubt that this will happen. On the other hand, Spanish troops have replaced the Internationals on the Aragon front, and the Fifteenth Brigade, one of the real shock brigades which did supremely well in the last drive but lost heavily at Fuentes de Ebro, is now back in the center again."

As November drew to a close and mid-December approached the pattern of Franco's military plans became clearer. Huge concentrations of Italian and Moorish and native troops were observed north of Guadalajara and in the Aragon. It was evident that the insurgents planned great simultaneous offensives toward Guadalajara and southward to Madrid, and eastward against the territory gained by the Republicans in the fall. Action was expected daily, but the days passed with the usual *sin novedad* leading the war dispatches. Spaniards attributed the delay to the weather. Snowfall—the heaviest in twenty years—had covered Central Spain, and a blizzard raged in the rocky hills and wide unprotected valleys of Aragon. It seemed that the heavy winter was really going to hold up all operations till the spring.

But just as everyone was beginning to accept this as a fact, the news came which shattered the quiet and made the Spanish Christmas really a *Buena Noche*—a night of rejoicing. Teruel, after a stunning and swift offensive through snow and gale by purely Spanish units of the Republican Army, had been captured and was in the hands of the Government.

The Americans received the news in the little Aragonese towns of Alcorisa, Agua Viva and Mas de las Matas, to which they had been moved on December 10th. Word reached them of the capture of the provincial stronghold at 10 o'clock in the evening of December 25th—Christmas Day, a full year after the first of them had set out for the war. At once both the soldiers and the civilians of the town began a joyous snake dance, singing and shouting and, un-

TERUEL: SPAIN'S VALLEY FORGE

mindful of any possible rebel air raid, carrying burning torches as they sang and danced through the streets.

The Americans remained in these towns for another week, training each day, waiting for word to move on. Social life was full after the capture of Teruel, with endless fiestas, dinners, pre-Christmas and after-Christmas celebrations following each other in rapid succession. "All of this," wrote Lamb, back with the Lincolns again as second commanding officer, "added to the splendid morale, for we had many new men who had been added after Fuentes de Ebro and had seen no action although they had been with the battalion for several months. The towns themselves were hospitable, helping in all sorts of ways to make our stay comfortable. The discipline of the men was something I had not known before, coming as I did from the Division hospital at Grañen. Apparently the long training period at Ambité and Albarez had been a good one, and the veterans in the battalion were well-seasoned and sober soldiers."

A lull settled over the battalions a few days after Christmas. Many were looking forward to the New Year's Eve dance which was being arranged by the American nurses of Dr. Barsky's mobile hospital stationed at Alcorisa, where brigade HQ was located. But Major Galleani, brigade staff officer, bet everyone who would take him up a good dinner that the battalion would be fighting before the day of the dance came. Those who accepted the bet lost. On the morning of December 31st the entire brigade received orders to proceed to Teruel. The insurgent counter-offensive had already begun.

The brigade arrived at the town of Argenté on New Year's Eve, after nine hours of journey, cramped and crowded and freezing, in a motor convoy over the bleak Aragon mountains through raging snowstorms and blizzard, in an icy gale which frequently reached a velocity of fifty miles an hour. The men tumbled out of the camions and bedded down for the night in the battered houses at the edge of the town. This, like every other village in the vicinity, was almost completely bare of inhabitants (perhaps forty families, out of a population of 1,500, remained) and greatly damaged by shells and aerial bombs. Before daybreak, since further air attacks were expected, orders came to camp on the flatlands two kilometers away. It was a miserable day for the troops; unable to move about and keep themselves warm because of the incessant air alarms, they had to camouflage themselves as well as they could by hugging the flat white blanket of snow. At least 10 per cent of the men suffered from frostbites and numbness from the cold.

The Lincoln Battalion's next stop was Fuentes Caliente. The brigade was separated, spread out and concentrated at several points of a wide, undefended front. What was feared at the time was a rebel thrust at the vulnerable points of Argenté (where the MacPaps remained) and Fuentes Caliente, a thrust which, if successful, would enable them to cut Loyalist communications with the town of Perales

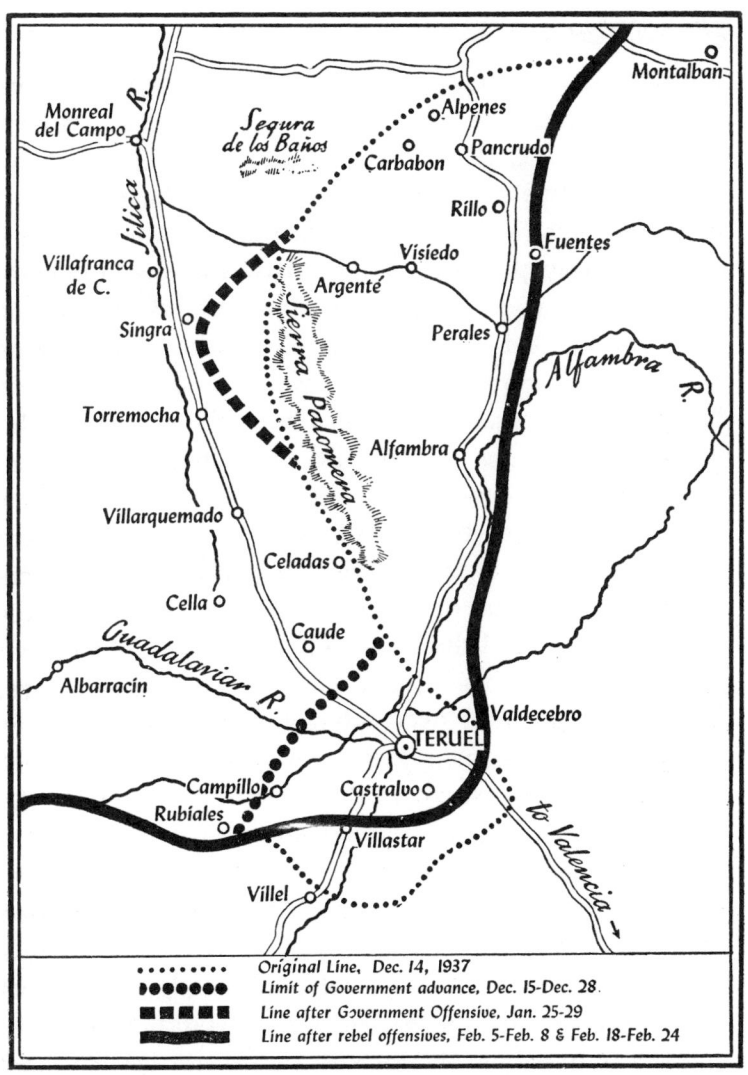

TERUEL

and thereby force the Americans to leave the positions protecting the road which ran through to Alfambra, the main highway into Teruel from the north.

The MacPaps remained in Argenté until January 6th. It was impossible to sleep, even to sit still in the intense cold. The only way the men could keep warm was to dig—dig anything, anywhere. There was tremendous difficulty even in preparing food. Everything—meat, beans, bread—was so frozen that it could not be thawed out. The staple food became hot soup, and that had to be swallowed hastily, because it became ice, frozen solid, ten minutes after it was removed from the pot.

On January 4th the Lincoln Battalion left for Cuévas Labradas, five kilometers south of Alfambra, where it was quartered in a cold, drafty railroad tunnel on the heights above the road and the town. The call to action came the following day. That night the Americans marched eight kilometers westward over submountainous terrain to the broad plateau overlooking the rebel-held town of Celadas. From their positions, where they reinforced a Catalan battalion, part of a brigade protecting an extensive front, they could see clearly into Celadas, lying in the valley which extended westward toward Teruel. The town was the scene of intense enemy activity, centering around a commissariat, several kitchens and the general supply dump of the Fascist forces. The orders given the Lincoln Battalion were to prepare to defend the Heights of Celadas against attack.

For the first two days the Lincoln activity was confined

to digging and constructing fortifications, with occasional sniping and machine-gunning at the men and mule trains passing down the valley whenever they came within range, usually at 1,500 to 1,700 meters. On the third day fully three brigades of the enemy, in a series of waves, attacked a Spanish Loyalist brigade to the south, using heavy and intense artillery fire, but with no success. From the battalion positions the entire action was like a performance of puppets. The Americans could see the numerous figures of the enemy marching down the valley, out of its range of fire, taking positions, wave after wave, and hurling themselves at the Republican positions on the Lincolns' flank. The artillery barrage covered the plateau behind the lines; all calibers of shells dropped closely on every square foot of ground in an accurate geometric pattern. It was the first time the Americans had witnessed a big-scale bombardment laid down by the newly arrived Italian guns. The aviation was always present, circling around for ten or fifteen minutes, then dropping their loads.

The attack, resumed on the following morning, petered out before noon. Shortly after, a small detachment of rebel forces attacked the left flank of the Lincolns. Apparently a company or two of the enemy had scaled the plateau between the Americans and their nearest neighboring troops two kilometers away, surprising them with a volley of rifle fire. Captain Detro, back again in command of the battalion, ordered the first company to counter-attack. Captain Lamb was assigned to lead them out, clear the plateau

THE LINCOLN BATTALION

and establish the line as far forward as possible in order to protect the main force against any similar action on the part of the enemy. The company deployed beautifully, spreading like a fan across the plateau under fire, infiltrated as though on a training maneuver, and after thirty minutes of brisk fighting routed the enemy and established its own line five hundred meters out and only a few meters from the downslope leading into the valley.

In the ensuing days the cold swooped down again, and it became impossible to dig into the frozen rocky ground. Casualties from frostbite and cold began to mount sharply. From then on, Altas Celadas was familiarly called the North Pole. The cold stopped all action except for occasional sniping and the wild bursts of shooting at night.

On the tenth day after their arrival at the North Pole, the Lincoln Battalion was relieved. The English battalion came up through a sea of mud to take up their positions, and the Americans filed out, swearing with each precarious step, back to the tunnel. A tubful of hot and oily soup, the ingredients of which were unidentifiable, awaited them.

2

Within another two days the Fifteenth Brigade was on the move again. It was January 14th, a full month since the Spanish troops, clad in rags and wearing thin, rope-soled *alpargatas*, had moved swiftly through the snow against Teruel. Two great columns—Lister's Eleventh Division and another Spanish division—had moved pincerlike in a simul-

TERUEL: SPAIN'S VALLEY FORGE

taneous advance from the northeast and southwest, establishing contact midway between Campillo and Concud. The movement, which had enclosed the rebels in a circle of iron, practically sealed the fate of Teruel.

The planning of the operation was no less brilliant than its execution. Fortified by the most skilful German military engineers, Teruel had been considered impregnable. Yet the Republican troops, separating the original two columns into five smaller and more mobile ones, completed the whole series of operations with relatively few casualties. With the exception of Concud, none of the strongly fortified rebel positions was attacked frontally. The Republican command had felt out all the weak spots in the insurgent line of defense and driven wedges deep into the enemy's rear. Thus isolated, and attacked from the rear, the strongholds fell with little resistance, and three columns entered Teruel simultaneously from the north, northwest and south.

Franco immediately countered by moving ten thousand Italians and perhaps fifty thousand additional insurgent troops from the Guadalajara front and from the other Aragonese sectors. New Italian batteries were dispatched by the dozens for the counter-offensive, and the skies above Teruel were blackened by swarms of German and Italian planes. At this point, with the rebel counter-offensive already in full swing, the Fifteenth Brigade moved southward to a position just outside of Teruel itself. The MacPaps, in reserve since Argenté, preceded the Lincolns and left the road at Kilometer 3 to cut across country and take up positions occupied by a thinned battalion of the Eleventh Brigade which had just completed a furious action, during which they had met a Fascist thrust head-on and beaten it back. The Lincoln Battalion replaced another of the Eleventh Brigade units whose lines defended the hills to the left and rear of the MacPaps. The Twenty-fourth (Spanish) Battalion had already been placed at the outskirts of the city, stretching a thinly fortified line across the valley cradling the Saragossa road, and ending on La Muela de Teruel, a toothlike lump which carried on its back the scratches and scars of two opposing lines.

Insurgent light artillery peppered the Americans' lines, and in the evening the Lincolns moved into the territory guarding the northern outskirts of Teruel.

The MacPaps meanwhile deepened their trenches on the hills to the north, while the enemy began its attack against another huge hill, El Muleton. For five days shells and trench mortars fell continuously into their positions, killing and wounding many of the Americans and Canadians in the battalion. At one point the enemy trenches on the extreme left flank were only forty meters away and on higher ground, and they were able to hurl hand-grenades easily into the MacPap trenches, which were soon abandoned. The battalion was placed at an extremely dangerous spot, on the peak of an almost sheer cliff which dropped at an 85-degree angle behind it, so that the men would have been hopelessly trapped had the enemy suddenly and successfully attacked.

TERUEL: SPAIN'S VALLEY FORGE

The insurgents, unable to take El Muleton in frontal assault, moved southward and broke through. Between February 16th and 19th, they slowly advanced toward the MacPap positions. Using an entire army corps, and with their artillery and aviation far superior to that of the Loyalists, they decimated an entire battalion of the Thaelmann (Eleventh) Brigade and succeeded in storming El Muleton. Then began the attack against the MacPaps' left flank. Slowly, crushed before the force of the Fascist counter-attack, at a disadvantage because the rebels held higher and dominating hills to the north from which they could rake the battalion hills with steady fire, the MacPaps relinquished two hills on two successive days. Accurate German artillery marksmanship took a heavy toll among the defenders. In one small company, the Third, forty-five out of fifty men were hit, ten of them killed in one day of battle.

Meanwhile, guarding the walls of Teruel, the Lincolns fortified the approach to the valley along the railroad embankment, sent out raiding parties each night, engaged the enemy in sniping contests, threatening their flanks on both sides of the valley. In the course of the days the Lincoln casualties mounted—and from the same cause: the enemy occupied higher ground and possessed superior equipment. Trench mortars were the Americans' greatest dread. They made no sound until they were directly over the men, and then only a swift sound like tearing paper, and the explosion. Artillery wounded several, and snipers accounted for the rest. Larry Kleidman, the battalion's chief of fortifications, was killed by a mortar bomb, and Phil Detro, trying to cross a street between two factories without using a shallow communicating trench ("It's got to be deeper than six feet five to protect me properly," he drawled) was mortally wounded. Again Captain Lamb assumed command of the battalion. Yet the Lincoln Battalion was comparatively unmolested. The Twenty-fourth suffered heavily from trench mortars while the MacPaps took the brunt of the action concentrated on the left flank. They were pounded by artillery fired as accurately as rifles, and in such inconceivable concentration that the crest of the hill defended by their third company was leveled by no fewer than six feet.

To the men who held these positions the destruction of the hilltop was not surprising. They were chalk hills, so weak that trenches and machine-gun pits could be completely demolished even by glancing shells. The defending machine-guns and rifles were almost useless; the chalk dust continuously clogged the mechanism. In holding these positions the men had to hold on by little more than sheer nerve. Saul Wellman, who had been commissar of the MacPaps since Joe Dallet's death on October 13th, added a new job to the many which commissars had filled in the past: he became, as one of his men said, "a traveling machine-gun mechanic," going up and down the lines repairing the choking guns. After a burst of twenty bullets the mechanism would jam; a cartridge would be wedged tightly and uselessly in the firing chamber, held rigid while the entire gun was crammed with the dust. There were no trees, no

TERUEL: SPAIN'S VALLEY FORGE

vegetation on the hills. The surface was completely bare, and Teruel was always visible down below.

When the Americans had first reached Teruel, the surrounding terrain bore the marks of the early fighting and of the brilliant initial Republican attack. The rebels had constructed fortifications facing the road leading into the city: deep trenches, machine-gun posts constructed of steel rails and concrete, and a complete system of communication lanes. The graphic story of the first days of attack was told *behind* the former Fascist lines, where hurriedly constructed foxholes and parapets faced in the opposite direction. And the attempts to bomb the attacking Loyalists out of existence were evident in the pitted land, in the shell craters and in the duds of various sizes and dimensions that got underfoot at every step and covered acres of ground in every direction.

Teruel itself had been almost completely demolished. It had been a city of 12,000 people, a minor metropolis of the Aragon, and the Americans saw, in the vestiges of walls still standing and the wreckage strewn wide, the remnants of luxurious modern apartments. Outside of Teruel, beyond the walls, stood the old and ramshackle mud huts of the peasants, the adobe walls crumbling. It appeared to have been a very rich city; there were modern stores in abundance, a luxurious Singer Sewing Machine shop, kodak and jewelry stores. While stationed on the outskirts of the town the Lincoln men discovered a big hat shop, well stocked with sombreros, and soon 90 per cent of the men in the battalion were wearing sombreros instead of their cotton and flannel berets. After Bruneté most of the Americans had—either by choice or necessity—discarded the steel helmets, and they considered the sombrero greater protection against sunlight and cold than their former headgear. Protection against bullets was not even considered by them; they had too often seen the tin hats perforated by bullets, and Leonard Levinson, of the MacPaps, still carried with him, as a souvenir, a helmet neatly drilled at Fuentes. Only the fact that it had been much too large for him had saved him from more than a superficial skull wound. The battalion lived and slept in the houses in town. Food was plentiful, and the well-stocked stores supplied fantastic clothes to take the place of their ragged uniforms. It was not unusual to see hundreds of men walking about in patent-leather shoes, striped vests, and an odd assortment of trousers, coats and ties. Commissar Fred Keller of the Lincolns himself set the new note in military attire when he appeared in striped morning trousers, heavy riding boots, a serviceable sheepskin-lined coat and a huge black sombrero. A huge 38-caliber pistol, swinging at his side, completed the costume. Captain Lamb, his men said, remained the only military-looking person around.

3

Relief for the entire brigade arrived on February 3rd. The Forty-sixth Division, the Campesinos—so called because their commander, Valentin Gonzales, was known

TERUEL: SPAIN'S VALLEY FORGE

throughout Spain as "El Campesino" or the Peasant—took over the brigade sector with its disciplined men and energetic officers. The Lincoln Battalion filed out of the lines, stumbling over the rutted ground past the city, and marched south on the paved highway leading to Valencia and the orange groves along the coast. Scheduled to go into rest and reorganization, the brigade assembled at Kilometer 19, outside of La Puebla de Valverde, in the concrete fortifications and covered trenches built as secondary lines of defense. All the battalions were to be sent to the town of Belmonte, in Madrid Province, and the English had already left by camion. Two days later the Americans boarded a train and rolled out toward Valencia. A broken boiler plate several kilometers down the line held them overnight and part of the next day. Then with a new engine, the trip was resumed.

The MacPaps remained behind to wait for another train, which arrived on February 7th. Just as the men settled back in the hard compartments, easing themselves for the long and slow journey, telegraphed orders were received to stop the train and to proceed back to Kilometer 19 to await further orders. The same message greeted the Lincolns on their arrival in Valencia, and reached the English in the haven of Belmonte, where they had already spent two restful days. All reserve and secondary troops were ordered back; the insurgents had begun their second counter-attack, had broken through the Government lines and taken Argenté, Perales and Alfambra, north of Teruel.

THE LINCOLN BATTALION

When the brigade had been entirely reassembled it was sent northward about seventy-five kilometers toward Segura de los Baños. A diversion movement was being planned by the Loyalist command, a series of attacks in the north strong enough to force the enemy to remove its advancing forces in the south, the forces which, by breaking through the series of hills which formed the Sierra Palomera, were endangering the entire Aragon front.

The brigades went into the attack during a snowstorm, on the night of February 15th, after careful and detailed instructions had been given every man. It was known in advance that the action was to be a long one, and each soldier went into battle carrying a two days' supply of iron rations and three days' rations of cognac, corked tightly in ancient canteens. The plan was daring: the Thirty-fifth Division, composed of the Fifteenth and Eleventh Brigades, were to strike from Segura de los Baños at the heart of the Fascist communications over which poured the troops and materials for their Teruel counter-drive. The two brigades were to assault the rebel fortifications at Atalaya and Sierra Pedigrossa, which overlooked the town of Segura, and from there to battle southward, sweeping over the enemy forts, and to take possession of the apex formed by three main roads converging. The task of the assault was given to the Fifteenth Brigade, which was in far better condition than the Eleventh. The latter had practically been cut to pieces in the defense of Teruel and El Muleton, and was assigned to the job of acting as a rear guard against any sur-

TERUEL: SPAIN'S VALLEY FORGE

prise flank attack that might develop after the movements of the Fifteenth Brigade got under way. Simultaneously with the launching of the attack on the heavily fortified outposts by the Fifteenth, the *marineros* (marines)—later discovered to have been led by pro-Fascist officers—were to circle the brigade's right flank and penetrate in a spreading movement ahead and to the Fifteenth's left until they made contact with a similar force sweeping up from the opposite direction. Failure would endanger the entire maneuver, the lives of a division of men as well as the precious complement of arms and equipment they carried.

The height of the enemy fortifications made a frontal assault impossible. The tactic chosen was to march the brigade past the lines and to launch the attack from the rebels' rear. The MacPaps were to lead the way up the slopes, skirt the enemy's left flank and attack Atalaya. The Lincolns were assigned to follow close behind, not to wait for the successful completion of the MacPap venture. Instead, they were to skim by the left flank of the enemy on the tail of the first battalion, continue south and scale Sierra Pedigrossa. The Twenty-fourth and British Battalions were to follow and push on toward the lesser fortifications, farther to the south, lying within the apex of the crossroads. It was a movement of great importance, designed to surround and annihilate the opposing forces, and it required not only most careful and delicate planning but flawless precision in operation. In order to achieve the sur-

THE LINCOLN BATTALION

prise necessary for success, the attack was launched at night.

The battalions moved out in darkness on the night of February 16th, leaving their own fortifications, proceeding out into no-man's land, across the broad valley and up the steep slopes of the insurgent heights. Not a man spoke. Machine-gunners, under their heavy burdens, kept the grunts down to whispers. The MacPaps were in position by the time the Lincoln Battalion reached the summit. Their attack began just as the Americans passed them, in complete silence, going south. Telephone lines were cut on the way.

Just at daylight the Lincolns reached their take-off point for the assault. It appeared to be an almost impossible job. The height was protected by two companies of infantrymen, four heavy and eight light machine-guns and two 81-caliber mortars. Protected by barbed wire on all sides, the insurgents maintained their positions until early afternoon, when another assault swept the Americans successfully up the slope, over the shattered and cut wire entanglements and into the enemy trenches.

The English and the Twenty-fourth Battalions, the latter minus one company which had broken through the barbed wire with the Lincoln Battalion, forged ahead. Lines were reformed, facing the enemy, and defense positions established. The next day the Americans fought off a counter-attack, inflicting severe losses on the enemy. The fighting, which lasted for three full days and nights, had captured four important hills over a small but strategic two-kilometer front.

"From a simply physical point of view," the MacPap commissar, Saul Wellman, says, "this was one of our most difficult and exhausting actions. It was a constant grind that lasted for seventy-two hours, with no time to eat or rest. The entire operation depended on speed, perfect coordination, simultaneity of attack, and the all-important surprise element. In taking the four hills the brigade carried out one of the most difficult troop maneuvers: that of moving a large body of men and attacking enemy positions at night."

On February 19th the brigade was taken out of its newly won positions and rushed back toward Teruel at the peak of the Fascist counter-offensive. It was already realized that Teruel would have to be evacuated; the constant unrelenting shower of shells and aerial bombs was more than flesh could withstand. After a short stay on the North Pole, the men were moved back to Kilometer 19 on the Teruel-Sagunto road to cover up the retreat of the Campesinos, who had been surrounded in Teruel and who were even then fighting their way through the rebel encirclement. Between the brigade and the Campesinos were Lister's crack troops, covering the area from Kilometers 3 to 10. The Lincoln Battalion was sent up in advance of the rest of the brigade to prepare positions for resistance in the event that the insurgents broke through Lister's lines. But they failed to break through, and the Fifteenth Brigade was not used again. The men returned to the concrete fortifications outside Kilometer 19.

In a swift account of the entire campaign, written shortly after its completion, by Captain Milton Wolff, who had left the command of the machine-gun company of the Lincolns to serve on the brigade staff during the two months of the Teruel fighting, some of the more personal and intimate highlights of the battles were described:

"The first day of 1938 we got moving orders and went up to relieve the troops at Teruel. In passing, we learned from them that they had suffered more casualties from the extreme cold than from anything else. On the Heights of Celadas we suffered our first casualties of the action in the form of several severe cases of frostbite. Our main source of warmth was our supply of cognac, and we had to divide that between the water tanks of our machine-guns and ourselves. Who said Valley Forge?

"Here begins the story of one Bill Titus, lieutenant and commander of Company Three. I knew very little about him, but for some strange reason I watched him and was with him as much as I could be until the day he was killed. All I know of Bill was that he was from Buffalo, that he was very much American, that he knew more about plays and poetry than anyone I have ever met, that he was loved by the men he commanded, and also that he had more courage than I have seen anyone display in Spain. One night, Bill, Sid Levine and I took a stroll up to the enemy outpost outside the town of Celadas. It was all we could do to keep Bill from going into the town singlehanded and starting something.

"Then we went to Teruel. We Americans had a fairly easy time of it . . . except that Phil Detro was the target of an explosive bullet. He died later in a hospital. He had been a flyer when he left New York for Spain. A long, lanky Texan, a few inches taller than I, he was a Democrat who couldn't see the point of being a Democrat in a peaceful democracy when another democracy's life was being attacked. He had been in the National Guard for a number of years, and he had studied journalism at Rice and Missouri. He was always cool, always had the answers to the tough ones.

"Bill Titus went out into no-man's land to capture a white horse, a saddle, a bridle and a fancy riding crop complete, all of which he presented to Freddie Keller. Keller was spending his days finding food for the battalion and conversing with the nuns who had remained in the sanatorium for the mentally deranged in Teruel. A Catholic himself, Freddie struck up a real friendship with these hardworking nuns, and finally convinced them that they and their patients would be much safer in Barcelona. . . .

"Later we went north to a place called Segura de los Baños. Segura, with its peasants whose livelihood depended on their sheep and pigs, peacefully carried on its civilian business, though right below the town which was on a hill lay the valley where there were trenches, barbed wire and machine-guns. Segura was a most peaceful gateway to hell, and one white night we marched through it, down into the valley, past the barbed wire, around the rear of the enemy's positions and laid siege to their hilly fortresses.

"It is here that the story of Bill Titus ends. With a grenade in each hand, he hurdled the enemy's barbed wire and met his death on their bayonets. We took two companies of Fascists and we stayed there in the snow while the Fascists bombed and shelled us incessantly until we were on the verge of cracking under the strain. We didn't crack—and we repulsed their furious counter-attacks. We had still to meet that pressure under which no man could stand up."

8

THE PRESSURE NO MAN CAN WITHSTAND

AT THE END OF FEBRUARY, AFTER TWO MONTHS OF ALMOST incessant fighting, the brigade moved back, away from the lines, to Hijar. The men were tired. Not only casualties, but the cold and the mud of the long campaign had sapped their strength. A thousand small ailments, which had been overlooked during the warmer months and in the excitement of the winter's actions, needed immediate attention. Old wounds, apparently healed, plagued many who had fought and slept in the damp and snow at Altas Celadas, who had not rested during the three-day assault at Segura de los Baños.

There were many who had been through most of the major campaigns of the war and who badly needed rest. Among them were some of the key officers of the brigade and the battalions. Within a few days six of the leading officers left. Lieutenant-Colonel Copic, brigade commander, was given thirty days' furlough, and he proceeded first to Barcelona and then to Madrid. Captain Lamb and Commissar Keller of the Lincoln Battalion went to Barcelona on similar leaves; Malcolm Dunbar, a young Englishman who had been commander of the brigade's anti-tank battery before becoming Chief of Operations for the brigade, accompanied them. Brigade Commissar Doran departed for Valencia to undergo an operation for a sinus infection which had been bothering him since the fall, and Captain Wolff went off to seek dental treatment at Benicasim, the large hospital center on the Mediterranean coast north of Valencia.

These departures necessitated rapid changes in command, and fortunately there were sufficient well-trained and experienced men in the battalions to take over the posts. Since October, 1937, Major Johnson had been in charge of the training base, and under his guidance almost 2,000 new men—Americans, Canadians, Britons, Spanish—had been given expert instruction. He had also directed an officers' school to which veterans of previous battles and the most promising of the newcomers were sent. The flow of recruits to the brigade never ceased during the late fall and winter months; during Teruel and up to the middle of March more than 1,000 such men in all were to reach the brigade. They supplied the man power needed to replace the hundreds of wounded, sick and dead. Their presence enabled the Lincoln Battalion to continue to function as a battalion despite its constantly heavy losses.

THE PRESSURE NO MAN CAN WITHSTAND

After a few days in Hijar, the entire brigade was again moved closer to the front. The Lincolns were sent to the scene of their earlier Aragon conquest, Belchité; the English went to near-by Lecera and the MacPaps and Spanish to Letucs. The battalions spread out over the open fields during the day, when airplane raids were most likely to occur; at night they returned to the towns to sleep. In these positions the new commanding officers took over.

Major Merriman, as Chief of Staff, was the highest ranking officer left after Copic's departure. Doran's place as commissar was filled by young José María Sastré. Dave Reiss, of Paterson, New Jersey, who had led the machine-gun company through Teruel, succeeded Lamb as commander of the Lincoln Battalion, and Eric Parker, fresh from the training base where he had been commissar, assumed the same post in the battalion. Similar replacements were made, through necessity or expediency, in the companies, sections, platoons and squads. By the end of the first week of March the reorganization of the brigade and the battalions was complete. The Lincolns, 550 strong, again went through the paces of rest and reorganization. But this was to be the briefest rest it had ever experienced.

2

On March 9th the insurgents, concentrating all the man power they could gather from the north, from the center, and from the newly arrived Italian divisions, went into action along a wide front extending from Huesca to

THE LINCOLN BATTALION

Teruel. Ten divisions of men—including 50,000 Italians and 30,000 Moors—launched the offensive. Against the few and widely scattered artillery batteries of the Republic, Franco pitted his new Italian and German batteries, manned by 10,000 German and Italian army technicians. Eight hundred war planes, hurriedly dispatched to Franco after the Government forces had captured Teruel, took to the air in mass flights, opposed by only the sixty planes on the Loyalists' side. As the Fascist artillery pieces laid down their initial barrages, hundreds of swift Fiat tanks were lined up, and additional rebel divisions stood by their swift, motorized equipment, ready to swoop past any gap in the defending lines.

The Americans were still supposedly at rest when the break-through occurred. Their first indication that the front had been ruptured was the strange and thoroughly unexpected sight of men running back along the road and over the hills. Some of them were in army uniform, and when the Lincoln men stopped them, they spoke vaguely of a break-through. Somewhere, they said—they weren't sure just where—a gap had been created for the insurgents. Bitterly, they mentioned treachery within the Loyalist Army itself. It was not until days later that they learned that the insurgents had pierced the lines at La Puebla de Alberton, thirty kilometers northwest of Belchité.

Meanwhile the fleeing soldiers revealed that they were artillerymen, that the enemy had so thoroughly surprised them that they had been forced to destroy their guns, flee-

THE RETREATS

ing with the locks of the cannon they had not had time enough to blow up.

On the evening of March 9th Major Merriman ordered the Mackenzie-Papineau Battalion to proceed to Azuara, about nine kilometers west of Letucs. The Lincoln Battalion was to remain at Belchité, where it was to be joined by the British and Twenty-fourth Battalions.

The Americans were the first to go into action. The battalion proceeded several kilometers northwest of Belchité, where it established its lines in hilly country near a deserted monastery. Paul MacEachron, who had quit Oberlin College to volunteer in the International Brigade, led a group of six men to an outpost position almost a kilometer away. The Americans were given a sector to the left of the road leading to La Puebla de Alberton, and the British were given orders to take up positions on the Americans' right flank. But they did not arrive until daybreak of the following day. By that time, the enemy, moving swiftly, had advanced to within a few kilometers of the lines, and the entire sector was under rebel observation and fire. The British could not advance over the open plain to the Lincolns' flank under this fire, and the Americans were left to hold the first-line positions without help.

The enemy attack began with daylight. Its fury had not been equaled in any previous battle of the war. Planes swooped over the entire sector, dropping their loads of bombs, then diving to strafe the men in the lines. The artillery opened up simultaneously, sending the shells shrieking into the Lincolns' positions. Smaller caliber shells, fired from the tanks massed behind the insurgent positions, were deadly in their accuracy. In the first hours of the attack the battalion suffered its first major casualties: a single shell, exploding directly on the command post of the battalion, killed Dave Reiss and Eric Parker, commander and commissar, the latter witnessing his first action, and wounded five members of the staff, Frank Rogers, Albert Prago and Yale Stuart among them. Here at last was the beginning of the pressure no man could withstand.

With their flanks thoroughly exposed and with no possibility of aid arriving soon, the orders were quickly given to fall back beyond Belchité, and the men, still under savage fire from cannon, planes, tanks and machine-guns, retired past the town. The insurgents advanced relentlessly.

Twice the battalion attempted to reform its lines east of Belchité and both times the ferocity of the rebel onslaught smashed the attempts. On the evening of March 10th the battalion evacuated the outskirts of the town. Orders were given for the line of march, but the confusion was so great that the Americans split up and went off in two directions. In the confusion a platoon stumbled into a large enemy force; its members were captured and some of them killed. One group, with Major Merriman leading them, headed for Lecera; the other, with John Gates of the brigade commissariat among them, pushed on to Azaila. At every point of their march the men faced the same threat, the greatest disaster that can ever befall an infantry unit—the turned flank.

THE LINCOLN BATTALION

Wherever the Americans stopped to dig in, they discovered that the enemy had already swept beyond them. First they proceeded to Hijar, where the aerial bombardment was the most inhuman they had ever undergone; then they returned to Albalaté, where they tried to establish a line of defense. The other half of the battalion, which had moved toward Lecera with Merriman and most of the brigade staff, was still unheard from.

The MacPaps had in the meantime arrived at Azuara, to which they had been sent to reinforce two brigades of the marines. The front was already crumbling, but the Mac-Paps took up positions in the center of the line, flanked on either side by the marines. By 11 o'clock in the morning of March 10th the enemy had already reached the high hills beyond the town. From these hills they began a powerful attack, preceded by an intense artillery bombardment which was later followed by an airplane attack. As at Belchité, strafing followed the release of the aerial bombs. They were small hand aviation bombs, thrown out of the planes by the boxload. One American counted twenty-two dropping simultaneously from a single plane. The first casualties were suffered as the MacPaps scrambled into hastily constructed trenches. Their flanks began to give way under the violence of the attack, but they held their ground. During the heaviest moments of the bombardment Joe Gibbons, the Chicago steel worker who acted as quartermaster of the battalion, brought food up to the men who had eaten nothing since they had left Letucs. Milton Epstein, Company Three commissar, joined the first-aid men and brought back three of the wounded under fire. The ever-present Abe Smorodin sped back and forth from battalion HQ to the different companies, bearing messages. Archie Kessner, a young New Yorker who like Smorodin had been with the MacPaps since its first action, darted about under fire with instructions from the battalion commissar.

The battalion's funds and papers and other personal possessions had been left in one of three long wooden barracks a few hundred meters away. From their positions the men saw shells drop among them, splintering them. When they tried to retrieve some of the papers, they found them under crosspiles of wood, riddled, torn, useless. Wellman's military tunic had been blown three hundred meters away by the force of the explosion. The entire area was littered with the fragments of the battalion funds—all in paper pesetas. They were found in tiny bits, as if a maniac had torn them to shreds.

At 1 o'clock news arrived that the *marineros* on the left flank were retreating. Immediately Captain Niilo Makela, a Finnish-Canadian, and Lieutenant Jack Thomas were dispatched with a company of men to hold the open flank against the enemy. They succeeded, suffering only one casualty. But he was one of the best-loved men in the battalion, small, courageous Joe Kaplan, of the tanned face and sharp blue young eyes that made him appear ten years younger than his thirty years. His popularity could be gauged by the fact that the men paused in the heat of so violent an attack to think of him at all. Their only consolation was that his death had been instantaneous; the bullet had entered cleanly, between his eyes.

Azuara had to be evacuated, and the battalion took up positions on the steep cliffs back of the town. Meanwhile Joe Gibbons had been sent out to contact brigade headquarters, from which no word had been received since the previous night. He failed to reach HQ, but he did stop a car bearing General Walter, commander of the Thirty-fifth Division, and sped back to the battalion with orders to evacuate the site without delay. Gibbons returned at dawn of March 11th, after the men had been busily digging fortifications all night. The retreat began at daylight, twenty minutes after the order arrived. All were evacuated with the exception of two machine-gun crews, directed by Leo Gordon, commander of the machine-gun company and brother of Joe Gordon, who had fought at Jarama more than a year before. Leo Gordon had been wounded in the face by flying shrapnel splinters during the battles around Teruel, and after having been ordered to hospital (he had refused at first to leave), he had returned within a few weeks to his post. The two guns which he commanded had been placed on an open spot on a cliff which could not be reached in daylight; it was under direct enemy fire. The crews had supplies of water, food and ammunition enough to last for twenty-four hours. When the evacuation orders came through, Captain Makela and Commissar Wellman tried to reach them, but the entire face of the cliff was under enemy artillery and machine-gun fire.

"We shouted, fired our pistols," said Wellman, "trying to attract their attention, but we were unsuccessful. There was too much noise in the air for them to notice us. We watched two of the men try to crawl out along the ledge which formed the road on the side of the cliff, and saw them immediately cut down by enemy fire. We remained there for almost a half hour, but seeing it was hopeless, we left and rejoined the battalion. Probably all of them died, holding their positions to the very end. We know that those two crews held up the enemy advance at that spot between eight and twelve hours. From a point twelve kilometers away, we could see through our field glasses the overhead shrapnel bursting against that cliff. . . ."

At four in the afternoon the battalion reached Lecera, re-establishing contact with the brigade. There they first heard of the ordeal the Lincolns had undergone, and of the deaths of Reiss and Parker. Two hours later they took up positions as a reserve battalion of the division to cover the flank of the retreat. As night fell the Eleventh (German) and Thirteenth (Polish) Brigades began to march by in the direction of Albalaté. Then, very slowly, remnants of the American and English battalions of the Fifteenth Brigade filed by. None knew where the brigade staff could be found. Rumors were persistent that the entire staff had been surrounded and captured. First-hand reports were scarce; the air was thick with a jumble of wild and unchecked rumors, all of which told an exaggerated story, but a story which in its very wildness revealed the extent of the rebel advance.

The first hour of March 12th the MacPaps began their forced march to Albalaté. They followed the road, and after a few kilometers they spied a tall figure at the side of the road. "It was Merriman," said one of the Americans who met him there. "Tall, smiling Bob Merriman. When I saw him I felt so happy I almost forgot we were retreating. They had told us he was gone, missing, maybe dead, and when I approached him I felt as if I were approaching someone risen from the dead. I felt so good to see him I threw my arms around him and kissed him. He told me that Pete Hampkins, of the brigade staff, had been captured, together with some others. He himself had managed to get out by driving his car over an open field, breaking through the Fascist sentries; some others had escaped in an open car.

"There he was, as always, waiting on the road for us. Merriman never fell back if he knew there was still a single group of men unaccounted for."

The MacPaps reached Albalaté, thirty-three kilometers away, at dawn of March 12th, meeting the Lincoln Battalion in its lines outside the town. Al Kaufman, a New York seaman, and John Gates, of the brigade commissariat, had already been appointed commander and commissar, respectively, of the battalion. No sooner had the MacPaps arrived, however, than the enemy steam-roller swept on,

THE PRESSURE NO MAN CAN WITHSTAND

past the town, and again the Americans gathered their equipment and started on a forced march over the hills toward Hijar. Setting up new lines outside of Hijar, between that town and Alcañiz, they fought on the spot for two nights and a day. On the very first night Captain Wolff and Commissar Doran returned, and were with them when they left the spot to move on toward Alcañiz.

The trek over the mountains was grim and silent and exhausting. Between Hijar and Alcañiz the men completed their own reorganization. As they approached Alcañiz, however, they faced the same tragic fact which had kept them moving from all of their previous positions: the enemy, using the main highways, mounted on horse or riding in camions and tanks, had beaten them, and the town was already under their artillery fire. The Fascist cavalry had attacked the Americans at their last position outside of Hijar, but the Lincolns had still been strong enough to repulse them. The long retreat had been a nightmare to the men; there had been moments of panic, yet they had reorganized their ranks and were still ready to fight off any direct attack.

On the following morning the message came that their left flank, held by the Thirteenth Army Corps, had retreated. This was the army corps in which the greatest treachery of the action had occurred, whose officers, many of them members of the POUM, had disappeared, leaving the entire unit lost and disorganized and leaderless before the advancing insurgents. The entire corps was later dis-

THE LINCOLN BATTALION

solved, but then it was known only that it was again falling back. The Americans were therefore instructed to proceed toward Caspé. Again they filed out into the hills. No one was certain that Caspé was still in Loyalist hands, or that it would be by the time they arrived. But there was nothing else to do but push on, and attempt to find a place where they could make a solid stand—even if it turned out to be a last stand.

3

News of the tragic retreat filtered slowly back to the cities and towns distant from the front. Reports came in a dozen forms, in semi-official messages from single army units, in boastful claims by Quiepo de Llano over Radio Seville, in rumors carried by thousands of retreating men. The rumors, at first borne by the most panic-stricken of the deserters, were by far the most ominous, and in the face of them the official Republican war communiqué was for a brief period of days almost impotent. The Fascists had swept through to the sea at Tortosa, said the soldiers who drifted back to Barcelona and Valencia. In the south the rumor spread that the insurgent advance had cut communications with the French mainland in Northern Catalonia. A thousand variations on the theme of imminent doom, spread by enemy provocateurs as well as demoralized soldiers, challenged the final resources of courage in the people who had withstood hunger and the pounding of Franco and his Italo-German allies for almost two years.

THE PRESSURE NO MAN CAN WITHSTAND

And Franco confidently announced that victory would be his before the spring of the year was over.

Yet the people rallied. In Barcelona, Madrid and Valencia the newspapers printed glaring banner heads: *No Céder un Solo Palmo de Terreno al Enemigo!*—Do Not Yield an Inch of Ground to the Enemy! Others repeated the single simple word: Resist—or they called upon the civil population to help fortify the positions still held by the Republican troops. Time is on our side, the Loyalists repeated, day after day, and if we can simply resist and hold our lines today, we will yet have our chance to win the war. Dolores Ibarurri, the inspiring Asturian Communist member of the Cortes known throughout Spain as La Pasionaria, called on the soldiers of the Republic to fight to the death before yielding. She repeated her words which had rallied the men and women of Spain at the very outbreak of the rebellion: "It is better to die on your feet than live on your knees!"

And in the midst of the panic the people of Spain rallied. Thousands, too old to serve in the army, marched to the front to serve in the fortification battalions, their hands gripping the wooden handles of picks and shovels. Thousands more rushed to the front before they completed their training to take the places of the exhausted battalions in the path of the oncoming rebels. Men with half-healed wounds left their hospitals to rejoin their units at the front. All the available man power of Spain converged before the Fascist troops.

Major Johnson hurriedly began to wind up the affairs

of the American training base at Tarazona, and the soldiers in training prepared to travel to the north. The American hospitals at Tarancon and Villa Paz and Castillejo called for volunteers for the front. Patients, medical personnel, ambulance drivers—all responded. From Benicasim and Valencia and Murcia, all the hospital centers which housed the American wounded of the Teruel actions, emptied as the men sped toward the lines. Hundreds of men, many of them declared *inutiie*, began their journeys back to the brigade.

In the ten days between March 15th and March 25th, all of the remaining Fifteenth Brigade officers on furlough and sick leave rejoined their men—Commander Copic, Malcolm Dunbar, Leonard Lamb, Fred Keller and a score of others. Traveling with full equipment over the hills, with Luigi Gallo, Commissar Inspector of the International Brigades, accompanying them, avoiding the roads which might mean ambush and annihilation, the Americans entered Caspé at twilight of March 16th. For the first time since they had retreated from Belchité six days before, they had arrived before the enemy. It was a spirit-saving fact; the men had grown tired of the constant retreats, the tiring forced marches from place to place only to find the flanks already gone, the enemy beyond them. It was the first time in the history of the Americans in Spain that they had witnessed a panic of such proportions.

Wolff, when he rejoined the men on the plains outside Hijar, discovered they were weary of running away, anx-

THE PRESSURE NO MAN CAN WITHSTAND

ious to meet the enemy face to face. "I went up to a group of men," Wolff said, "and before I could ask them where battalion headquarters was I noticed that they were digging their foxholes in a most peculiar fashion. They were digging them in such a way that they would be able to take up positions in them facing not only the front and the flanks but the rear as well. They were so tired that they were determined to dig in there and stay put. But it wasn't to be. . . . We tramped sixty kilometers before we reached Caspé, but this time we got there first."

At Caspé an official order placed Dave Doran in command of the brigade and of the entire sector. The arrival had been not a moment too soon, for the insurgents were rapidly advancing upon the city. Doran at once set out to organize a line of defense, choosing the boldest tactic of all, an attack against the approaching enemy, which had already occupied the great surrounding heights.

The Americans formed their line on the lower heights around the outlying houses, facing the insurgents, but the first rebel attack from the dominating hills drove them back into the streets of the city. That night Doran decided to counter-attack, which was a recklessly bold move to make with men who had been through almost a week of hellish fire and constant retreat. The men were demoralized almost to the point of tears. "If we could only meet them face to face," they repeated, "if we could only fight them, head on, not this running, this being surrounded and flanked." There were by this time only a hundred men left in the

THE LINCOLN BATTALION

Lincoln Battalion, which had gone into Belchité with 550, and approximately the same number in each of the other three battalions. In all, counting brigade staffs and services, the entire Fifteenth Brigade comprised fewer than 500 officers and soldiers. Yet the plan to counter-attack proceeded. "Whatever the cost," Doran told one of his staff members, "we've got to stop them here. If help comes, good. If not, we will at least have given the rest of the army a chance to dig in behind us."

The men were sent out to attack the insurgents along two roads leading out of the town. Along one the Lincolns marched ahead, passing a crossroads, where they encountered enemy fire. A small patrol advanced beyond the crossroad in the direction of a large building, discovered that the fire was coming from its windows, and returned to report. As they answered the insurgents' volleys, they heard a tremendous volume of firing behind them, but in the heat of the fighting they didn't pause to investigate it.

Meanwhile the MacPaps and English were counter-attacking along another road, against the heights held by the enemy. With the few arms still left in their possession the men held Caspé for two full days, constantly attacking, being thrown back, and counter-attacking. Against them were arrayed the hundreds of tanks and planes and motorized artillery batteries which had followed them, sometimes preceded them, during the many days of retreat. Most of the Americans' equipment was gone, strewn in the path of their retreat. Bombed trucks and ambulances, abandoned artillery pieces, and the bodies of the dead marked the staggering line from Belchité to Caspé. Only a few had been strong enough to lug their heavy machine-guns all the way; of the men who still remained to fight, few had heavier arms than their rifles, and some had lost even these.

The Lincolns were slowly forced back into the city, where they soon discovered the evidence of fighting in the streets of the town itself. At the intersection of two streets they came across the mangled and flattened bodies of six of their comrades; a dozen others lay about, wounded and bleeding. Captain Wolff, who had been with a group of the men patrolling the streets of Caspé, told them what had occurred: "We were supposed to be accompanied by a few of our own tanks, but it was a very dark night and somehow we lost them. Suddenly, coming down a side street just inside the edge of the town, we heard tanks approaching. We supposed they were ours, but we were taking no chances. The men huddled in the shadows, and John Martinelli, Sam Grant and I went out to speak with the foremost tankist. As soon as I got close I knew I had made a mistake—it was a Fiat. We weren't sure about the next step —there were more tanks coming up behind this one. The machine-gunner of the tank opened his turret top and asked me, in very bad Spanish, 'From what part of Spain, you?' I told him, in my very best Spanish, 'Salamanca,' and then turned and shouted in English to the men to take cover. The tankist cursed in Italian and started to close the turret top, but not before Grant had had time to take a shot at him. I ducked and the tank opened fire. The range was a short one, and he succeeded in catching a group of Americans who had not heard my warning and still thought the tank was ours. The rest of us spread out and ran for cover. I looked back in time to see the tank run over the prostrate bodies of the wounded men."

Their morale shaken, the men were given the job first of patrolling the city, and then of guarding its outskirts against any sudden surprise attack. They spread out behind the railroad tracks, their guns leveled against the enemy which occupied positions several hundred meters on the other side of the tracks. At the same time, another group of Americans, Canadians and English attacked, under a full moon, a section of the rebel line on the hills southwest of the town. The few Loyalist tanks fired heavily, and under the barrage the men rushed furiously and impetuously forward, hurling hand-grenades, and succeeded in dislodging the rebels from their positions. Not for long—strength and materials were too unevenly matched. The next Fascist counter-attack drove them back into Caspé. But by then the Twelfth and Fourteenth Brigades—all fresh troops—had come up to reinforce the Loyalist lines. The fact that they too subsequently were hurled back was secondary. The important thing, later recognized even in a Nazi military journal published in Berlin, was that the stand made by the Fifteenth Brigade at Caspé did permit a momentary stabilization of the secondary lines and did enable other sec-

THE PRESSURE NO MAN CAN WITHSTAND

tions of the army to prepare for the next onslaught of the insurgents.

On March 18th, after three days of ferocious fighting, three days under constant, racking bombardment, the Lincolns left Caspé. The Lincolns had been ordered to stay outside the town until further orders, and Gates kept the men there for twelve full hours after even the two fresh brigades had retreated, waiting for the word that did not arrive. Finally, with the enemy almost upon them, they moved back. The Americans were the last to leave Caspé, just as they had been the last to move out of Belchité.

4

After a day of cross-country marching, over hills and past rivers, heading generally eastward, the Americans crossed the new Loyalist lines on the border of Catalonia, and found the rest of the brigade gathered at the town of Maella. In a few days they moved back to Batéa, and then, when the fighting became heavy along the new front, the entire brigade was sent for rest to the village of Corbera. No other unit on the southern sector had so heavily met the impact of the insurgent advance, no other had fought as staunchly as the Fifteenth Brigade at Caspé. The men were therefore relieved while the Twelfth and Fourteenth International Brigades moved up to the front lines.

Again, as at Teruel in January, Franco had broadcast the news of the complete annihilation of the Americans. During the long retreats the men had themselves seen their

THE LINCOLN BATTALION

numbers dwindle after each forced march, and feared that they were the sole survivors. At Maella, Batéa and Corbera, however, they discovered that comparatively few of the missing men had been killed. A number had been captured. Of the fate of Dave Reiss and Eric Parker, or of Paul Mac-Eachron and Jack Corrigan and the others who had held the farthest outpost at Belchité, there was little doubt. But many of the other missing men soon turned up. In the confusion of the first days of the retreat, when the battalion had itself been divided and mixed with other units, they had gone off with different battalions in other brigades, fighting rear-guard actions similar to those the Americans engaged in, all the way back. Others, lost in small groups, had made their way back to Tarragona and other coastal cities; a number had even reached Barcelona. While they rested, the lists of hospitalized Americans reached them, and they discovered scores of others were alive. Losses had been heavy, but not as great as the band of less than a hundred which had retreated from Caspé had feared. Once in Catalonia, the last large group of recruits from Tarazona arrived—165 Americans, Canadians and Englishmen. More than sixty of them were Americans.

The Americans returning from Barcelona brought with them the news of the most horrible attack on an open city that modern history had yet recorded—the three-day aerial bombardment of the Mediterranean port which had begun on the evening of March 15th, while the Americans were fighting at Caspé, and had continued with almost bi-hourly

THE PRESSURE NO MAN CAN WITHSTAND

attacks of terror from the skies until the afternoon of the 17th. Gigantic bombs had been dropped, not only in the waterfront areas and in the crowded streets of Barrio Chino and the maze of thickly populated sections diverging from the Ramblas, but in the central areas of the town as well. Huge aerial torpedoes had struck the wide Calle de Cortes, and the Paséo de Gracia. The bombs used on the second day had been so powerful that they had completely demolished the houses on both sides of a block on the Calle de Cortes. The dead alone had reached the staggering total of 3,000, with many bodies still buried under the debris. And the final squadron of planes had dropped not only bombs, but leaflets too, before they returned to the Italian aviation base at Mallorca. "If your Government does not surrender within two hours," the leaflets threatened, "we will return hour after hour until we will have completely demolished Barcelona."

While the Americans rested at Corbera the second phase of the rebel offensive began in the north, with the insurgents sweeping the thinly held Loyalist lines back from Huesca and Saragossa to the shores of the Segré River, a stream which flowed into the Ebro. They were stopped at Lerida by the veteran Forty-sixth Division, the Campesinos, who duplicated and bettered the feat of the Americans at Caspé by counter-attacking and stopping the insurgents cold.

The brigade rested for only two weeks, at a period when the enemy continued to whittle away at the defending lines. The retreats of the early part of the month were the key to the military situation. Everyone understood that the stand-by orders might arrive at any minute.

During the two weeks at Corbera the Lincoln Battalion trained under the leadership of Captain Wolff, who assumed command for the first time, and of John Gates. The rest period, short as it was, accomplished several improvements. The men were refreshed, and their anger at the drubbing inflicted on them in the retreats began to reveal a bit more of humor and less of haunted feeling of the long running marches. They were ready to go back into action, if only to repay the enemy for some of the running they had been forced to do. Secondly, they received a new shipment of arms, desperately needed, which helped greatly to restore the general morale; until then the men without guns had felt dejected and helpless. The days of the retreats still haunted them.

During this period a number of other brigades bore the full brunt of the enemy's renewed attacks, and soon they were in no condition to remain unsupported. They had resisted the renewed insurgent attacks east of Caspé, begun a few days after the Fifteenth had fallen back. The only news the Americans received was auditory; the intensity of the battle could be gauged by the subdued, distant sound of the booming of the guns.

The men were well aware of the enemy's plans. Gandesa appeared to be their new objective, and they were beginning to push down the two main highways which forked

THE PRESSURE NO MAN CAN WITHSTAND

into the single road leading into the hub of Gandesa and then outward toward Villalba de los Arcos, Mora de Ebro and Tortosa. In the period of disorganization following the retreat, the Republicans were left with very few forces to carry on an adequate defense. What the Republic was attempting to do, and what it did in reality, was to parry the enemy thrusts with its shock forces in head-on battle. The brigades defending Caspé moved back slowly under the terrific pressure of the weight of men and material and their own weakness and fatigue engendered by the continuous action since the disasters following Teruel. They were now defending the lines from the secret fortifications constructed by the Catalonians, fortifications which had never been marked on the military maps nor mentioned in the dispatches to the distressed Republican forces in the area. In addition, the increasing number of troops in the enemy concentrations brought new threats to the defending lines, which were thin and scattered.

The insurgents again pursued the tactic which they had successfully employed in the previous actions. Converging columns were dispatched toward a central strategic point, in this case Gandesa. If one of the attacking columns were held up by any Loyalist concentration of men and effort, it could be almost certain that another column would break through, accomplishing in this way the encirclement of the Republicans and, if the latter were lucky, their withdrawal. It was a case in which the Republic simply had not enough men or heavy arms or planes needed to cover all points of danger.

As the rebel attacks began to bend the defending lines the Fifteenth Brigade received orders to move, and on March 30th the battalions filed out of Corbera, through Gandesa and up the long road to the fork which led to Calaceite in the south and Batéa in the north. The brigade was then split up to cover an unusually wide sector. The MacPaps and English proceeded toward Calaceite while the Lincolns went beyond Batéa to help defend the road from two tributaries converging on it from Caspé and Nonaspé. The Americans' new positions were situated in an arc several kilometers inside the angle formed by the roads to both of these towns. The Eleventh Brigade, in action before the Americans, had placed its two remaining battalions at strategic points. One was defending the Caspé road and the terrain to the left. The other, the Edgar André Battalion, established lines in defense of the other road winding in from Nonaspé, which contained a concentration of rebel troops for the enemy flank on that front. The Lincolns were in the hills between, loosely connecting the gap between the scattered battalions of the Eleventh Brigade. This sort of defense left much to be desired, for a kilometer and a half of undefended hills lay between the extreme left outpost of the Lincolns and the battalion of the Eleventh Brigade. To the Americans' right, another two kilometers of wooded hills were a possible entry point for the enemy as far as the road itself,

THE PRESSURE NO MAN CAN WITHSTAND

where the Edgar Andrés, with a total strength of only eighty men and a few officers, anchored the Lincolns' flank. The one reserve company of the American battalion was used for patrol duty in the hills and forests to the right of the Nonaspé-Batéa road.

The Lincolns marched into position the morning following their departure from Corbera. After occupying the defensive points marked by the brigade staff, they pushed on a kilometer ahead in a rapidly organized attack to dislodge a swarming contingent of Fascists on the hills to the north. The small attack as a maneuver was successful. Not only did the Lincolns push their lines forward to better defensive positions (not marked on the superponibles, which were the only maps received from the brigade) but they inflicted heavy casualties on the enemy, which was caught unorganized and unprepared for battle. The remainder of the afternoon was spent in checking the maneuvers of the Fascists, who attempted to infiltrate around the Americans' right flank to occupy the hills between the Lincolns and the Edgar Andrés. By nightfall the battalion was digging in at the crests of its newly occupied hills, little dreaming that the Fascist break-through had already occurred, and that the next few days would witness the swiftest and most confusing action of the war, an action in which three-quarters of the soldiers in the brigade were to be lost, captured and killed before the remnants could fight their way back to safety on the other side of the Ebro River.

Reporting to brigade HQ on the second night, brigade

THE LINCOLN BATTALION

and battalion officers received the staggering news that the attacking forces from Alcañiz had smashed through the Republican defenses in the Calaceite sector. The British had been caught in the midst of the sweeping columns; while still in marching formation and unprepared, they had walked into a Fascist tank park and had become the mass targets for point-blank fire from a company of Italian whippets. Walter Tapsell, British commissar, and Frank Ryan, the Irish leader, were captured here. Captain Dunbar, twice wounded, barely escaped. The route of communications was in view of the insurgents, since the battle was ranging a short distance away from the Caspé-Alcañiz fork, and the road itself was under intense artillery fire. Though none of the Americans was fully aware of the extent of the break-through, the Lincoln Battalion was already completely encircled.

The divisional sector had been divided in two: Copic, Merriman and Dunbar were with that section of the brigade around Calaceite, and Doran was in charge of the Batéa sector, with the Eleventh Brigade and the Lincoln Battalion under his command. Leonard Lamb, Fred Keller and two privates on the brigade commissariat, Joe Brandt and Bill Ellis, remained with Doran.

On the morning of April 1st, Major Merriman rode through the battle around the fork in the Gandesa road in an armored car, bringing word to the Lincolns that they were to withdraw without delay. The new positions they were to occupy were tentatively set for defense of the main

Gandesa road. Joe Brandt was sent to contact the Lincolns to inform them of the order while Captain Lamb left for the Edgar Andrés to remain with them until their men were evacuated. Communications were immediately established between the battalions in the line. The Thaelmann and its companion battalions in the Eleventh Brigade were to pull out first, to be followed by the Americans and, finally, the Edgar Andrés.

No sooner had Lamb reached the Edgar Andrés with the original order than a division dispatch rider brought fresh and more menacing information: the Gandesa fork had already been taken by the enemy. The men were to retreat through Batéa to Villalba de los Arcos and establish contact with the other units near Gandesa itself. Meanwhile the withdrawal operations were going slowly. The battalions on the extreme left were delayed because some light artillery pieces had to be moved out under their protection. Toward afternoon additional information arrived. Batéa was no longer safe; enemy patrols were already in town, and the men were to march to Fifteenth Brigade HQ and from there set out across the hills to Villalba.

As evening fell and the first three battalions were well on their way, the Edgar Andrés pulled out of line, only to learn at the last moment that Villalba was in the hands of the enemy, whose tanks and motorized columns had already pushed around to the entire defending sector's rear. Roads were no longer safe, and the methods of retreat so bitterly learned in the early days of the month—over the hills like a roving band of guerrillas—was the best, if not the only guarantee of survival.

Wearily, the same night, the Lincolns began their long march through what was already enemy territory. The men were silent and tired. A strong advance guard of one company, with Bill Ellis as the brigade representative, set out to feel the way in the general direction of captured Villalba. But contact was lost at the very beginning, and a new advance guard had to be formed.

The battalion skirted Batéa, running the gauntlet of a night artillery barrage on its edge, marching throughout the cool hours intact. At dawn they reached the heights, the fertile hills overlooking Gandesa. With the battalion were Major Merriman, Dave Doran, Fred Keller and Lamb.

With motorized equipment the Fascists had advanced rapidly. From their vantage point the Americans could see their troop concentrations, camions, tanks and ambulances at the western gate of the town. From the northeast, troops were marching from Corbera. Their motorized columns had swept through Villalba de los Arcos and had taken Corbera during the night. The road from Villalba to Gandesa, a kilometer to the Americans' left, was filled with enemy concentrations pouring down from the north.

That Gandesa was still partly occupied by Republican forces was apparent, for intermittent fire played between the town and the forces surrounding it on three sides. The battalion officers believed that the Tortosa road, leading southeast, was still open. They could see the bursts from

THE PRESSURE NO MAN CAN WITHSTAND

the enemy artillery attempting to stop communications. The Americans' only salvation then appeared to be in breaking through from behind the ring of besieging troops to gain entrance to the town and join the defending forces. They watched the Fascist tanks, artillery and truckloads of troops rolling into the outskirts of the town, and then the decision—to attack and cut their way through—was made.

The attack got under way at 10 o'clock in the morning. The Americans swept forward in a broad front. One company advanced on the right flank, engaged the enemy in running combat and melted toward the town. The commander and commissar, Melvin Offsink and Irving Keith, were killed, and Fred Keller was wounded.

The remainder of the men, center and left flank, were stopped dead by batteries of machine-guns on all sides. The battalion had been observed in movement and the enemy was prepared. Fortunately they themselves had launched the attack and taken the initiative. Given a little more time the enemy, in an organized attempt, would have made their plight far more hopeless. The Americans retired section by section to a small hill farther north, where they hoped to wait until nightfall, where they hoped, too, that the enemy, busy as it was besieging the town, would not again attack. They planned, under cover of darkness, to make their way across the stretch of road between Corbera and Gandesa, to the highway leading to Tortosa.

At 6 o'clock that evening a troop of insurgent cavalry bearing banners charged the Lincolns' position. What was left of the battalion after the losses of the day opened a concentrated fire. There were still some machine-guns left, and it took no more than a few minutes to convince the attackers that their charge was futile. The Americans' only chance then was to hold tight until darkness and then to make their break to the northeast in the direction of the Ebro River.

The minutes between the setting of the sun and the coming of darkness were the longest the men spent that day. The enemy artillery opened up against their hill, but before they could get the range the sudden Spanish dusk fell, and the men eased off the hill in single file, making their way silently through the enemy troops, across the Villalba road and up the heights to the west of Corbera. They avoided those hills where the bonfires flared. There were many of them, all indicating insurgent troop encampments. "It would be useless," Captain Wolff said later, "to describe my feelings or the feelings of the men as we made our way through the dark in hostile, unknown territory. . . . But this I believe: that there wasn't a man who made that trip who didn't feel death walking by his side."

Toward midnight they approached Corbera. The groves which the Americans themselves had occupied a few days before were filled with enemy soldiers. As the men crossed the vineyards in darkness they could hear the stirrings, coughs, snores and whispered conversations of the Fascist troops. By that time the ranks of the Americans were sadly thinned out. In the scramble to cross the Villalba road in

ERNEST HEMINGWAY TALKS WITH HUGH SLATER AND
MATTHEW MATTISON (LEFT) OUTSIDE HQ

A BATH IN AN IRRIGATION DITCH

A DETAIL AT REST

THE PRESSURE NO MAN CAN WITHSTAND

small groups, and scaling the cliff on the opposite side, contact was completely lost. Numbers of men found themselves wandering, thoroughly out of touch with the vanguard. The machine-gun company was one of these groups. John Gates and George Watt, who had been wounded at Fuentes de Ebro six months before, led the largest, composed of 150 men. When the road was crossed Doran, Merriman, Lamb, Wolff, Fred Keller, Joe Brandt and a Chicagoan named Ivan were together.

A group of about thirty-five men approached Corbera. Ivan was in the lead, followed by Lamb and Brandt, with Merriman and Doran following. The other soldiers were lined up behind. What happened was so sudden and startling that few of the survivors' stories afterward jibed. Unwittingly they marched into a force of German and Spanish troops. Ivan was challenged by a terrified guard, who yelled, *"Cabo de Guardia, Cabo de Guardia! Rojos! Rojos!"* (Corporal of the guard, corporal of the guard! Reds! Reds!) in a weird, hysterical voice. He fumbled with the bolt of his rifle and then fired into the group, which broke, running to the right. Ivan and Brandt ran ahead. Lamb called out to Merriman, "I'm cutting directly across!" There was a steep embankment about twenty feet in height down which Lamb, followed by two other Americans, slid; then all three made a mad break for the hill opposite. Merriman and Doran took a different direction, rushing, whether they knew it or not, toward the insurgents. Brandt and Ivan heard a series of shots ring out of the darkness into which the two highest-ranking Americans of the brigade had disappeared. Then finally the order: "*Manos Arriba!*"—hands up! That was the last ever seen of them.

5

The men were now hopelessly scattered. Singly and in small groups they clambered up and down the hills on the last long stretch toward the river. Enemy sentries were everywhere. From Belchité to Caspé the Americans had marched together over long exhausting distances. This time they could not afford to waste their time in walking. They rushed on, scaled cliffs, dropped down steep terraces, hid in shrubbery when the enemy was near, broke into sprints across open valleys. The blood pounded in them, they gasped, dodged, ran. Many, stopping to rest for a moment, sank to the ground and whispered, "I can't go on, I can't go on, even if they kill me, I can't keep it up any longer." One American, a thin, wiry seaman who had fought in every battle since Quinto, went mad; his companions were forced to leave him, raving and unmanageable, as an enemy force advanced on them from an adjacent hill. Lou Cohen, a New York office worker who had been in the group surprised by the Italian tanks at Caspé, fell back from his group as they struggled up a series of stone terraces. He was not seen again. The others plodded on, hopelessly, but still forcing their last reserves of strength and nerve to keep their feet moving, automatically.

THE PRESSURE NO MAN CAN WITHSTAND

Remnants of the British Battalion, fleeing after the enemy tanks had ambushed them at Calaceite, made their way to the road running southward from Gandesa to Tortosa. There a small group of Canadians, Americans and Englishmen, led by the wounded Brigade Chief of Operations, Malcolm Dunbar, made a stand similar to that which Doran had led at Caspé. The entire group, which included some French, German and Spanish volunteers, first entered Gandesa, but were driven out by overwhelming fire. From there, with the Canadians and Americans headed by Sol Rose, Henry Mack and Leonard Levinson, who became adjutant commander of the MacPaps during the retreat, the group, numbering 200 in all, took up positions on a hill dominating the roads leading east to Mora de Ebro and south to Tortosa. A few light machine-guns, rifles and hand-grenades made up the complete complement of arms, but with these the 200 men held up the enemy for an entire day while the men behind them slowly retreated. Long trains of enemy supplies were stalled on the road while the small group held the strategic height. Planes and artillery rained bombs and shells upon them, tanks advanced against them but were turned back, a cavalry detachment sent against them was decimated by the fire of their last cartridge-pans. Only at nightfall, after holding up the enemy advance an entire day, did they fall back, scatter and head for the river.

A group of nine Americans and six Canadian members of the Mackenzie-Papineau Battalion formed a scouting party, led by Carl Geiser, who had become commissar of the battalion when Saul Wellman had been sent away on sick-leave after reaching Batéa, and headed east through the hills to locate the enemy. Making their way through a valley, the men came across a large group of men lying about on the side of a hill a few hundred meters away. They looked like fellow soldiers of the Fifteenth Brigade, and they became reasonably sure that they had contacted their own unit when an officer ambled down the hill toward them, speaking in English. While his men waited behind, Geiser approached the officer. The usual questions were asked—"What brigade? What part of Spain?" But Geiser did not answer. As the two men drew close to each other, Geiser looked at the officer's tunic, and realized he was facing the enemy. Just above the officer's breast was an emblem with the words "23rd of March." That was the name of one of the Italian regular army divisions in Spain. Geiser looked up, past the officer's shoulder, to the hill where the Italians were still lying about. They had not changed position. But this time he saw the muzzles of four machine-guns leveled against his group from strategic spots. "You see," said the Italian officer, speaking suavely, almost gently, in a low voice, "you had better surrender." There was nothing else to be done. "You are fortunate," explained the officer as they marched back for several kilometers, "you are fortunate that you have fallen into our hands, not the Moors or the Tercio." Yet when they arrived at the first town all sixteen were lined up against a wall. A firing squad hovered around, not many paces away. A priest walked back and forth before them, his Bible open in his hands, and a doctor whose Red Cross band glared violently in the intense sunlight stood by, fingering his stethoscope. The Fascist officers asked each of the men a number of questions: "What brought you to Spain?" "What nationality are you?" "What are your politics?" "What is the strength of your brigade? How many effectives still in action? How many machine-guns? Other arms?" Although the captured men were not permitted to speak to one another, they answered all questions alike. They were Americans—or Canadians. Politics? Anti-Fascist. Volunteered to fight in Spain to preserve its democratic government. As for the brigade's strength and arms, each insisted that, since he was not an officer, but merely a soldier in this or that squad and platoon, he knew nothing about them. For a terrifying twenty minutes they answered these questions, their backs against the firing wall. Then, because, as they afterward learned, the information asked of them had already been supplied by a Portuguese informant who had deserted the MacPaps the day before, and because international prisoners were then being taken alive to be used in exchange for Italian and German prisoners in the Republic's hands, they were sent back, through Alcañiz and Saragossa, to the concentration camp at San Pedro de Cardenas, sixteen kilometers east of Franco's capital at Burgos.

Those who escaped death and capture during the rout

did so by the merest of margins. A group of Lincoln men, including tall and rangy Luke Hinman, Alvah Bessie, a novelist, and Herman Tabb—both of the latter had reached the battalion after the withdrawal from Caspé—fled rapidly through the hills past Gandesa, paced by Hinman. Once they entered the camp of an Italian unit, the men asleep on the earth and the officers in pup-tents. There was no other way than to proceed rapidly and silently through the enemy encampment. Bessie stumbled against a prostrate body and was sleepily cursed in Spanish. Sentries discovered them as they were leaving the encampment, spread the alarm, but by that time the men were clambering up the terraces of a near-by hill. They reached Mora de Ebro, still in Loyalist hands, late in the afternoon of April 2nd and crossed the bridge to Mora la Nueva a few minutes before the Republican troops dynamited it to stop the enemy advance at the river.

A group of Americans, Canadians and English in the communications corps of the Fifteenth Brigade, still lugging their heavy spools of telephone wire on their backs, ran into a company of the insurgents. They were about to ask the usual question—"What brigade?"—when they heard one of the soldiers mutter, "They look like Republicans." The spot was a tough one, but one of the Canadians saved the situation and the lives of the entire group. He approached a Fascist sergeant and asked for a light. When asked to name his unit he replied *"Transmissiones,"* casually pointing to his equipment. The sergeant seemed satis-

THE PRESSURE NO MAN CAN WITHSTAND

fied. In the darkness the communications men mingled with the Fascists, sitting down among them. And when the company moved off, they followed behind, lagging, pantomiming the laying of wire. When the last of the men before them disappeared behind a bend in the road, the communications men hurriedly took to the open country and melted away into the darkness before their absence could be noticed. Another communications group, meeting a battalion of the enemy, fell into step behind them and followed them several kilometers along a road, knowing they were headed in the direction of the Americans' retreat. When the battalion marched past a fork in the road, the group swung down the opposite lane and made their way to safety.

Captain Wolff, after reaching the other side of the Villalba road, found himself alone. "I made an effort to find some of the other men," he says, "but met with no success. I dropped off what I had taken to be a three-foot-high terrace. It turned out to be a drop of some fifteen feet, and when I hit the earth I knew I was alone. For four days I watched Italian legions marching along Catalonian highways, accompanied as always by their scores of artillery pieces and tanks, and in the air by their planes. As I lay concealed in the fields one afternoon near a town (I traveled only by night) I watched Moorish troops seeking quarters in that town. At first I didn't connect them with the women's screams and scattered shots that I heard. But then it dawned upon me—a picture of what must be taking place in those Spanish houses as the Moors broke in.

"I got what little food I could from the friendly Spanish peasants, who shook their heads in bitter sorrow as their women-folk sobbed softly by their sides. I received information from them, and they in turn inquired about their son's fate in this or that military unit of the Government forces. They expressed doubts about my being able to swim the river. The enemy had opened the dams farther up and the river was in flood. The peasants asked me to stay until the river became more navigable. On the fourth night I swam the river near Cherta, and two days later I joined what was left of my battalion—thirty Americans and as many Spaniards."

Captain Lamb, after breaking away from the spot near Corbera where Merriman and Doran had rushed into ambush, managed to push past the guards on the hill ahead. With the two soldiers at his heels, he made for the next height. The sound of confused conversations in pidgin-Spanish was audible all around. On the new height the three were again challenged. "I cautioned the soldiers to drop down, but with the naïve trust of new men—they had reached the battalion only a few weeks before, and this was their first action—they wanted to see if the sentries were 'friends.' Despite my warning they walked to the top under the order of *Manos arriba*. That left me alone to continue my wanderings. I read the North Star as conscientiously as I had ever read a shirt for lice. Afterward I headed in the

THE PRESSURE NO MAN CAN WITHSTAND

direction of the river. For four days I traveled, sleeping in the hills, fed sometimes by friendly peasants; and at other times I ate the berries and the still-green almonds on the trees." Finally he reached the river, and a new problem faced him. He couldn't swim. For hours he walked up and down the bank. Late that night he tried to cross by crawling along the twisted steel girders of a dynamited bridge. Halfway across, his pistol swung against the steel, and the clatter echoed loudly across both sides of the river. A few machine-gun bursts were fired from the western side. He lay still, breathing heavily, not daring to move, caught between the enemy and his own side. Later, when the moon dimmed, he attempted again to crawl forward. After a few more yards he reached the break in the steel skeleton of the bridge. From the shore it had seemed to be only a few feet wide, but now he saw the break was several yards. The flood-waters rushed by below him. Silently he made his way back to the enemy shore. The next morning he decided he had to risk everything to make the crossing. Spotting several figures on the other side, he shouted to them, asking for a boat. They told him to continue up the shore. There he found a group of Spanish guerrilla fighters ferrying men across in small rowboats. He crossed the river near the village of Garcia and rejoined the battalion a few hours after Wolff had arrived.

Fred Keller received a bullet in his left hip in the fighting near Gandesa, but the powerful, chunky former commissar of the Lincolns carried on. He was with Wolff after they made the dash across the road, but though he heard him shouting later, he did not see him again. With sixteen men about him, he came head-on against a large rebel force, marching along the road with banners flying and band playing. They felt capture was certain. But the troops did not pause, and they continued across the hills toward the town of Fatarella, where from the heights outside the town they spied a great column of cavalry cantering by. One part of the group, led by Al Kaufman, the sergeant who had commanded the Lincolns for a short while betwen Albalaté and Caspé, was caught by a section of this cavalry column. The men scattered in an orchard, as the horsemen followed them. "It was like a pig-sticking contest," said Keller, who witnessed the bloody scene. Kaufman and the others, outnumbered and separated, were sabered as they ran.

That night Keller and his group hid and slept in a cave. The next morning they continued eastward, reaching the river bank between Asco and Flix. While the men hesitated to enter the cold and swift current, Keller, fully clothed, swam to the opposite shore to show them it could be done. Then, leaving his clothes behind, he swam back to rejoin the men. He wanted to be the last one to cross. As he stood, dripping, on the enemy side again, a Fascist cavalry patrol suddenly appeared and opened fire on the group. They broke and ran. A few entered the water but were riddled by automatic rifle fire as they began to swim.

THE PRESSURE NO MAN CAN WITHSTAND

The others were shot as they ran. Keller and a Canadian companion saw it was useless, and put up their hands.

Taken to Flix, they found themseves among many prisoners distributed in a number of houses under the watch of only a few guards. Keller waited his time. Late in the afternoon he saw his opportunity. Walking over to one of the few guards, he asked for something, just as he had done several times before. As the sentry turned around, he swung his fist solidly. The sentry went down, stunned, and the Canadian, grabbing his rifle, brought its butt down on the man's head. Together they broke through the door, past the houses and down toward the river. All night they wandered through the hills, aided by the darkness. Then, as the sun rose, they reached the river shore again. The glare of the rising sun was in Keller's eyes and he was sure it would make it easier for him to escape. Hesitating only a second, he plunged into the water. It was a long swim this time; there was a bend in the river at that point, the distance to cross was greater, and the wound was more painful now. But he made it. As he turned to shout to the Canadian on the other bank, a group of enemy guards appeared and shots rang out. The Canadian disappeared into the foliage. Keller was given clothes and sent to a hospital.

The hundred and fifty men led by John Gates and George Watt had safely passed through strongly held enemy hills when one man had voluntarily surrendered to keep the entire force from being discovered. As they proceeded toward the east, enemy planes and artillery spotted them, and they were bombed and, as Gates afterwards described it, "sniped at by Fascist artillery." Under the incessant pounding the force was separated into smaller groups. Watt went off with one band of men, Gates with another. As the latter approached the town of Pinell, he was challenged by an insurgent patrol. "Lewis Gayle and I," said Gates, "ducked behind a stone wall and moved off. Blackie Maprahlian, commander of the Third Company, ran off in another direction. His body was later washed ashore on the Ebro near Tortosa. Another one of the men walked straight toward the enemy patrol and was captured.

"Gayle and I reached the river. There were no boats, so we looked around the shore and entered a stone house near the river. As we entered we heard someone say, 'Who's that?' in English. I recognized Watt's voice. He and six other men had been sleeping there. All nine of us decided to cross the river before dawn. Only four of us made it—Watt, Joe Hecht, Gayle and myself. The other five either turned back or were drowned."

Naked and shivering, they made for the road and stopped a truck, from which they salvaged bits of clothes—a shirt, a coat and two pairs of ragged trousers. They were dressed in these odds and ends when they reached the remnants of the brigade.

Every man who regained the Loyalist shore had a similar tale, and everyone contributed a variation in the pattern of flight, hiding, hunger, fear and exhaustion. To recount each experience is impossible. But one last incident must be told.

THE PRESSURE NO MAN CAN WITHSTAND

It is the most heroic, the most self-sacrificing single deed of all. And its hero, fittingly enough, was a Spaniard—one of the Spanish commissars in the Lincoln Battalion—named Copernico, a diminutive figure only an inch or two over five feet in height.

Just past Gandesa, the men of the Lincoln Battalion led by Gates and Watt were making their way through a valley. It was dawn and the men could hardly be seen. Suddenly, from a near-by height, a voice shouted "Halt!" Immediately Copernico answered with the same word, "*Halto!*" The voice again called back, "Who are you?" Copernico asked the same question, "Who are *you?*"

"And for what seemed hours," said one of the soldiers in the group, "Copernico played with them while the men passed silently by, out of range. It was getting lighter and the last few men were filing past when the order came to approach. It was certain that they were Fascists on the hill, for one of them had just shouted in German, 'Eighth Division.' As slowly as possible, Copernico drew out his white handkerchief and walked up the hill. He had given himself up just to save the last few men, as he had saved the rest."

9
"WAITING, WAITING, WAITING..."

By April 12th the survivors knew that no more of their lost comrades would be returning to the brigade. The men of the four battalions rested in their dirt and sand dugouts and in the long and narrow ravines formed by the heavy rains of many seasons. Except for a strict rotating guard at the staff headquarters—a stone house on the crossroads east of Mora la Nueva—and an occasional scouting and observation detail along the river front, there was little to do. Yet the brigade was still in the lines; the losses of the retreat had been so enormous that even a unit as literally decimated as the Fifteenth Brigade had to remain in the lines. While some battalions occupied positions along the river front, the others rested several kilometers away. Only at night did the reserve battalions work; then they marched to the hills overlooking Mora la Nueva with picks and shovels, ready to dig.

In the fields adjacent to the road which, bisecting the main highway from Mora to the coast, led to the little vil-

"WAITING, WAITING, WAITING..."

lage of Darmos and beyond, the Lincoln Battalion—what was left of it—pitched camp. Aaron Lopoff, former adjutant to Blackie Maprahlian, was in command of the Americans during those first days when the men were staggering in singly, in pairs, dirty, half-naked, with bleeding feet. Lopoff, who had won his lieutenant's stripes in previous battles with the American battalion, was a silent and serious figure, and in those first wretched days the survivors were glad he was among them. Dark of face, with smoldering moody eyes, this twenty-four-year-old New Yorker gathered the straggling men around him in a loose but compelling discipline. He issued his orders quietly and firmly, understanding the state of mind that prevailed. Like each of them, he had lost his closest companion in the last desperate retreat.

Then Captain Wolff, the first high-ranking battalion officer, returned after eight days behind the enemy lines and took over command, with Lopoff as battalion adjutant. Later Captain Lamb returned and was given command of the First Company. George Watt was appointed commissar.

Company One consisted of one section of Americans, numbering fewer than forty men, and a Spanish section with about thirty-five others. And that, on April 12, was all that was left of the Lincoln Battalion.

Lieutenant Howard Goddard, the young Californian who had suffered several severe chest wounds during the Aragon offensive of the previous year, returned to become Lamb's adjutant. Two commissars, William Mayer for the

THE LINCOLN BATTALION

Americans and a young Madrileño for the Spaniards, completed the entire officer personnel of the battalion.

The scenes that occurred as the men returned were emotional to a degree never before known among the Americans. Each missing man who appeared was immediately surrounded, embraced, kissed. Two close companions, reunited after one of them had been given up as dead, would stand silently, hands clasped, each fearing to speak lest the words break the tension of pent-up fear and joy and shock, and end in tears. Many wept unashamedly. The affection and fellowship loosely spread over five hundred men became intense when concentrated on a few dozen. More than four hundred were gone, and those who remained were precious beyond any possession, beyond any friendship or love, even, across the Atlantic, three thousand miles away. This had happened before, during every battle, as the ranks had thinned, as men had fallen before bullets and shrapnel. And those who remained had crowded much into the brief exchanges of words in the midst of the continuing battle, eager to say as much as possible before the remaining faces, friendships, voices disappeared. But never before had the dead and the missing reached the terrifying total of the retreats. Never before had so few faces reappeared.

The exhausted men and those of the sick who were not seriously ill enough to be sent back to a hospital continued for almost a month to go through the motions—and not only the motions, but some of the work as well—of a battalion at full force. After a little more than a week in the

BARRICADES IN MADRID

SANDBAGS FOR MADRID TELEPHONE BUILDING

HERMAN KLEIN AND VAUGHN LOVE

A MACHINE GUN CREW MOUNTED ON A TROOP TRAIN

"WAITING, WAITING, WAITING . . ."

fields around Darmos or, when it rained, in an old meetinghall in the village itself, the Lincolns went off on their first real service since the retreats. At dusk the order to stand by was given. When darkness came the men lined up in one of the little village streets; and at midnight, under a bright full moon, the whispered order to march went from man to man along the length of the line.

Twelve kilometers they marched, southward to a deep and hidden valley a few kilometers from the river. Here, resting and training during the day and marching to the river shore to dig trenches in the loose sandy hills at night, the men spent their next two weeks. It was here too that several of the wounded and ill survivors of the retreats rejoined the battalion, among them Herman Tabb and Alvah Bessie. Here, too, John Murra, who had "deserted" from his rear-guard post in Albaceté, showed up. The other three battalions were spread out along the river shore from Garcia to Tivisa—one brigade holding a front-line trench sector fifteen kilometers in length. It was the river, of course, which made this thin scattering of man power possible; but there was also the fact that the enemy was still almost as tired and disorganized after its as yet unconsolidated advance as the Republican troops were worn out after their retreat. There was little firing from either side —occasionally a single nervous rifle crack, now and then an abrupt but soon silenced machine-gun burst. The valley in which the Lincolns were stationed lay directly below a steep ridge, in the trees of which was a Republican artillery battery that fired desultorily across the river. This occasionally drew answering artillery fire from the enemy, the shells on one day landing uncomfortably close to the Americans' positions. But for the greater part of the time it was quiet, and the men were grateful and took full advantage of the rest.

Toward the end of the month marching orders were again given, but again, instead of going into action, the small contingent made its way back to its former encampment in the fields near Darmos.

The three months which followed were as trying an ordeal as any under which the Americans had labored during all of their time in Spain. Not even fortification work was given to the men to relieve the tedium. Had the survivors foreseen the three deadly long months of inactivity at the time they had recrossed the river, they would have sighed long and contentedly in anticipation of the rest. Tired as they were at the time, they could not possibly have imagined how long and dull the coming months were to be. Only the long trench vigil of the original Lincoln Battalion at Jarama even approached this period in its feeling of endless, purposeless waiting and infinite boredom.. Yet the Americans at Jarama had always, at least, been within sight of the enemy trenches, always in the front lines.

No sooner had the Americans returned to Darmos than a large group of Spanish conscripts joined them. There were about four hundred and fifty in the group, most of them youngsters of eighteen, nineteen and twenty, many

"WAITING, WAITING, WAITING..."

with the faint fuzz of adolescence on their upper lips and chins. They were part of the huge new conscription in progress throughout Spain—Premier Negrin's great effort to enlist all the available men of his country in the fight against the limitless war material of the Fascists. They were part of Negrin's answer to the defeatists on the Republican side, who were frantically urging capitulation as the insurgent troops, stopped in the north at the shores of the Segré and Ebro Rivers, were continuing their push toward the province of Castellon, south of Catalonia, and the sea. To inspirit the hard-hit people Negrin issued his famous slogan: *"Resistir es Vencer!"* (To resist is to conquer.) In addition to the draft, he called for 100,000 volunteer soldiers and 50,000 fortification workers in Catalonia alone. In his dual post as Premier and Minister of National Defense, the latter taken from Prieto after the disasters of March and early April, he was to rally the army for one more last, great offensive and keep the people defiant and unbeaten for almost a year after Republican Spain's own appeasement clique had declared the war was lost. Yet, courageous and hopeful as he was, Negrin was a realist. In his communications to the General Staff of the army after the insurgents reached the sea on May 15th, he stressed the truth and the warning of La Pasionaria's words at the Spanish Communist Party's plenary sessions in Madrid: "The situation is grave. We cannot afford to lose another inch of ground."

Many of the young, new recruits who joined the decimated American battalion were from Valencia and Alicanté, on the southern Mediterranean coast. Others were Catalans, schoolboys and young farm and city workers. They arrived with huge packs—gaily colored blankets, small valises, innumerable changes of underclothes and socks, and carefully wrapped odds and ends of food prepared for them by fond if impractical parents. They delighted in speaking with the Americans—their interest in and admiration for all things *norteamericano* were endless and boundless. There was one, particularly—Hilario was his first name, nineteen years old and a Catalan—who delighted in singing outlandish renditions of American jazz. For a while he was battalion bugler, and whether he played his horn or sang, his tunes were invariably a combination of jazz and *flamenco*. He was an artist with his horn, and often he woke the men at dawn with *Minnie the Moocher*, and sometimes, at night he played *Star Dust* instead of Taps. He hated the army tunes; he loved what he called "hot jhozz." He was always asking questions about Benny Goodman (the way he pronounced it was Ghudeman), what was he like, how were his politics. "A great musician," one of the Americans told him. "I've heard him play a dozen times. Politics? I don't know exactly, but his quartet once played at a TAC concert to raise money for Spain, long ago, in the spring of 1937." Hilario's eyes would gleam with pride and professional solidarity: *"Un hombre muy simpatico,"* he would say, *"muy formidable*. After our victory, I will be the

"WAITING, WAITING, WAITING..."

Bennie Ghudeman of Spain." Hilario lived to be almost twenty years old.

The arrival of the young recruits finally gave the Americans something definite to do: the responsibility of training these young and raw Spanish and Catalan soldiers was theirs. They adopted the young *quintos* as brothers, they told them. Actually, despite the very slight differences in age, the relationship was more like that of fathers and sons. Murray Goldstein of Nebraska and Roy Sheehan of Ohio anchored a small tarpaulin against a small hazelnut tree over a wide leveled trench; their inseparable companion was Pedro, a small eighteen-year-old boy from Alicanté, who was being groomed for a post on the company staff. As "brothers," the three were supposed to mingle continually, the Americans acting as instructors for Pedro in military technique, and they in turn learning as much as possible from Pedro of his people, customs, language, traditions. Joseph Shenkir, a lanky red-headed lumber worker from Oregon, was made corporal of a light machine-gun squad. All the soldiers under his command were Spanish youngsters. They trained incessantly under this tall and unruffled veteran until there was not a single one among them who could not handle the new Czech Brenn automatic gun as effectively as his leader. He spent the siesta hours with them, reading and translating aloud the clippings from his native papers, which friends in Oregon sent to him; the Spaniards in turn read the Catalan and Castilian press to him. When Joe was killed, in the first few days of the Ebro offensive, his squad was inconsolable—he had been one of the few among the Americans who had learned enough Catalan to enable him to carry on protracted conversations with those among them who had been reared in the north, with those to whom the sharp clipped speech of Catalonia was more natural than the more melodic and vowel-softened syllables of the rest of Spain. All of this instruction, it should be noted, was "extra-curricular," voluntary and additional to the regular battalion and company maneuvers, arms practice and lectures.

With the arrival of the Spanish recruits and the gradual return, as the days went on, of other Americans—from hospitals, rest camps, units dissolved because of lack of materials (anti-aircraft and artillery batteries)—the battalion again began to assume normal contours and full fighting strength. Numerically, with five companies and more than 700 men among its effectives, it was a larger battalion than ever before. There was, however, one major difference: the new Lincoln Battalion, unlike its predecessors, was overwhelmingly Spanish. The ratio was now approximately three and a half to one. And the Americans quickened the pace of their job of training Spanish officers and men to take their own places after the vague and distant next battle which would undoubtedly claim its share of casualties among the leading personnel—Spanish officers and men to step into the shoes of the Americans when there would be no more Americans left in Spain.

With the unit at full strength, changes were again made

"WAITING, WAITING, WAITING..."

in the commands. Wolff and Watt remained commander and commissar. Lamb, as head of the First Shock Company, was automatically second-in-command of the battalion, and a Spanish commissar replaced Bill Mayer, who, as a veteran machine-gunner, was transferred to the Third Company to help in the military training of the young Spaniards. Aaron Lopoff was placed in command of the Second Infantry Company, with Nikolas Kurkuliotis, a Greek who spoke no English but fluent Spanish, as commissar. The Third Company was placed in charge of Teniente Abad Garcia, a small fighting-cock of a Spaniard, with Larry Lustgarten, an American, as commissar. Company Four was entirely Spanish in personnel and command, and the machine-gun company trained under Mike Pappas and Commissar David Drummond. Yale Stuart, Jarama veteran who had recovered from his wound of March 10th, returned to become chief of the headquarters company, and a Spaniard, transferred from another battalion, became Captain Wolff's adjutant.*

The first of May was a holiday for the men. Contests were held: infiltration, during which the young Spaniards covered the hundred-meter distance on all fours with a speed which in battle, Wolff hoped, might compensate for their inexperience, hand-grenade throwing, target shooting, a dozen additional events. The prizes were chocolates,

* I have identified by name only those of the Spanish members of the Lincoln Battalion who were killed in action. The others may still be alive, and to name them would be to expose them to the reprisals and the "merciful brutality" of the Franco regime.

cigarettes, pipes, tobacco and odd bits of wearing apparel taken from packages addressed to Americans who were either dead or missing. Citations for outstanding work during the last action were conferred on a number of men, among them Lewis Gayle, the battalion's first-aid man, and Dick Rusciano, who received the new rank of lieutenant. While the soldiers were out in the fields, two old friends showed up at battalion HQ, Herbert L. Matthews and Ernest Hemingway. Both, as always, came bearing cigarettes and a few precious books, and both were greeted as old friends whose very presence was more cheering than a hundred gifts; they personified, to the Americans in Spain, the best qualities of the distant, civilian world with which they were the Americans' most constant links. They, in turn, went off with renewed confidence, with stories of a battalion rebuilt to full power and spirit within a period of less than a month after one of the grimmest disasters of the war.

One afternoon, about a week after the May 1st fiesta, a young man in khaki, looking fresh and clean, showed up outside of battalion headquarters. He was immediately recognized by some of the men who had seen him among other newspaper correspondents a few days after the retreats. It was Jim Lardner, son of the famous American writer. He had trudged the mile or more from brigade headquarters to the battalion and arrived, neat and almost spotless in his new soldier's clothes, with a brand-new rucksack in which he carried, among some other articles, a French grammar,

"WAITING, WAITING, WAITING..."

a Spanish-English dictionary and grammar and a copy of *Red Star Over China*. It was just past midday, and in the clear sun some of the men were throwing a baseball outside the little stone hut which housed the battalion *estado mayor*. While he waited for Wolff to see him, he stood about, talking shyly with Yale Stuart, Martin Sullivan, Harry Fisher and a few others of the headquarters company.

As they talked Wolff's orderly brought out a scared rabbit that he had caught earlier in the day and delivered, with much relish, a neat rabbit punch. Everyone was used to this, and the jerky movements of the rabbit on the ground, its neck broken and blood oozing from its mouth and ears, went almost unnoticed. But Lardner went a shade paler and turned his eyes away. Stuart noticed this and quickened the conversation, but Lardner said little.

In the hut Wolff was informed of Lardner's arrival. He didn't answer. George Watt repeated the words, adding, "You know who he is, Ring Lardner's son." Wolff looked up for a moment, then shouted in the great, booming voice that he used when he was very pleased, or angry, or embarrassed: "Yeah, I know! What do you expect me to do about it?" Then, more softly: "Put him in Company Three." The message was quickly delivered to Lardner, who got his big pack together, walked off toward Abad's dirt cave, and was immediately assigned to his section, platoon and squad.

In the days that followed, Lardner's pack dwindled in

size to almost nothing. He kept only his Spanish-English dictionary and grammar; other reading material he borrowed from the men in his company, particularly from the two who became his closest friends, John Murra and Elman Service. Slowly he ripped his extra under-shorts to pieces; cloth-strips for the cleaning of his rifle were precious, and like everything else, scarce. He picked up the rifle studiously, as he had probably picked up his math books at Andover and Harvard; and he mastered it just as thoroughly. He learned how to handle the light machine-gun, went out on practice maneuvers and to the rifle-range with his company day after day during that long hot summer that reached its peak in the Ebro offensive. Shy and awkward and deliberate in speech and movement at first, he slowly relaxed, made friends among the men, and was soon completely accepted and liked by all who knew him. Despite his late arrival, he was in a way the prototype of the American volunteer in Spain. Hundreds of the men had been students and young professionals who, like Lardner, had carefully examined their own motives and impulses before they had discarded their civilian clothes to carry guns in defense of the Spanish Republic.

The fact that he had enlisted so late in the war, and that he met his death so soon after entering his first real front-line action made him both typical and unusual. There had been so many others who had died in the very first moments of battle, so many who, had they lived, would have joined the list of the men who rose to leadership and to al-

"WAITING, WAITING, WAITING..."

most legendary proportions. But they died, like Paul Sigel and John Lenthier and a hundred others, in their first advance.

Hundreds of other Americans provided the steady and unspectacular base of all the Lincolns' actions in Spain. They did their job quietly and well, were wounded in battle after battle, and always returned. They were the rank and file, the men whose very presence was the strengthening element in battle, the men, like Archie Kessner and Jerry Cook, who remained strong and predictable in their courage and steadiness throughout the long war. Men like Benjamin Goldstein, the young Philadelphia butcher-shop worker who wouldn't go to officers' training school. "My own mother couldn't make me go to school," he shouted when they wanted to send him off, away from the lines, "and if she couldn't, nobody can! I stick right here!" And Earl Steward, the small blond boy from Montana—or maybe it was Nevada; the facts are already growing dim in the memory—who would walk away when an off-color story was being told, but who fought through action after action till he dropped of fatigue during the retreats. That rank-and-file soldier without whom there would never have been a Lincoln Battalion, who remained a rank-and-file soldier whether he got his corporal's or sergeant's or lieutenant's chevrons, was somebody like tall Bob Collentine, of Milwaukee, or Lee Levick, both of whom died at Belchité in 1937. His name was every name on the Americans' rolls: Carl Cannon, Abe Osheroff, Jim Hill, Martin

THE LINCOLN BATTALION

Sramek, Tom Page, Herman Tabb, Bob Rogers, Don Thayer, Jack Penrod, Joe Bianca, Sam Spiller, Morris Taubman, Roy Sears, Norman Berkowitz, Jim Cody, Arthur Witt, Jack Shaffran, Nat Gross, Pat Roosevelt, Ruby Kaufman, Jules Deutsch, Tom Lloyd, Vaughn Love, and almost three thousand others.

2

Lardner had been with the battalion for less than two weeks when, in mid-May it moved again, this time on the road toward Lerida and Balaguer, along the Segré River, where a new Government attack was planned. The Lincolns arrived at a spot near Mollerusa, on the Lerida-Barcelona highway, not far west of the important junction of Tarrega, when the offensive, in which the Fifteenth Brigade was to have been used as a second echelon, was stopped dead during the first attempt to cross the river. For a week the men remained in huge open barns near Mollerusa, resting mostly and keeping out of sight of the enemy bombers which came over three to six times daily, dropping their loads on near-by territory, but never finding the huge concentration of troops below them.

To these barns came Vincent Sheean, then writing for the New York *Herald Tribune*, Joseph North of the *Daily Worker* and Leigh White, of Reuters. Sheean came not only to check on rumors of the offensive, which were circulating freely but vaguely in Barcelona, but also to deliver a pair of spectacles to Jim Lardner, whose other pair

"WAITING, WAITING, WAITING..."

had been smashed during a practice maneuver. The three correspondents spent part of a frolicsome afternoon in the Company One barn, emptying several canteens of sour wine, singing barroom ballads with the boys, talking and taking messages home for them. Just when Vincent Sheean was being introduced to Roy Sheehan, Captain Lamb's adjutant, Harry Hakam, the veteran soldier and communications corps man and jack-of-all-trades, offered the visitor a swig from a small canteen which he dug up from its hiding place deep in a straw pile.

"Here's something," Hakam said. "Have a swig."

"What is it?" asked Sheean. "Wine?"

"No," said Hakam. "You'll find out. Just take a sip of it."

Sheean brought the canteen to his nose.

"Doesn't smell like anything on earth," he said. "Thanks anyway."

The rest of the men crowded around Hakam, but he wouldn't offer the canteen any more. He was hurt. It was goat's milk, a kilo of which he had succeeded in buying at a near-by village by the simple expedient of courting the dairyman's daughter for two successive days and evenings. Oh, it really was love this time, said Harry, but, gee, you have to be practical. Sheean insisted he would have nothing to do with the canteen. Instead he said he wished Hemingway were there, "Professor Hemingstein with his six-quart whiskey flask." And after Sheean had left, Harry went around from barn to barn, making the rounds of all the headquarters, repeating, "Imagine, I offer the guy a drink of *milk* and he won't have none of it! Imagine, *milk*, *real* milk. And he turns it down!"

It never occurred to Harry Hakam, nor to dozens of others in the battalion, that what was a rare luxury to the half-starved soldiers and people of Spain was a commonplace to men who came from the world outside, where everything was plentiful, a commonplace to be accepted or rejected on the basis not of need or starvation for good food but simply of preference.

3

After this abortive offensive the entire brigade was returned to rest—real rest, not the usual reserve lines—at a spot in the little valley near Marsa. Two kilometers over the mountains was Falset, the ancient Catalan town where once a week the men took turns in visiting the local movie house to see films, some of them produced as recently as 1930.

Here, among the ripening vineyards and the still-green hazelnut and almond trees the men relaxed, falling into the easy routine of rest and training. Within a few weeks the earth was dotted with small, grave-like trenches, the single habitations of the soldiers, and with large lean-tos against the trees which could easily shelter five or six men apiece. Others dug in against the side of the terraces or against the hill itself, still others built huts which they covered with branches, layers of cloth and soil and leaves. On the earth

"WAITING, WAITING, WAITING..."

inside they spread pine needles, and made niches for candles in the rock and soil walls.

Here, too, newspapers—*periodicos murals*—blossomed forth, on trees, or terrace walls, or against the sides of the few stone huts in the fields. Anyone who wanted to could write articles for the papers. The chief artist and illustrator was a man named Manheim, a professional artist from the West Coast, who was in charge of layout and art-work for the battalion wall paper. James Lardner, now a squad leader and corporal, contributed one of the prize verses to the Company Three wall board when he registered his and the entire battalion's sorrow over the fact that the other three battalions had rated truck-transportation from Mollerusa to Marsa while the Lincolns, as usual, had been forced to march a good part of the distance. Using the marching-words "*oop au ay arro*" (a military corruption of the first four Spanish numerals, *uno, dos, tres, quatro*) and setting his words to the tune of "Tit-Willow," Lardner composed the following sorrowful but unbowed lyrics:

> *In the hills by the Ebro the Fifteenth Brigade*
> *Marched oop au and oop au ay arro*
> *And they kept right in step while their officers brayed*
> *Loudly "Oop au and oop au ay arro."*
> *Oh, the MacPaps and British and Spanish as well*
> *Get no practice in marching, it's easy to tell,*
> *And compared with the Lincolns they're lousy as hell,*
> *Singing "Oop au and oop au ay arro."*

THE LINCOLN BATTALION

*Yes, the Lincoln Battalion gets more than its share
Of oop au and oop au ay arro,
But because our morale is high none of us care,
Singing "Oop au and oop au ay arro."
Oh, we don't give a damn for a ride in a truck;
If the others get carried it's just their hard luck;
For as long as we're marching, we don't give a ....
Singing "Oop au and oop au ay arro."*

Life for the battalion settled into the dullness of training, siesta, training, eating and sleep. Each company, allotted a separate stretch of earth along the curling road, sank back into a dull and almost exclusive routine of its own. Only at varying intervals, when full battalion and brigade maneuvers were held, did all the men of the different companies mix and mingle. Once back at camp, however, the tiredness fell back upon them and ploddingly they went through the motions of their own little sections, platoons and squads.

Summer had arrived early to the hills and valleys of Southern Catalonia. The June days were scorchers; sometimes even the nights were hot. When the men climbed the steep hill above the hamlet in which Dr. Simon's medical unit was located, they could see the Mediterranean clear and vast and blue before them. Sometimes they imagined they could see the Balearic Islands beyond and, by turning half south, the broad flatness of the Ebro delta near Tortosa. But only a few climbed the hill. Most of the men preferred to lie back against the thin trunks of the hazelnut trees,

"WAITING, WAITING, WAITING..."

looking up toward the huge wooded hill surmounted by a great stone nipple of white cliff over whose summit the clouds broke and poured Niagara-like every evening; and on late afternoons the face of the rock glowed pink against the dropping sun.

In the valley below the hills the men plodded and sweated on. Occasional meetings and discussions punctuated the routine. To the young Spaniards, who were now beginning to look upon themselves as veterans, the most interesting were the small informal company lectures on the United States, on Abraham Lincoln and George Washington, who they were and why the Americans had named their own battalions after them. A new group of American volunteers joined the battalion at Marsa, the first group that had come to Spain for many months, the first Americans to join the battalion since Jim Lardner had showed up in May. It was a small group, perhaps six in all, but it was proof that interest in the United States in the Spanish war, although it had sagged for a time under the impact of Franco's huge territorial gains, was still very much alive. More astonishing to the men, however, was the return of seven Americans who had fought at Jarama and in later actions of 1937 and who had been invalided home. The seven were Joe Rehill, Bill Wheeler, Walter Kowalowski, Joe Cuban, Joe Gordon, Joe Cobert and Al Tanz. "It's O.K. for the rookies," many of the veterans said, "but *you* guys, you've been through it, you've been plugged, you know what it's like. What the hell did you have to come back for?"

Joe Rehill, writing in *The Volunteer for Liberty*, explained:

"I have been asked time and again 'What made you boys come back to Spain?' Some comrades, I am sure, must think that we had committed a crime and came back as fugitives from justice. I want to say that the reason was, and is, the desire to see Fascism defeated here, in Spain, before another country, possibly ours, becomes the next battlefield of Democracy versus Fascism.

"It is true," Rehill added, "that there are many veterans back in America today. A number of these have also tried to return, but unfortunately the doctors did not think them fit. In fact, some reached Paris, only to be rejected by the medical commission there."

About this time, news came drifting in from Barcelona, news heavily larded with exaggerated rumors, with vague tales about a new commission soon to be named by the League of Nations, a commission whose sole job it would be to repatriate the Americans remaining in Spain. And in the quiet and boredom of their prolonged training the Americans spent their days talking and their nights dreaming about the forthcoming evacuation. The news accounts in the Barcelona papers, which reached the camp daily, did little to dispel these rumors, little to factualize the sources and the possibilities of so complete a withdrawal. The commission, it seemed, would count heads, of volunteers in

"WAITING, WAITING, WAITING..."

Loyalist Spain's army, and of the "volunteers" on Franco's side. All that the Americans could do was to speculate, and this they did freely, although most of them admitted to themselves that they could expect little from the Non-Intervention Committee. Even if they had originally been innocent of any knowledge of international political intrigue (and in this respect most of them were wise beyond their years), by this time they surely understood that the notorious Non-Intervention Committee, but for which the war might speedily have been won by the Republic, would do nothing to bring about an equal withdrawal of all foreign fighters in Spain. They knew, too, that the foreigners on Franco's side were members of the regular armies and air corps of Italy and Germany, not volunteers, and that neither Hitler nor Mussolini, deeply sunk in the Spanish war, could permit their departure without jeopardizing the outcome of the war, without losing the political, economic and strategic control of Spain which had been the original cause of their huge troop and arms shipments.

What kept some of the Americans hoping against hope was their homesickness, their ever-plaguing memory of the retreats, and their feeling that they were no longer a large enough fighting force to play any decisive part in the future course of the war. Of the 2,800 Americans who had reached Spain, there were now fewer than 200 in the Lincoln Battalion, about fifty or sixty in the MacPaps, a dozen in the British and Spanish battalions and perhaps two dozen more on the brigade staff. In addition there were about

THE LINCOLN BATTALION

200 Americans in the transport, medical and other services, and about 150 scattered through Central Spain, cut off from Catalonia and the rest of the Internationals. In all, there were perhaps 750 Americans left; of the other 2,000, a large number had been repatriated, and the rest were wounded or dead.

Yet the men hoped, speculated, referred constantly to their Spanish-English dictionaries as they read the Barcelona papers—and the training went on. More, the tempo of the training was accelerated and maneuvers were systematized to a degree previously spoken about, but only spoken about. Much of it was directly attributable to the arrival of one man, an Asturian under whose guidance and leadership the Fifteenth Brigade staff was soon to achieve the most precise and competent military cohesion it had ever known.

Major José Antonio Valledor had been one of the leading active figures in the Asturian revolt of 1934. He was in prison under a death sentence passed by the Lerroux-Robles Government when the victory of the People's Front Government in the elections of 1936 set him free. Joining the army in Asturias, he fought as a soldier for many months, then became successively a battalion and then a brigade commander in the Army of the North. After the fall of the North he had hidden in the mountains and attempted to cross the border into France. Wounded twice by Fascist sentries, he was taken back to prison, where he escaped death by hiding his identity. After five months of heavy

"WAITING, WAITING, WAITING..."

labor he again escaped, made his way into France where he reported to the nearest Spanish consul, re-entered Spain and was assigned to the Army of the Ebro. Late in May, 1938, he succeeded Lt.-Col. Copic, who was leaving Spain, as commander of the Fifteenth Brigade.

Like most of the officers in the Republican army Valledor was a young man, not more than thirty-one. He and twenty-four-year-old John Gates at once formed a close friendship, the fiery Asturian and the sober young American immediately coming together to plan the increased efficiency of the brigade for the time, which they knew would be soon, when the Army of the Ebro would go into action again. Together they worked out long, overnight maneuvers for the entire brigade, while Gates turned his attention more actively to the job of dispelling any false ideas the Americans might have of imminent repatriation. He was tough and unbending in the process, but he felt that was the only way to end a state of mind which would impair the morale and fighting spirit of the brigade in the actions which were sure to come. He appeared at meetings of every battalion, speaking harshly and with bitterness about the Non-Intervention Committee, flaying the men who put any hope or trust in its doings. "When the time comes for us to go, it will be on the decision of the Spanish Government, not through any plans of those whose only hope and deeds are, and have always been, to weaken the Republic. I'll go home myself when the Spanish Government tells me to; until then I'll stay on and fight." Many of

THE LINCOLN BATTALION

the men resented the sharpness of his words, especially when he called the most incorrigible of the repatriation speculators cowards, but none of them could deny that he, as much as any American in Spain, had the right to utter them. His record was among the best of any volunteer in the entire army. Originally elected by the men of his group as commissar for the American section, he had been on the Cordoba front for seven solid months, rising successively to company commissar, then battalion and finally adjutant brigade commissar. When called to Albacete in October, 1937, to take Bill Lawrence's place as base commissar for all the Americans in Spain, he was acting brigade commissar on the Cordoba front. Had he remained, he would have been in line for the post of division commissar, for the Eighty-sixth Mixed Brigade, to which he had been attached, was soon enlarged and turned into a division, and Lt.-Col. Morandi, the Italian officer with whom he had worked, became divisional commander. In citing Gates' record on his departure from the Cordoba front, Morandi had declared he was "the political and organizational spirit of his (original) company, which in all of the battles engaged in at the Pozoblanco front demonstrated great fighting courage and a truly anti-Fascist spirit. . . . All of the (later) missions that were entrusted to him were satisfactorily carried out. . . . He has gained a high reputation. . . . His transfer to more important work is felt very keenly by the brigade because we lose in John Gates a true comrade and an excellent commissar in every aspect." In Albacete Gates had felt out of things; the work was responsible and difficult, but his thoughts were at the front. In the early months of 1938 he finally got himself transferred to the Fifteenth Brigade, and he had been in all of its actions since then.

The battalion swung into the new training. Booklets were distributed, entitled "How to Cross Rivers." Night maneuvers were invariably alike: the four battalions would converge at the bank of a mock river, then the men would mimic the crossing of the river in boats, in complete darkness, and after reaching the theoretical opposite shore, would rapidly storm the heights.

For six full weeks this training continued. The pattern of the next action was clear. The only question remained: when?

4

In July some of the men received two-day furloughs to Barcelona. The brief change of scene helped, even though it was not really a vacation. The city lived under the terror of continual bombardments from the air, just as Madrid had been under constant artillery fire. But the chance to sleep in a clean bed, to visit a cinema, to receive more accurate news of the world outside Spain, compensated for the sleepless nights and the brevity of the leave. One American returned with an account of his stay which illuminated the temper of the people.

"Somehow," he wrote, "it had been easy to understand the men in the army rallying after smashing defeats, standing up under terrific punishment and going back for more, ever determined to resist, to fight. But it was much more difficult to understand the determination of the civilian population of Barcelona. They had gone through horrible bombings, they had seen their homes, schools, hospitals, churches and markets smashed to earth by Italian and German bombs. They suffered from cold, for fuel was non-existent, and from hunger, for food was very scarce. Yes, Chamberlain and Daladier and American neutrality starved and froze the women and children of Spain while permitting German and Italian planes to snuff out their lives. Yet these people weren't through with their fight for freedom, for independence. With dogged will, they worked in the factories, making arms and ammunition for their army.

"In one factory which produced 75-mm. shells, I met a pretty Spanish girl. She was seated at a wooden table upon which were several shells, and she was busy with one of them. She seemed to be about eighteen when she smiled up at me. I noticed that there was a wooden crutch leaning against her chair. I asked her about her working hours and her wages, and she answered, 'What matter how much or how long?' Pointing to the shell, she continued,. 'The important thing is that this has the address of a Fascist on it.'

"I discovered later that she had lost her leg up to her knee and that her mother and younger brother had been killed by a bomb when their house had been hit some months back. And indeed 'What matter how much' when there was so little that money could buy? The people of Spain

"WAITING, WAITING, WAITING..."

remained loyal to the last to the Government they had elected."

The midsummer heat was deadly when, on July 20th, I received a two-day furlough to Barcelona, partly for rest and partly on assignment from the brigade. I was to bring all brigade material on hand to John Tisa, who had taken my place as editor of *The Volunteer for Liberty* early in April, when I had left to join the battalion. I found Tisa, busy and imperturbable as ever, immersed in his work at the International Brigade commissariat building in the palm- and flower-lined Pasaje de Mendez Vigo, and after a few hours with him I proceeded to the stamping grounds of the foreign press, the mid-Victorian Hotel Majestic on the Paseo de Gracia, midway between the Plaza de Catalunya and the broad and beautiful Diagonal. There, for the first time in many months, I rested in a real, civilized bed after a luxurious shower in a tiled bathtub. Later in the day I ran into Leland Stowe, whom I had not seen for almost a full year, since the August before when he and Ralph Bates had been at the International Brigade headquarters in Madrid. It was good to see him, youthful as ever, his face tanned and shining under his white hair. His presence—he was spending his vacation in Spain!—compensated for the absence of Herbert Matthews, who was on the Valencia front, where the insurgents were pushing southward toward Sagunto. In the evening we went for a long walk along the darkened streets of Barcelona, looking in vain for a wine shop.

THE LINCOLN BATTALION

But the Government nine-o'clock curfew decree was scrupulously kept, and we walked for many blocks, dodging the piled-up earth and stones where air-raid shelters had been built at every other street corner.

Late the following day Joseph North returned from a short trip to the brigade—he had left Barcelona the day before, at the same time that I had started northward from Marsa—with exciting but not altogether unexpected news.

"The brigade moved last night," he said. "I'm not sure, maybe it's just another maneuver. But I think it may be the real thing."

We spoke for half an hour. I asked many questions, and North told me that not only the battalions, but the entire brigade staff had moved. The communications corps had gone with all its equipment. Finally, when he said that the battalion kitchens were preparing to move, I was sure it was the real thing.

On the morning of July 23rd I rejoined the brigade, now encamped in a huge gully not far from Torre de España. After reporting to Gates, I continued on to the Lincolns, who were encamped in the farthest corner of the gully. The men were excited, now that action was imminent; the very daring of the approaching offensive roused them out of the lethargy of the previous months. The Spaniards ran about shouting, *"Ay, las barcas, las barcas!"* (Hurrah, the boats, the boats!) The Non-Intervention Commission was completely forgotten. All thoughts were concentrated on

"WAITING, WAITING, WAITING..."

the coming offensive about which, as Wolff said, "the men all knew, and the Fascists knew but couldn't believe."

At brigade HQ, Major Valledor and John Gates were gathered with the staff: Malcolm Dunbar, now Chief of Staff, Howard Goddard, Chief of Operations, and his assistants, Owen P. Smith and Manuel Estevas. Word had just come from Divisional Headquarters (where José María Sastré, Doran's former assistant, now was commissar) concerning the brigade's part in the offensive, and the plans were being checked. Later a meeting of battalion officers and commissars was held, and all was ready.

Late on the afternoon of July 24th, a letter arrived from home, addressed to one of the Americans, with a clipping from the New York *Times* of July 11th. The story was an interview with the American volunteers who had been captured in March and early April and who now, the men learned for the first time, were held prisoners in the concentration camp at San Pedro de Cardenas, fourteen kilometers from Burgos. The clipping reached the battalion just as Captain Wolff, gaunt and tired after a long conference at brigade HQ, called the men to assembly in a level field near the command post. He waited, putting off his talk as the men gathered around one soldier who read, in a loud voice, the names of the seventy-odd prisoners, most of whom had long since been given up as dead. While they cheered, happy to find that so many were still alive, and while some, failing to hear the wanted name read, walked off sadly, Wolff mounted a terrace about four feet above the field on which the men were sprawled. Joe Gordon still scanned the clipping, slowly, carefully, with painful concentration, looking for the one name which meant more to him than any of the others. But he came to the last name listed, and the name of Leo Gordon was not among them. He handed the clipping back to its owner and walked slowly away. By this time Wolff had raised his hand, twisted the strap and holster of his huge pistol from his shoulders, and stood facing the men. Dressed in his pair of far-too-short khaki overalls, his officer's stripes pinned loosely to his shirt, he looked more like the young Abe Lincoln than ever.

"Men," he said, "I've called you together because everything is set. You all know for what. Before another day is over we'll be in action again. You all know the reasons for this offensive. We've got to stop the Fascists' drive toward Valencia, we've got to divert their troops and planes from the Levante front. If all goes well we're going to roll into action the same way we did in our maneuvers back at Marsa.

"This is the big effort we've got to make now. If we succeed—and we will if we stick together and remember everything we've learned in the past—we should penetrate deep into enemy territory. We know the lines across the river are thinly held. This action has been thoroughly planned. We've got all the information anyone would want to have before entering an action like this.

"One thing you've got to know. We won't have any of

"WAITING, WAITING, WAITING..."

our planes to help us, not for at least three days. They're all on the Valencia front, and they can't be spared. And we have very few anti-air batteries. And we'll have no artillery of our own for some days, until we can get them across the river. You understand why. But I just wanted to let you know what to expect and what not to.

"Now remember: stick together. Remember the most important thing of all is to maintain discipline and contact. Contact—remember that word. They cut us off near Gandesa last April because our companies separated and lost contact with each other. That must not happen again. If we keep together, we should take back much of what we lost during the retreats. For us it's more important than just taking back a few towns. We can drive them out of the spots where we lost Merriman and Doran and all the others. And we can change the whole complexion of the war. But we've got to stick together. That's all, comrades."

Then, lifting his right arm, his fingers bunched in a fist, he bellowed:

"*Viva el ejercito popular!*
"*Viva las Brigades Internacionales!*
"*Viva la victoria final!*"

10

THE EBRO OFFENSIVE

An hour after midnight, on July 25, 1938, the army of the Ebro went quietly into the offensive which stopped the advance of Franco's troops on the Mediterranean coast, gained five hundred square miles of territory along a ninety-mile front, recaptured more than a dozen towns lost during the retreats, and tied up the insurgent armies on a single sector for four long months. By nightfall of the third day more than 6,000 prisoners had been taken. The towns of Flix, Asco, Mora de Ebro, Benifallet, Pinell, Fatarella, Ribarroja, Miravet, Corbera and a number of smaller villages were in Government hands, and the key town of Gandesa was surrounded on three sides. The offensive, launched along the great bend in the Ebro River from Amposta, south of Tortosa, to Mequinenza, in Aragon, stunned not only the insurgents but the entire world, which since the cutting in two of the Republic had conceded rapid victory to Franco. Yet the offensive had not been

THE EBRO OFFENSIVE

planned as a decisive one; its main objective had simply been to halt the rebel advance toward Sagunto and Valencia by diverting Fascist troops and planes to the north.

The night was quiet and the river flowed silently when the first wave of men crossed. The silence was only slightly broken by the plash of oars as the first boats, each bearing eighteen or twenty fully equipped men, were rowed across by Spanish sailors and fishermen, men from Galicia and the conquered North. The men of one battalion swam across, holding their rifles high above their heads as they made for the opposite shore. Once the crossing had been made the fighting began, but so great was the surprise that the first landing parties quickly overcame the resistance of the enemy at every important defense post on the riverside. The inland push began.

The Fifteenth Brigade went over with the second wave of Republican troops. The sun was mounting and artillery fire was sweeping the approaches to the river as the Lincoln Battalion, marching along a dried stream bed from Torre de España, emerged on a sandy strip of shore below Asco. As the First Company dashed forward to enter the waiting boats a huge tri-motored bomber approached. It coasted staggeringly low over the men as Captain Lamb, with eighteen of his company, shoved off in the first boat, the one with the reassuring name "All Right" painted on its bow. As the rest of Company One crowded into the remaining boats the bomber glided lower, directly above the men. Immediately the Lincolns opened fire on it with rifles and light machine-guns. One gunner especially popped calmly away at the big plane while Lt. Garcia Abad, his company commander, steadied the gun on his own shoulder. Through the fire, and while the plane continued to circle overhead, Captain Wolff's six-feet-two loomed at the river shore, directing the men to the boats. Enemy artillery was still in action at Asco, and once a chunk of shrapnel the size of two fists shrieked down and plopped in the mud fewer than five feet away from him.

The volume of fire from the battalion was terrific; a dozen bullets must have hit the plane, but not at any vital spot, for it continued beyond the shore to unload its bombs upon the men following the Lincolns along the dried stream bed. Later it returned to bomb the MacPaps, who were storming Asco, and to strafe the last of the Americans crossing to the enemy shore.

By the end of the first day, the battalion rested on the crest on a hill overlooking the town of Fatarella, waiting for the Eleventh Division, which it had been instructed to contact on its right flank, to show up. By nightfall, after the First Company had advanced over two additional heights, the entire battalion moved ahead, and on the morning of the following day it entered Fatarella. The men already were guarding ten prisoners, all of them taken by the First Company, which had also cleared Fatarella of its remaining Civil Guards during the night. Every man in the company, from Captain Lamb and Commissar Murray

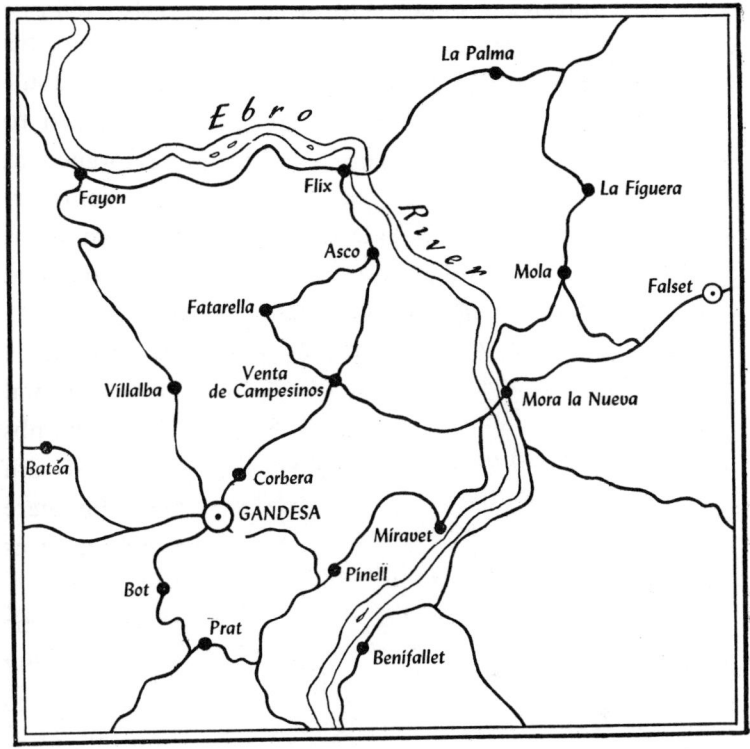

THE EBRO OFFENSIVE

THE LINCOLN BATTALION

Goldstein down, had new uniforms and pistols, taken from the *Guardia Civil* headquarters of the town.

The advance had been so rapid that contact with the brigade had been lost. Wolff, Watt and Lamb, out of sight of the men, exchanged anxious and significant glances. Lt. Donald Thayer, who had been sent to contact the brigade, had not returned, and Yale Stuart, accompanied by two members of the headquarters company, set off on the dual mission of returning the ten prisoners and re-establishing communications with the brigade command post.

At midday several battalions of the Eleventh Division marched into Fatarella, along the same highway on which Fred Keller had seen the enemy cavalry column advancing almost four months back. The terrain was familiar to the few survivors of the retreat still in the battalion; the hills and roads abounded with landmarks of special significance to them: here was a clump of trees where one had hidden overnight, there an olive grove where another had seen his companions killed. But the general mood of the men was joyful; at last they were repaying the Fascists in their own coin.

The battalion pushed on down the road, leaving Fatarella in the hands of the Eleventh Division. After two kilometers an armored car pulled up and announced that an enemy force was scattered in the wooded hills ahead. The entire battalion deployed against the hills on both sides of the road, and within an hour it had taken 250 additional prisoners. Two sections of the Third Company, headed by

THE EBRO OFFENSIVE

Sergeant Joe Taylor, a Negro, and Corporal Jim Lardner, were sent off to escort the captured men across the river.

Donald Thayer returned on the morning of the third day, with news and instructions from the brigade. After marching ahead three kilometers the Lincolns deployed again against enemy positions on the hills ahead, just outside the town of Villalba de los Arcos. The action from that point on was recorded in detail by the brigade commissariat representative to the staff of the battalion:

"Advancing perfectly, we drove the insurgents from their original wooded height, then over another hill, where our command post was established. Before nightfall we had chased them off still another hill ahead—and the battalion moved up again. On the new hill the first heavy fighting began.

"Lieutenant Paulo, commander of the Fourth Company, had been wounded in a night skirmish along the road, and at the end of the first day in the hills below Villalba Captain Lamb fell wounded, with a bullet through his side. All of the wounded men lay on stretchers or blankets below a fig-tree some 200 meters behind the lines where John Simon, the battalion medico, had set up his first-aid station. Low-flying bullets whistled past, inches above their heads. Jack Hoshooley lay next to Lamb, and beside them were Herman Tabb and young Wilfred Mendelsohn, who had reached Spain less than two months before. Tabb and Mendelsohn had both received head wounds—the latter a vicious hit which had plowed through the side of his skull. He regained consciousness only once before he died.

"From then on the Lincolns attacked time after time. The enemy had already been reinforced by a thousand members of the *Tercio*, Franco's infamous Foreign Legion. In one morning attack a section of Company Three remained out in no-man's land from dawn until nightfall, when Bill Wheeler, aided by Jack Shaffran, carried the wounded men back to safety. Tom Page was among the wounded—a bullet had punctured his chest—but he puffed calmly away at a cigarette butt, refusing aid, waiting for Doctor Simon to finish bandaging John Murra on the adjacent stretcher. Murra had suffered a painful and dangerous wound. The bullet had pierced one lung, and the day in the hot sun had badly weakened him. He had lost so much blood that the men felt he was sure to die. Yet he insisted on describing his wound and his pain to Simon in the most accurate and thorough of medical terms, elaborating on the possibilities coolly and methodically until Simon convinced him that silence was essential if he was to conserve his strength."

Simon worked calmly and swiftly during the action, soon moving his post up to a point directly behind the lines and a few yards in back of Wolff's command post. The twenty-five-year-old battalion medico was not really a doctor; he had left medical school in Philadelphia almost two years before to go to Spain, had served in almost all of the battles since Jarama, and had been a front-line doctor, with the rank of captain, for a longer period than any other medical man in Spain. The men respected him for his courage and competence under fire.

During the next two days there were frequent attacks—action heavy at all times. The commissars of the First, Second and Third Companies were wounded, and sent away from the lines despite their protests. Murray Goldstein's arm and leg had been hit; Hal Smith received a bullet in the same hand which had been badly wounded at Bruneté; and Larry Lustgarten was struck high on the chest by shrapnel. The enemy was firing everything in its possession against the hills held by the battalion—trench mortars and artillery shells as well as bullets; shells and aviation bombs rained in the valley behind the hills. The fighting was so heavy that by evening of July 29th there were fewer than 400 men of the original seven hundred still in action. Kurkuliotis, the Greek commissar of Company Two, was dead; his body lay in an exposed spot below the crest of the hill, facing the enemy. Joe Cuban, one of the seven Americans who had returned for a second enlistment, had been killed on the third day. The stream of wounded men through Doc Simon's post never stopped for long; and those whom Simon couldn't stop to treat were taken care of by Lewis Gayle, the battalion's chief first-aid man. The words of the wounded were strange to listen to: the Spaniards cursed silently, many of them kept repeating the words "Madre mia" over and over again; and some of the youngest ones wept. A tall and rangy Tennessean, one of the toughest men in the battalion, looked up from the stretcher where he lay painfully wounded, with a bullet in his stomach, and with a weak voice repeated dully: "God damned crazy thing, war, god damned silly business. Just because two people have different ideas, they gotta shoot each other. . . ." Joe Taylor, back from the trip across the river on which Jim Lardner had been wounded by aerial shrapnel, hummed an old Negro folksong, "The Preacher Went Down to the River to Pray," as the stretcher-bearers carried him away, a bullet in his shoulder. Another, wounded in the chest, kept anxious eyes on the doctor as his wound was being treated. "Do you think I'll live, Doc, do you think I'll live?" he repeated.

Word reached the men of the serious wounding of Yale Stuart as they rested on their first hill below Villalba de los Arcos. Stuart and his two companions had succeeded in reaching the brigade, had turned over the ten prisoners under their guard, and were walking along a road on their way back to the battalion when they were ambushed by a stray group of rebel soldiers. The hills were filled with many such bands; the Loyalist advance had been so rapid that not all of the territory taken had been completely cleared of the enemy. Shots rang out, and the bullets whipped past the three Americans. Stuart, in the center, dropped to the ground, his left forearm smashed. But he called on his two companions to answer the fire. All three opened up and in a short time the enemy band was scattered. Joe Gordon and Morris Mickenberg, who had ac-

THE EBRO OFFENSIVE

companied Stuart, later rejoined the battalion and told how, looking ruefully at his shattered arm, Stuart's lips had set in the hard smile so familiar to the men, how he'd cursed a bit and shrugged his shoulders. The arm was later amputated above the elbow.

On a hill adjacent to the Lincoln position another American—one of the most competent and mature and kindly of all in Spain—died as he directed the fire of a machine-gun in his company. He was Arnold Reid, a twenty-six-year-old American who had worked for many years in South and Latin America, and who had joined the Spanish battalion of the Fifteenth Brigade in order to strengthen the work of the many Latin Americans in its ranks. The Spaniards, especially the young *quintos*, had loved the quiet young man who became commissar of their machine-gun company; who knew their language and songs and traditions as well, if not better, than any of them, who treated them like a kind and just father. The Lincolns heard of his death for the first time when Joseph North, first of the correspondents to reach the Ebro lines, visited the battalion during a momentary lull in the fighting on July 29th. The news stunned them more than the news of any death ordinarily did; they had respected and looked up to him in the same way that they had respected Eric Parker, who had died at Belchité; the two were extraordinarily alike, in their firmness, their underlying gentleness, their great knowledge of many things. And they remembered what Jim Lardner had said of Reid after he had returned from the corporals' school where Reid had been commissar: "That man knows more than anyone I've met here of what it's all about."

There was a day of comparative quiet after the battalion moved from its positions below Villalba to a point north of Gandesa. But it was a much needed bit of rest, for the following two days were to be among the toughest of the first part of the campaign. The Lincolns did not attack, but bore the brunt of a Fascist bombardment which lasted far into the night and morning of August 2nd. My notebook contains the following brief account of the action:

"Moved across hill at 3:30 A.M., took up positions under artillery fire on side of hill behind Spanish battalion. At dawn our command post moved ahead to our former observation post, which directly faced the enemy. Our own artillery opened up, and at 11 A.M., after a short barrage, the Spanish moved up, went through our lines, and into attack. We proceeded to our take-off positions, overlooking what was immediately christened Death Valley. Enemy artillery bombarded us all day. Three times our own planes came over, bombing Gandesa. They told me the town was three kilometers away; it appeared to be much closer.

"In the evening the enemy again shelled the valley and the slopes leading up the hill. Moors and members of the Tercio were in the enemy lines, facing us. The place stank with the smell of dead and decomposing bodies. Enemy shells looped over our ridge and into the valley behind, killing many of the wounded who were being evacuated and men who had gone down to the waterhole to fill their canteens. Shells screamed directly overhead as we lay against the rock wall of a terrace; some dropped ten, twenty meters away. Hugged wall. As dark came, enemy began to use tracer bullets in their rifles and machine-guns, and shelled the hillside methodically, the shells tracing a horseshoe against the sides of the bottle-neck-shaped gully. Bullets were always in the air; the reddish and pink tracer bullets seemed to move slowly and weirdly. Sounds of men screaming '*Socorro, socorro!*' (Help, help!) and groaning '*Madre mia*,' kept up all night, with just intermittent lulls; always the noise of rifles, machine-guns, hand-grenades and artillery. Men were dead by the hundreds—mostly the enemy's —and the bodies stank when you came close to them. . . ."

When it was all over, and comparatively quiet again, Frank Stout was carried away, with trench-mortar fragments in his stomach and groin, on a wing-like contraption slung over a mule's back. The sight of the mule disappearing down the valley was strangely peaceful and rustic. And John Rody, the first-aid man who had carried a score of the wounded up from the open valley, sank to the ground under a fig tree, completely exhausted. "Longest day I've ever spent," he said.

After the fighting at Death Valley the battalion moved to a new position just outside Gandesa, relieving a battalion of the Thirteenth Brigade. The MacPaps were on the Lincolns' left flank, with the English just beyond them. Both battalions had suffered heavy losses in a series of frontal

THE LINCOLN BATTALION

attacks against a height which dominated the town and the surrounding area. The Lincolns remained there for three days, holding the lines in the face of artillery and constant trench-mortar fire which, because of good entrenchments, did slight damage. In reaching the positions the Americans passed through the same valley, outside Corbera, where Merriman and Doran had last been seen. (Later, the people of Corbera showed Gates and other men of the brigade staff the exact spot where the Fascists had lined up and shot many of the Americans captured during the last days of the retreat.) Enemy planes were always overhead, but they concentrated their bombings on the communication lines, especially the hastily constructed bridges over the Ebro, and the men in the lines suffered only a few casualties from their activity.

On the night of August 6th, after thirteen days of constant fighting, the Lincoln Battalion moved away from the hills overlooking Gandesa. As they filed through the main street of Corbera they held their noses. The town had been brutally bombed and shelled by the enemy; not a house remained intact. The corpses of mules and horses lay disemboweled and bloated in the street, and the odor of decaying flesh rose from under the fallen stones and beams of many houses. Just as the last company approached the outskirts of the town the enemy artillery went into action, and for a few hundred paces the men marched at double-time. Then they left Corbera behind. The first phase of the Ebro battles was over.

THE EBRO OFFENSIVE

2

The olive field where the men remained in reserve for eight days was a few hundred meters away from the main Mora-Gandesa road. Great squadrons of enemy planes came over constantly, making real rest impossible. Yet for the first few days the men slept almost continually. With the tension of the fighting over for the moment, they no longer forced themselves to dig into their reserves of strength and nerve. When they were not sleeping, they talked and griped about the food and the lack of cigarettes and the scarcity of letters from home. Or they went over the details of the thirteen days of battle, mentioning names of men who lay buried where they fell, saying merely, "Too bad, he was a swell guy." The casual reaction to death was familiar, almost a ritual now. It appeared always when death was intimate, when, as Wolff said, it "walked always by your side." Bernard Sall, John Gates' little chauffeur, who had been in Spain as long as any of the Americans, explained how he felt about it:

"You don't think anything about a guy being killed; even if he was your best friend, you just click your tongue and say 'Too bad.' Blood doesn't mean anything if you've been in action. I saw five hundred men being carried out on stretchers, and if I'd felt torn up about them, as I was at first, what good would I be in this war?"

As their strength returned, the Americans talked about the men who "had done good jobs" during the action. The phrase was their synonym for the civilian term, hero, which they scoffed at and uttered only in moments of sarcasm or banter. The list of Americans who had been proposed for citations was long: Luke Hinman, the battalion's chief of scouts; Sam Spiller, Company Two runner; Luchell McDaniells, the smiling Negro whose accurate grenade-throwing had earned him the nickname *Fantastico* from the young Spaniards in his section; Gerald Cook, Tom Page and Gabby Klein; Yale Stuart, and Lt. Henry Mack of the MacPaps. Others were Harold Smith, Bill Wheeler, Archie Brown, Frank Stout, and the two tireless communications men, Harry Fisher and Martin Sullivan.

One day, Al Stone of the MacPaps visited the Lincolns to inquire about his friends. Stone had been commissar of the American hospitals at Tarancon, Villa Paz and Castillejo, but had given up his important post to join the battalion. "I didn't come here to work in a hospital," he said, "and if I ever go back, it'll be only as a patient." He found many still alive. The law of averages had been true to itself in the fighting, and for every six Spaniards wounded or dead there was only one American.

Yet the battalion was only half the size it had been when it had crossed the river on July 25th. About 350 men were still listed among the effectives, and the companies were entirely regrouped, reorganized and under new commands. Companies One and Two had suffered more losses than any other, and so the two were combined, first under the joint command of Lt. Lopoff and Lt. Rusciano, and then under the sole direction of Lopoff. Archie Brown, a Californian who had reached Spain late in May, became commissar, while Harold Smith, who had succeeded Kurkuliotis before the action, was transferred to the battalion staff. Company Three was headed by Bill Wheeler, who had taken over the command on the death of Abad Garcia, and Donald Thayer still led the Fourth Company. The machine-gun company had emerged with far fewer casualties than any of the other units, and its original command was still intact. Because the ranks had been so greatly depleted during the very first days of fighting, and because the Lincolns were, as always, doing shock duty, the Special Brigade Machine-Gun Company had been assigned to the battalion. Its commander, a Spaniard, and Wellman, its commissar, had both been wounded during the first few days; and now Jack Cooper, a Cleveland auto worker, was in command, with a nineteen-year-old Spaniard acting as his commissar.

Cooper had undergone the unusual experience of being captured, together with thirteen of his men, during the second day of action, being held prisoner overnight, and then turning the tables on his captors by glibly talking them into surrendering themselves. "The Fascists," he explained afterward, "were in a pretty panicky state. Their observers had sighted many of our troops on a number of adjacent hills; and when their own aviation came over, I decided to worry them still further: 'Don't worry,' I told them. 'The planes are ours—Republican.' In addition to their general strain and panic, they had been without food for three days. They had eaten only nuts and whatever fruit they could pick off the trees, and they had been out of contact with their own forces for the same period of time. All of them were pretty well exhausted.

"While we waited to see what what would happen, their six officers conferred and decided their game was up and that their safest course would be to turn themselves over to us. It had been dark most of the time we had been held prisoners, and it wasn't until we marched them to brigade HQ that I discovered that there were two hundred and eight of them! I didn't know until that minute how big a haul we had made."

The story of Cooper's feat was hilariously funny to the Americans, some of whom remembered the old, silent movie *Shoulder Arms* in which Charlie Chaplin had ventured out into no-man's land and returned shortly after, leading a couple of platoons of German prisoners. "But how?" the commanding officer had asked him. Charlie had shrugged his shoulders and lowered his eyes. "Simple," he had modestly replied. "I surrounded them."

But Cooper was not the only American who had been captured. Lt. Howard Goddard had been chugging along in the sidecar of his motorcycle, bound for Fatarella in search of the Lincoln Battalion, when both he and his motorcyclist had been taken prisoner by a group of fifteen young Spaniards. The incident had been witnessed from a near-by hill, and word soon spread to all four battalions. Distorted in the retelling, the rumor spread that Goddard and Minuto, his motorcyclist, were dead. The tale which capped everything was a vague, untraceable story to the effect that the two dead bodies had been seen. Only the return of the young Chief of Operations and his motorcyclist, leading the fifteen prisoners, had scotched the wild stories of his death. Goddard explained that all of them had been part of the Mora de Ebro garrison which had scattered after the Republicans had crossed the river and been told to push on to Fatarella. "I explained it was no use their going there; the town was already ours," Goddard told his fellow staff members at brigade HQ. "They said that didn't matter, that they'd go to Corbera. When I told them Corbera was also ours, their faces showed they knew they were in a tough spot.

"I advised them that there was no sense shooting us—our troops were all over the sector, and they themselves would be captured before long. While we argued, with their spirits perceptibly drooping, we kept marching. Presently we ran up against the spot where the Lincolns were fighting a couple of companies of the enemy. By that time we were pretty friendly. I had assured them that prisoners of war are not harmed by our side.

"Their corporals talked it over with the men, and they reached a decision. Shortly afterward they stacked up their rifles and made a pile of their hand-grenades. Then they gave back my pistol and turned themselves over to me as prisoners.

"After surrendering they seemed completely happy for

the first time since we had encountered them. They sang songs as we marched back to headquarters and informed me that all of them, with the exception of only one, had relatives on our side whom they were very anxious to see."

Men who had been only slightly wounded returned to the battalion during the days when it rested in the olive grove, bringing the man power a bit further on the road toward its original strength. Here, too, arrived a small group of new volunteers from the United States, the first since the six men who had joined at Marsa. The veterans accepted them almost stoically; they were too tired to ask many questions. They knew they would soon be in action again.

One day in mid-August, a familiar figure, neatly dressed in a light summer uniform, walked up to the tree under which Wolff and the other battalion officers lived and slept. Two of the older and tougher of the English battalion veterans gaped at him as he passed, paler than they had ever seen him, and moving slowly. One of the Englishmen shook his head, breathed deeply, then blew his breath out in a half-whistle. Turning to his companion, he said, still shaking his head, "Tough man, that Lamb, tough man." Wolff and the other men of the battalion greeted Lamb with mingled anger and relief; the battalion could well use the veteran officer, but Lamb was so evidently in need of further rest that officers and men alike shook their

PAUL MACEACHRON

JOHN GATES

GEORGE WATT AND ABAD GARCIA

YALE STUART

A WALL NEWSPAPER

A GROUP OF AMERICANS, APRIL, 1938

heads and told him he ought to "get the hell back to the hospital where you belong."

Lamb's wound, covered with bandages, was still half-healed. He had left the hospital on a one-day leave to Barcelona and had continued on to the front. If the hospital records are still preserved, somewhere in Spain or Southern France, he is still listed as a deserter. But the Republican authorities were used to such "desertions"—their books recorded thousands of such cases.

With Lamb, who had arrived in the car of a newspaper correspondent, were two visitors who were new to the Americans. One was a man with a grave, tired face and large, sad, bewildered eyes; his gray hair made Ernst Toller, the exiled German poet and playwright, appear far older than his years. The other was a tall, lanky young man, about the same height as Captain Wolff. He was Daniel Roosevelt, a nephew of the President. The two trudged up the dusty wagon-path from Major Valledor's headquarters to the fields where the Lincoln Battalion rested, then went from group to group, talking with the men. Then, under Wolff's tree, they ate the stew of *garabanzos* and strings of tough meat, and drank the water and sour wine from some of the tin mess plates stowed against such an emergency in the orderly's great sack. They spoke for a long time, the young man diffident and casual in his questions, the writer searching, painfully sincere. Finally they moved off to a tree under which their auto was parked, where they waited for their young English chauffeur to return. As they rested there, talking with Lamb, Bessie and a number of other men in the battalions, the enemy planes, which had been over innumerable times that day, returned. As many as twenty-seven bombers flew over the encampment; and each time, the two visitors looked up, calm but apprehensive, past the leaves of the tree into the clear sky. Now and then, as the bombers passed directly above, they flattened themselves, slightly, almost involuntarily, against the earth. And each time Lamb assured them that the planes would pass, that the angle was wrong, that there was no danger. The planes returned another time as the group waited; this time Lamb looked up, shading his eyes from the sun. Turning quietly to Toller and Roosevelt, he said very calmly and casually, "All right, now lie back, flat." His practiced eye had spotted what the others could not have seen. In a moment there came the horrible, tearing sound and the great rush of air as the bombs fell; then the explosions just beyond the hill to the right of the battalion positions. In a few moments they saw the geysers of smoke and dust rise above its crest, against the horizon. "All safe now," said Lamb. "Better get going."

We crossed the river at dusk that day, seven of us crowded into a small Matford sedan. In the front seat were Toller, Joseph North and the chauffeur; crowded in the rear were Roosevelt, Captain Wild, the commander of the British Battalion, Peter Kerrigan of the London *Daily Worker*, and I. After an hour all talking ceased. All of us, jumbled together, tried to sleep. It was four o'clock in the morning when we reached Barcelona.

Daniel Roosevelt, who had entered Spain with a bagful of clothes, left a few days later with just the ones he was wearing. He gave Saul Wellman, still in the International Brigade hospital at Mataro, his moccasins, which were far sturdier than the *alpargatas* the young commissar possessed. The rest of his things he distributed among other wounded men.

Toller, who was preparing to leave for Madrid, gave me a pair of binoculars for Bessie and asked me to pick up a copy of *I Was a German* from his hotel-neighbor and give it to Lamb. "When I get back," he said, in his slow and careful English, "I'll bring more books for your comrades, and you can take them back to the front." When I began to thank him, he stopped me. "Tell them I give them these things with *my* thanks," he said.

Before he left, he wrote a short piece for *The Volunteer for Liberty:*

"I am glad and proud to have spent a day with the American volunteers who, worthy of the tradition of Abraham Lincoln, defend the independence of the Spanish people against foreign invaders, the freedom of the democratic world against Fascist aggressors.

"The strongest impression I have had in Loyalist Spain has been the heroic attitude of the people, who fight and resist, who go hungry without complaining, courageous anti-Fascists who remain democrats in their daily life under war conditions.

"I have watched here, in a time of war, a tolerance in cultural, political and religious questions which one does not very often find in democratic countries where there is peace.

"More and more people in the world recognize the significance of the Spanish war. You—and your fellow volunteers from other lands—were the pioneers. You were the first to bestir the sleep of the world."

3

The brigade spent only eight days in reserve. The first enemy counter-attack had begun on August 3rd, and savage fighting was to continue along the entire Ebro front for almost four months. To repulse these attacks at the most vulnerable and dangerous points was the job of the Ebro Army's shock first-line units, of which the Fifteenth Brigade was one of the most efficient and effective. Even now, with a force composed overwhelmingly of Spanish recruits, the presence of the few Americans, Canadians, and British, and their officers and commissars, transformed the well-trained but inexperienced brigade into a stubborn and courageous fighting force.

When the young Spaniards had taken up their positions on the hill below Villalba, they had remembered only the instructions about adequate cover. They had dropped at points well below the crest, their rifles tilted at angles which

THE EBRO OFFENSIVE

would have sent stray bullets far into the fields behind the enemy's lines, never into the insurgent positions themselves. They were timid, over-cautious, afraid to expose themselves. Wolff smiled and shook his head when he saw them. "Infants," he said. He and Lamb went up and down the line, walking intentionally erect to show them how needless was their fear. With the aid of all the company officers, they approached individual lying figures, lifted them at their shoulders, tapped their backs reassuringly, and explained that their fire-power depended on their ability to see the enemy. Of course there was some danger, they explained; but how could they ever win the war if they took no risks? Little by little, one after another, the young *quintos* were reassured, and they fought splendidly in every action afterward.

On August 15th the Lincoln Battalion relieved a division of Lister's army corps on the Sierra Pandols. As they climbed the steep mountain, they saw they were mounting almost solid rock. There were no parapets or fortifications; trenches could not be dug in the stone; burnt shrubbery provided slight camouflage but no protection. The hill—Number 666—had been retaken by the men of the Eleventh Division only the day before, and the bodies of the dead lay unburied, among the broken bits of scattered rock and steel shrapnel which littered the surface.

The brigade occupied a series of three overlapping hills. The Lincolns, on Hill 666, were at the most advanced position. On their left flank, slightly behind them, were the

MacPaps, and the Spanish were further to the left. The English battalion stayed in reserve, about four hundred meters behind the Lincolns.

"We stayed in these positions," said Luke Hinman, "until August 24th. The enemy was located on higher hills to the southwest, looking down on us. We scraped the ground to try to dig ourselves in, but it was useless. A day after we arrived, we attacked. But the Fascists were well entrenched, and we couldn't get beyond their barbed wire. They were lousy with machine-guns and their positions enabled them to chuck hand-grenades right down on us.

"Retiring to our own hill, we spent our nights fortifying ourselves, stringing up barbed wire, piling loose rocks up to protect our machine-gun posts, and filling sandbags. We had very few bags to begin with, and even if we'd had more we couldn't have used them, there was so little loose dirt around."

On the third day the enemy, having set their range perfectly, opened up with huge 81-mm. trench mortars and automatic artillery fire. What followed, said George Kay of the machine-gun company, was "eight hours of unadulterated hell." It was the heaviest and most brutal artillery barrage that the Americans had ever undergone, heavier even than the one which had almost wiped out a company of the MacPaps during the Teruel battles. The shells and mortars landed solidly against the Lincolns' parapets, blowing them to pieces. Direct hits on many of the machine-gun nests smashed the guns and blew the gunners to instant death. Emanuel Lancer, of the machine-gun company, luckily escaped death when a shell landed close to him; all of his clothes except his heavy American hiking-boots were torn from his body. Yet, except for slight shock and a number of scratches on his arms, he was unhurt.

The following day the intense shelling lasted for only two and a half hours, and during each of the twelve days the battalion spent on the hill it was shelled at least once a day. The shrapnel fell everywhere: on the surrounding hills, in the valley behind, and on the road used by the supply and kitchen trucks. Those were the hottest days of the entire summer; the sun beat down relentlessly on the heads and backs of the unsheltered men. There was little water, and the food could be brought up only at night, when it arrived cold and squashed after the long uphill climb along the narrow goat-paths. Several times during the fighting the English sent some of their men—especially those of their machine-gun company—to the hilltop to aid the Lincolns. On August 24th, after twelve days of constant shelling and aerial bombardment, of almost daily attacks against the hill, the battalion moved down and changed places with the British. On the following day the entire brigade again went into reserve, into rest which was not rest, since the men remained close enough to the lines to be under constant threat of artillery fire.

During the fighting on Hill 666, the Americans lost two veterans who were well loved and irreplaceable. One was Joe Bianca, the seaman and machine-gun company sergeant

THE LINCOLN BATTALION

whom the men called "the best soldier in Spain." A huge chunk of shell penetrated his groin as he crouched behind his stone parapet playing a tune on his machine-gun. The other was Aaron Lopoff, the commander of the combined First and Second Companies. A bullet struck him above his eye as he led his company into an attack against the enemy positions; he fell below the rebels' barbed wire. Sent to the military hospital at La Sabiñosa, on the Mediterranean coast, he died just as plans were completed at the central International Brigade headquarters to move him to a hospital in Southern France. Alvah Bessie, who had served as his adjutant all through the Ebro fighting, commemorated his death in a restrained but grief-stricken elegy which was printed in *The Volunteer*.

From August 27th until September 22nd the Lincoln Battalion remained in the fighting, moving alternately into front-line positions and reserve lines, but always under enemy fire. The men fought outside of Corbera after the insurgents had retaken the the town, and on Sierra Caballs, where the enemy artillery was almost as intense as that on Sierra Pandols. Wherever the line was threatened the Fifteenth Brigade, and with it, the Lincoln Battalion, was sent. The fame of the Americans, spread by Franco and de Llano in dozens of broadcasts during the course of the war, reached the battalion itself one night just before it was about to be relieved. From the enemy positions, just a few hundred meters away, came the voices of the opposing

THE EBRO OFFENSIVE

soldiers, taunting the men who faced them. One of the young Spaniards couldn't resist answering.

"Your filthy words are as weak as your bullets," he yelled across the lines. "Do you know to whom you're talking? We're the Lincoln Battalion!"

"*Si, si*," the Fascists shouted back. "We know *el Batallon Lincoln*. And we know your *commandante, El Lobo* (the Wolf)."

"You'll never drive us off these hills," the young Spaniard shouted at them.

"Yes," came the reply. "We know you're the Americans, and maybe we won't drive *you* off, but just wait till you're relieved. Then watch us!"

The young Spaniard emitted an expert (though inaudible to the enemy) Bronx cheer which he had learned from his American brothers, and in an excess of patriotism shouted, "That's what you think! Well, we're being relieved tonight. Then just see how far you can get."

In any army but this the youngster would have been shot. His childish and stupid taunt warned the insurgents, who brought their artillery into play just as the relieving battalion began to climb the hill to change places in the lines with the Lincolns. Luckily, few were injured, and those only slightly.

When Wolff was told about it, he bellowed in anger. But then he smiled, and said, "Those crazy infants! Didn't know what they were saying." He felt too pleased and proud that his battalion was esteemed so highly even by the enemy to punish the young *quinto*.

4

All of the Barcelona papers on the morning of September 22nd carried leading stories on Premier Negrin's announcement before the League of Nations at Geneva that every foreign volunteer fighting for the Republic would be removed from the front lines without delay and repatriated as soon as a League Commission could reach Spain to count all foreign heads and check on the repatriation. Hurriedly dressing in my old nondescript khaki uniform, I speared a ride on an army truck and crossed the Ebro late in the afternoon. The newspapers which printed Dr. Negrin's speech were crammed into my old rucksack.

I expected to find the brigade in the secondary positions where it had been for many days, but I arrived to find only a few men left behind. They told me the brigade was even then moving into action. Irving Weissman, of the Mac-Paps, led me over hill and valley for four kilometers to the new field headquarters, where I immediately sought out John Gates.

Shells were landing not far away and bullets were humming close and cracking overhead as he explained that the order to move up to the first lines had reached him that very afternoon, that the Lincolns were already on their way and that the other three battalions would follow them as soon as it became dark. Gates was seriously sick. He spoke in a hoarse, rasping voice, his eyes were bloodshot and feverish. His incessant activity during the past two months had brought back an attack of an old fever he had suffered on the Cordoba front, in the south, a year and a half before. He had just risen from the sick cot to which he had been confined during the days when the brigade had been in reserve positions—positions at which one man had been killed and six wounded during an aerial bombardment. Yet I could not help being impressed, more than ever before, by the enormous vitality of the little commissar who had never once spared himself in all the time he had been in Spain. Even then, with the news of Premier Negrin's speech just beginning to trickle through to the front, his entire heart and mind were in the fight, and his deepest wish was that the men in his battalions would be able to leave Spain "with the taste of victory on our lips."

This feeling was shared by most of the Americans. They were too busy to think of repatriation at the moment, too busy moving up to the lines to think of anything but the fight they were in.

Intermittent shelling, grenade-throwing and rifle fire continued all through the night. The Lincolns, holding a hill to one side of the road between Corbera and Venta de Campesinos (the entire range of hills occupied by the brigade was the Sierra de Lavall de la Torre), went into action a few hours before midnight. Jim Lardner, who had just returned from a one-day trip across the river, where he had had a painful tooth treated, was standing with a group of men under a large tree off the road near the brigade post when I last saw him. He was waiting to move up to the lines. It was almost dark, but there was the same glow and eagerness in his face and voice that I remembered his having when we had first crossed the Ebro. We spoke for a few minutes, then he took a few papers from his pocket. "Will you hold on to them?" he asked. "Just till this is over."

The men remained in the lines until midnight of the next day. There was no help for it. The lines had taken terrible punishment, and were in danger of cracking, when the brigade, which was closest to the danger spot, was sent up to hold until Spanish reinforcements farther back could replace them. It was just a matter of a day, possibly two.

But they were hours of heartbreaking fighting, during which the enemy Juggernaut of planes and artillery literally raked with iron and high explosive the area held by the four battalions. Again and again the communications men had to go out under the fierce barrage to mend the telephone lines shattered by enemy shells. And at dawn of September 23rd the brigade post was moved up again, this time to the triangle end of a small valley about a half kilometer from the front-line positions.

The insurgents did not begin their heavy work until a few minutes before 10 o'clock. But when they started, they unloosed hell over the entire sector. Their planes came over in waves all day long, some bombing, others strafing the lines. Once, in an excess of zeal and a slight miscalculation, they dropped an entire load of explosive on their own positions. But this happened only once. Their rapid-fire batteries never ceased for long, transforming the hills and valleys into a landscape of flying metal and huge, low-hanging clouds of smoke and dust.

Twice the enemy planes bombed the valley where the brigade post was located. Each time we took shelter in the deep dugouts under the rock of the hillside, with the entrances well protected by piled-up rock and soil and double rows of sandbags. Shrapnel, at least, could not penetrate the dugout in which I took refuge with David Gordon, Gates' aide in charge of the brigade commissariat, and his English assistant. The bombs, dropping ten yards away, shook the earth around us, and dust seeped through the small entrance and through chinks in the sandbags. We coughed and gasped for breath.

In an adjacent dugout were Gates and Major Valledor, who had reached the post just a moment before the planes had come over. Both were dirty, fatigued, worn out. They had been caught on the hilltop under a previous bombardment; there had been no shelter of any kind. The bombs had dropped around them as they hugged the earth; and now both were lying back against the walls, panting, smiling at each other and calling their escape a miracle.

After the bombardment Gabby Klein arrived with a message from Wolff. He brought with him, too, news which stunned the members of the brigade staff: Jim Lardner was missing. No one knew for certain whether he had been captured or killed, or whether he lay wounded out in the open land between the Lincolns' and the enemy's hills.

A little after midnight of the 22nd, shortly after Lardner had reached the lines, he had been chosen to lead a special patrol of three men with instructions to contact a platoon of twenty Americans and Spaniards on the battalion's right flank. The platoon had been sent out to occupy a low hill to the right and slightly ahead of the main body and had not reported to headquarters for two hours. Two other patrols sent to reach them had failed.

It was then that Lardner was chosen to locate the missing men. With him were two men, a young Spaniard and Anthony Nowakowsky, an American. Within two and a half hours Nowakowsky returned, alone. He said the three had gone out to the designated spot and, finding no trace of the missing platoon, had continued on several hundred feet. Proceeding silently and cautiously in the dark, they finally came across what Nowakowsky believed was an enemy listening post, but which might have been the enemy's main lines.

Lardner stopped his companions, Nowakowsky said. "You stay here while I go ahead and see who it is," the young corporal told them. That was the last seen of him. A few moments after he left them, some shouts were heard, then a flurry of rifle shots and grenade explosions. The young Spaniard was killed. Nowakowsky, under cover, was unhurt. Almost two hours later he returned to the battalion, on Hill 281, to report what had happened.

Three other Lincoln men—Harold Smith, George Cady and Jack Hoshooley—later arrived at brigade HQ and verified the details of the incident. The men were more than normally worried about Lardner, not only because he had become so well liked during his four months in the battalion, but mainly because Republican army observers had spotted the enemy executing captured soldiers directly behind their own lines during the whole of the Ebro actions. They hoped he was merely wounded, and that they would be able to recapture Hill 376, near the spot where he had last been seen, so that they might be able to send out searching parties. If he was a prisoner they wanted something—anything—to be done that might save him from execution.

I spoke to John Gates, and later to Milton Wolff, about it, and they agreed with my suggestion that the news be sent home that Jim had been captured. If he was a prisoner, then it would undoubtedly bring the State Department machinery into immediate motion, and thus possibly bring about his release. If he was already dead, why, then the story would focus the attention of the United States on the fact that there were more than seventy American prisoners in Franco's concentration camps. In any case, since no one knew exactly what Lardner's fate had been, it would be a last desperate effort to save him.

The Lincolns lost Hill 376 during the course of the fighting on September 23rd, and they had no chance to search the terrain below the enemy positions. The day was a cruel one. The air was never free of planes; the batteries of the enemy never ceased firing. Each death was the more bitter, since the men knew that relief was on the way, that this was the last action. Of the group of five Americans who had reached the battalion in reserve positions less than a week before, one was killed and two, Bob Rogers and Ted Baratel, wounded. These were the last American volunteers.

Most tragic of all was the death, on the afternoon of the same day, of Archie Kessner, the young American who together with Jesse Wallach and Abe Smorodin had been with the MacPaps through every battle of the war. An aerial bomb exploded not far from where a group of the MacPaps were lying, flat on their bellies. Shrapnel had hurtled through the air, missing the others but striking Kessner's side. He lifted himself slightly, put his hand to the wound, and sank back to the ground. "I was beginning to think," he said, smiling wanly, "they'd never get me."

At 11 P.M. of the 23rd, the staff sat around outside the hillside dugouts, waiting for the relief that was sure to come. A Cuban commander of a battalion of the Campesinos was already there, with word that the Forty-sixth Division was moving up. He spoke to Gates and Valledor; to Howard Goddard who had been acting Chief of Staff since Dunbar had been wounded at Sierra Caballs; to gangling, sandy-haired Owen Smith, who had taken over Goddard's old post as Chief of Operations.

AMERICAN SURVIVORS OF THE LINCOLN BATTALION

OFFICERS AFTER THE LAST ACTION

TOP-RANKING OFFICERS IN THE LAST PARADE, BARCELONA

FINAL REVIEW OF THE 35TH DIVISION, MARSA

THE EBRO OFFENSIVE

Shortly after midnight the relief battalions appeared. The men moved out of the hills, and began the long, straggling march away from the lines. Just before dawn on September 24th the last of the Americans crossed the wooden-planked bridge at Mora de Ebro. They had seen their last battle.

11

LAST DAYS IN SPAIN

BY THE END OF SEPTEMBER THE LAST OF THE INTERNATIONALS had crossed the Ebro, and the two divisions in whose ranks they had fought, the Thirty-fifth and the Forty-fifth, were scattered through the little villages around Falset. The Lincolns had returned to Marsa, but this time they slept in the town itself, not in the open valleys and countryside. For a week or two training continued; the young Spaniards, veterans now, were still with them, and there was only a slight relaxation of military discipline. The villagers brought out the last of their wine, fiesta followed fiesta in interminable succession. The International Brigade chiefs were seeking spots in Northern Catalonia where the men could live until the League Commission completed its repatriation check-up.

At the end of the month eight Americans were promoted in recognition of the work they had done during the twelve days of fighting on Hill 666 of the Sierra Pandols. The entire brigade—but particularly the Lincoln Battalion—had been cited after the action, and the proposals for promotion had been made on August 28th. The official orders came through now, when the fighting was over for them.

Heading the list was Milton Wolff, who received the rank of major. Five lieutenants became captains: Donald Thayer of Rochester, Minnesota, Howard Goddard of Los Angeles, Owen Smith of Durham, New Hampshire, and Jack Cooper and Henry Mack of Cleveland. Dr. William Pike and Dr. Julius Hene, both of the brigade medical staff, became Major Pike and Captain Hene. The fiestas continued.

Then, one day, the final official episode in the history of the Americans in the battalion took place. While twenty-five Government planes were locked in combat with fifty-five enemy chasers, some directly overhead and others over a wide sky area to the west, the four companies of the Lincolns lined up in the football field at Marsa. Before Major Wolff could read the orders of the day, the closeness of the planes made him give the air-raid alarm for the men to take cover. The planes passed overhead, their machine-guns clattering, and when it was seen that the dogfight showed no signs of abating, the companies lined up again.

The orders of the day were simple: all Internationals were to fall out of the ranks and re-form in one group in a far corner of the field. As the order was given the Americans stepped out. Wolff and Commissar Watt turned over their posts to their successors, two young Spanish officers

THE LINCOLN BATTALION

who had been trained by the Americans, and the Lincoln Battalion, for the first time in its history, was now completely Spanish.

I counted the Americans as they lined up to be photographed against a terrace wall at one corner of the field. Officers and men, there were sixty-one in all.

2

In Barcelona again, I hurriedly typed my dispatch on the loss of Jim Lardner and rushed to the *Censura* to send it off. While one of the censors read the story, Robert Okin, of the *Associated Press*, entered the pressroom. He had known Lardner, and it occurred to me that an *A.P.* story, appearing in hundreds of American papers simultaneously, would do more to save Lardner—if he was still alive—than any single dispatch. Hurriedly I gave him the facts, stressing the captured angle. For me, and for the rest of Lardner's friends in the battalion, the most essential need was for a prompt and thorough investigation on Franco's side. And Okin's story, which was the first to reach the States, did far more to launch that inquiry than mine could have done.

That was the last thing we could do about Lardner, the last thing we did except one. Late in November, while Lamb and I were rummaging through the store room of the Hotel Majestic, searching for a bag he had left there before the Ebro crossing, we came upon Lardner's valise. Taking it up to my room, we opened it, found two civilian suits, a number of other odd bits of clothing, a penknife and a

LAST DAYS IN SPAIN

few notebooks and letters. Since the Americans were soon to be leaving Spain, and since many still had no clothes except the ragged khaki uniforms they had worn for months, we gave the suits to two of them and distributed the shirts, ties, underclothes among a number of others. The penknife I gave to Elman Service, one of his two closest friends, who murmured an incoherent sentence of thanks as he took it. The papers I sent on to Vincent Sheean in Paris.

The fiestas continued. On October 16th the Thirty-fifth Division marched in the hills near Marsa and Falset before a group of army trucks which served as the reviewing stand. First came the men of the Eleventh Brigade—Scandinavians, Austrians, German and Dutch. Behind them were the Poles, Hungarians, Czechs and Yugoslavs of the Thirteenth Brigade. Bringing up the rear was the Fifteenth. They marched for the last time as soldiers in the Republican Army. The emotion of the day rose to the surface only once, when Merino, the twenty-five-year-old Division Commander, spoke his few final words of farewell. The answering *Viva!* echoed from hill to hill. The farewell took place in a valley dominated by the one mountain which the Americans would never forget: the huge pine- and scrub-dotted mass surmounted by the great white cliff over whose crest that day, just as during the many days when the Americans had trained their young Spanish comrades, the clouds broke and billowed downward. Finally there came the symbolic parting: after the reviewing officers—Merino, Valledor, Gallo, Sastré, Ludwig Renn and Colonel Hans—had passed up and down the three long lines of men in their final inspection, the Internationals marched off toward the east. The groups of armed Spanish soldiers, flanked by two small cavalry columns, went off in the opposite direction, to the west where ran the Ebro and where the fury of the enemy's counter-attacks still raged.

Three months to a day after the crossing of the Ebro, large delegations from each of the nationalities which had fought in the International Brigade gathered at a large estate not far from Montblanch to celebrate a last farewell with their former officers. Premier Negrin, who had spent the morning on an inspection of the front lines, arrived in a dark, dust-covered suit and heavy boots. The Americans mingled with the other Internationals in the huge courtyard as Negrin faced them from a balcony above. His voice was choked with emotion as he told them they represented "a miniature world plebiscite for liberty and right."

"You came," he said, "to defend justice and freedom because you realized that here in Spain the liberty of the entire world was at stake."

Colonel Modesto, commander of the Ebro Army, who followed Negrin to the rostrum, wept openly as he spoke, unable to control his voice. Tears streamed down his cheeks as he faced the men whom he had commanded in successive posts and battles throughout the most decisive periods of the war.

Then, speaking in behalf of the International Brigade, André Marty thanked "the Spanish people for the opportunity you have given to the men of the entire world to fight for the independence of Spain and the freedom of mankind.

"We shall return to our own lands," he concluded, "not to rest, but to carry on our fight for Spain wherever we may be."

When the speeches and ceremonies were over, the men adjourned to a huge dining hall of the estate to eat one of their last real Spanish meals. The highly spiced rice and meat was saturated with olive oil, but the men were veterans not only of the war against Franco and Italy and Germany, but of their early battles with the native food as well. The chunks of garlic did not disturb them any longer, and later they washed the whole feast down with wine.

Then, gathering informally in the huge courtyard, the Americans joined a group which surrounded Modesto and huge Enrique Lister, commander of the Fifth Army Corps. Lifting them from the ground, they tossed them high into the air, catching them as they fell. Modesto, incidentally, invited the sport upon himself. He was busy talking with a group of newspaper men and Government officials when, seeing the Americans tossing his heavier comrade-in-arms into the air, he excused himself and went off to join them. "Sorry," he explained, "but I have to join my friends."

THE LINCOLN BATTALION

The League Commission had arrived, and the Americans, Canadians and English waited impatiently for its members to reach them, count them and send them across the border into France. The English-speaking volunteers were more certain of their futures than those of any of the other nationalities. The Germans and Italians, as well as the men of many other European countries, could not be sent home to certain death or imprisonment; their only hope lay in being permitted entry to France or Mexico or any of a number of South American countries with which the Spanish Government was even then carrying on negotiations with the purpose of settling those of its volunteers who were now literally "men without a country." For the Americans the future was certain: almost all of them were native-born citizens, and it was only a question of how long it would take before the Commission got around to Ripoll, the little Catalan town in the Pyrenees foothills, where they were waiting. As the days passed, they became more grumpy. There was no fighting to do any more, and they wondered why the Commission took so much time to get to them. "They're probably looking for Russians," said Gabby Klein.

Leaves for Barcelona were now easier to secure, and the Americans made the Hotel Majestic their gathering place, just as the Florida had been in Madrid eighteen months before. They came for baths, for an occasional meal served on white linen tablecloths (though the meal itself was unsatisfying: a plate of soup with a few strands of green leaves thrown in, so watery that it was called *Mediterraneo;* a plate of stringy, suspicious-looking meat, and occasionally a few chick-peas. Nothing more). Most of all, they came to speak with the American correspondents, who occasionally provided not only conversation, but a few delicacies—Spanish onions, tins of pâté, and ham—purchased in France.

The Americans scoured the town for little gifts to take home for their friends, and those who had saved sufficient pesetas went from tailor to clothing store, getting their civilian outfits. Wolff arrived one day just as Jo Davidson, the sculptor, was fretting in his room, next to mine, because Premier Negrin had been too busy to sit for his head. When I walked into his room, he said, "Well, it's his (Negrin's) loss. But what am I going to do with this clay? I've got enough left for another head. Know anybody I haven't done yet who should be done?"

I reeled off a list of names: Pasionaria, Lister, Modesto. He had done them all. Finally I said, "Why not do Milt Wolff?"

"Who's he?" asked Davidson.

"The commander of the Lincolns," I explained. "He's twenty-three years old, a major, and he's been . . ."

The sculptor interrupted: "What's he look like? How's his head? Let me get a look at him."

We walked back into my room, where Wolff was sitting and reading. After the introductions, we went out into the hall.

"Fine head," Davidson said. "Tell him to be ready in an hour."

I went back and broke the news to Milt.

"Can't do it," he said. "I have to be back in Ripoll tonight."

"This is more important," I insisted. "Gates won't mind if you stay another day for this."

Finally he agreed. But he said he had to take care of something first.

In an hour he returned. When Davidson saw him, he put his hands to his eyes, and shouted "Why the hell did you have to go and do that for!"

Wolff had got himself a shave and a close haircut, thus taking away much of the roughness and shagginess which had made Davidson decide so promptly that he wanted to do his head.

The two disappeared into Davidson's room. "We'll try to remedy the barber's butchery," said the sculptor.

In two hours the head was completed. "Toughest thing I ever went through," said Milt. "He kept squinting up at me over his glasses. Like Santa Claus. Or like Karl Marx. And don't tell him, but when he modelled away at that clay, I felt he was pounding my head. I have a headache now. Got any aspirin?"

The day after Wolff left for Ripoll, another American arrived, bearing a note from him. "He told me to tell you that you made him miss something very important the other day," the messenger said. "Here, it's in this note."

LAST DAYS IN SPAIN

I opened the envelope. A thousand-peseta note fell out. The letter was written on official army stationery:

"Enclosed you will find 1,000 pesetas. I want you to buy a gift for my mother. She's fifty-three years old, has blue eyes, is old-fashioned and loves me very much."

It was signed "Major Milton Wolff."

Not all of the Americans were in Ripoll. Twenty-nine were still in the hospital at Mataro, and additional scores were scattered through the hospitals farther north, in Vich, Sagaro and other points along the coast. A dozen wounded Americans, so seriously hurt that they could not be moved, remained in the hospitals of Barcelona.

It was in Sagaro that the Americans first read the news that two American deserters were at home, slandering the International Brigades before a Congressional inquiry. All of them immediately drew up a letter, denouncing them and revealing what they knew of their records in Spain.

"In all justice," they wrote, "you should know about these two men. For the many months that Abraham Sobol was here, he did everything in his power to stay away from the front. He had, in our own vernacular, 'a yellow streak down his back.' He was arrested a number of times for drunkenness, and again in January of this year for pillaging and looting. He was freed with the understanding that there would be no recurrence of these actions. But he proved his final unreliability by deserting at the first opportunity.

"Alvin Halpern, the other deserter, was known to us as 'Hot-Air Al.' He saw no front-line service, and much less was he a captain, as he seems to claim. However, he did manage to get wounded slightly by a stray bullet three kilometers behind the lines. This man, like the other, never came over here to help the Spanish people in their fight for independence. As soon as he found out that there was more to war than glory, he skipped.

"Both men failed to live up to the fine American ideals and courage brought here by almost three thousand other Americans.

"We, the undersigned wounded American volunteers at Hospital Militar No. 9, declare that the statements made by these two deserting rats are untrue."

The letter was signed by Saul Wellman and Yale Stuart, of New York; Bernard Havins, of Chicago; James Bayne, Saul Friedberg and Griffith Washburn, of New York; John V. Murra, Chicago; Norman Perlman, New York; John Toutleff, Lansing, Michigan; Raymond Costello, Cleveland; Harry Shepard, Muskogee, Oklahoma; Eluard Luchell McDaniells, San Francisco; Louis Gnepp, Philadelphia; Mark Coad, Charlotte, N. C.; Isidore Hyman, New York, and fourteen others.

In the last months before their departure, all the Americans still in Spain knew that the mere fact that a man had crossed the Atlantic to go to Spain was not, as they had originally believed, a virtue in itself, nor proof of a man's true quality. Almost two years of war had torn all illusions from even the youngest of them, and they faced themselves and their fellow volunteers with clear, unsentimental eyes. They remembered, each one of them, how they themselves had acted in battle. There were few who could not recall moments when the strain had seemed too much to be humanly borne, moments when the body, sometimes even the mind, was on the point of cracking. But most of them —like most men in any war—had overcome their fears, had fought till the very end. More, they knew that their record as a group was better by far than that of the army during the World War; there had been few cases of shell-shock— the sign of a morally strong group of men. And there had been a number—but a comparatively small number—of desertions.

And now, on the verge of their leaving Spain, they knew what had caused these desertions. Among the 2,800 Americans who had gone to Spain, there had been a number of adventurers, careerists, who had gone not through any firm convictions but for excitement, power and glory. When the power did not materialize, when the glory failed to outweigh the muck and the strain, and when the excitement was not sufficient compensation for the danger that came with it, these men—not all, but some of them—had deserted.

Then there were the romantics, the escapists who were anxious to flee from problems they could not solve at home, and looked forward to the ocean voyage, the days in France, as an escape. Yet the very nature of this impulse which sent them to Spain prevented them from seeing sufficiently far ahead to foretell the hard work, the battles, the days when they would be faced with problems even greater and more terrifying than those they had left unsolved.

Finally, there were the honest, the "good soldiers," who just could not stand the pressure. Physical weakness made some of them crack under fire, and in some cases this weakness infected and distorted their entire outlook on the war.

The Americans could understand and sometimes forgive moments of weakness; they could be tolerant toward those who cracked under the strain, for they knew that each human being is differently constituted. They even forgave two men who deserted under exceptional circumstances after they had fought courageously for more than a year.

But they had nothing but contempt for those who attempted to justify their own cowardice by attacking and slandering their former comrades, the men who had suffered, who had remained in battle, had fought, been wounded, died—till the end.

In short, they knew now that the simple act of going to Spain had not been enough. Only in actual battle, under fiercest fire, under danger of death, could a man's convictions and true mettle be really, finally tested.

3

All of Barcelona turned out on October 29th for the last great demonstration in honor of the departing Internationals. Squadrons of planes flew overhead and patrolled the sea approaches to the city as the Internationals marched

LAST DAYS IN SPAIN

down the wide Diagonal, the great promenade and highway which cut slantwise across the new Barcelona.

The parade began at 4:30 P.M., shortly after Premier Negrin and his war cabinet, with the exception of those ministers who were stationed in Valencia and Madrid—arrived at the hastily but solidly built reviewing stand.

The entire foreign press was there. Matthews of the New York *Times,* Okin of the *Associated Press,* Weldon James of the *United Press* and dozens of others. Robert Capa, who had lost hundreds of priceless photographs when he discovered a flaw in his camera after the celebrations near Marsa and Falset, had spent an hour checking his camera, and now he darted back and forth across the wide street, focusing his lens under the hooves of the horses as the cavalry trotted past. It was child's play for him; not long before, when we had crossed the narrow footbridge across the Segré River, I had seen him go forward under falling shells, advancing with the soldiers, holding his camera before him as the others held their tommy-guns.

It was the most thrilling sight, we agreed, that we had ever seen. The planes flew overhead, dipping recklessly above the heads of the hundreds of thousands of men and women and children who lined the streets, perched on benches, hanging from balconies and from the palm trees that lined the avenue. As the Internationals went by, hundreds of girls in native costumes rushed forward, kissing them, pressing huge bouquets of flowers into their arms.

None of the marchers drew as much applause as the

THE LINCOLN BATTALION

Americans who paraded proudly behind Wolff, Watt, Lamb and Thayer. Their marching left much to be desired; the military click and precision were not there, but that was not strange. After all, Matthews wrote in his story of the day, "They learned to fight before they had time to learn to march."

The work of the League Commission dragged on. Finally, at the end of November, the arrangements were completed. I traveled northward to Ripoll, fifteen miles from the French border, where the men had been stationed for many weeks.

The entire afternoon and night of December 1st were spent in preparing for the departure of the first large group of Americans, which was scheduled for 10 o'clock the following morning. The population of the little town turned out in droves to help them. Those who had been unable to buy suits in Barcelona were issued native civilian outfits, suits with weird stripes of many colors, which many of the men balked at wearing. The sizes of the leather shoes which were distributed were small, suited to Catalans' feet; and many of the Americans were left out in the cold. Finally, they accepted the suits in good humor, vowing that they would change to other and less violently patterned clothes the minute they reached the United States.

While the final check-up was made, the men remained awake. The large town hall was open all night long, and the girls were kept busy preparing big kettles of the black, bitter, unsweetened liquid which was substituted for coffee in this, the third winter of the war. The few radios in town blared forth from the cafés where the men gathered, and in the large main hall Wolff and Lamb gathered the men together for final instructions. In the same hall the men exchanged their remaining pesetas for francs—not much, but enough to pay for cigarettes and chocolates for men who had had little of either for almost two years. The *carabineros* sent their band of two dozen brass pieces out into the streets to serenade the Americans on their last night in Spain. They made a strange, gnomelike sight, parading through the foggy, chilled, narrow streets in their hooded ponchos from which no faces were visible—only the flaring ends of their horns. They looked like twenty-four freezing little Santa Clauses; the sound and tempo of their music indicated how cold they were. Yet the Americans cheered them whenever they passed.

About three o'clock in the morning most of the men turned in. I found a huge bed, almost five feet high, in a little house next to the eleventh-century church which was Ripoll's prize antiquity and chief treasure. None of the Americans ever saw the inside of that church, nor even the bas-relief murals on the outside walls, for the citizens, fearing its destruction in an air raid, had sandbagged and walled it as thoroughly as the Madrileños had cemented their famous statue of Cybele.

THE LINCOLN BATTALION

The train arrived early the next morning—two full hours before schedule, which turned out to be the most significant thing about the departure. The entire population appeared to see the *norteamericanos* off. The engine and cars were decorated with great wreaths and strands of evergreen, banners and huge signs. Across the cowcatcher of the old-fashioned locomotive was a banner put up by the town's Popular Front which read: "Take with you the fervent embrace of Ripoll—*Hasta pronto, hermanos americanos!*" The moment when the train began slowly to move out of the station was a tense one both for the Americans and for the people who were seeing them off. The entire garrison of the town was on hand; everyone had his right hand raised in the Popular Front salute. Just as the tension reached its highest point an American broke it; leaning out of the window and pointing to a Spanish officer who appeared to be on the point of tears, he shouted, "Hey, guys, pipe that captain going tragic on us!" The men relaxed. Milt Wolff, forsaking his usual Brooklynese, waved his hand at Malcolm Dunbar on the station. "Hi, Dunbah," he yelled. "Cheerio!" Dunbar looked up, smiled, waved, and without losing a bit of his Oxford inflexion, answered with Wolff's favorite word: "Coit'nly."

For two hours the train moved slowly through the austere snow-capped hills of Catalonia, tunneled its way through jagged mountains, past numerous towns where people watched and waited at the stations for a last glimpse of the departing men. It was icy cold in the cars; no glass remained in the windows and the sun was hidden behind the steep hills. But the men sang, joked and nibbled away at the bread and sausages given to them at Ripoll—their last dry rations.

Shortly after ten o'clock the train pulled into Puicgerda. The mayor was there to greet them, to pronounce the last hail and farewell. Howard Goddard, whose Spanish was perfect, answered in the name of the Americans. Then the train chugged on to Bourg-Madame across the border.

I stayed behind at Puicgerda, waiting for the return train which would carry me back to Ripoll. An automobile breakdown prevented my immediate return. But it gave me the opportunity to be on the scene, waiting at the station, when the most incredible of all of Franco's acts occurred.

It was a few minutes after twelve o'clock—just the time when, according to the original schedule, the train bearing the Americans was to have entered Puicgerda—when two squadrons of Fascist planes appeared overhead and dropped their bombs on the railroad tracks a few hundred meters outside the station.

Franco had bombed and shelled Madrid on Christmas of both years during which the war had been in progress. He had never permitted a day of celebration, whether religious or civil, to pass without taking advantage of the crowds gathered in the first Republican capital to cause more than the usual amount of death, of carnage, of destruction of human lives and works. But this was the most astounding act of all. It was done openly. And since Puicgerda lies within a natural bowl in the earth, the correspondents, the members of the League Commission, and the entire populations of Bourg-Madame and Tour de Carol—all were able to witness the final deed which, had the train not left two hours before time, would have meant the death and maiming of more than three hundred men who were no longer combatants.

A week later, the second large group of Americans left for France. Only a few remained, scattered through Central Spain, Ripoll and the hospitals. They too waited for the day when, crossing the magic borderline, the subtle change in the atmosphere would enter them, and the war of bullets and steel would be left behind, and the war of nerves and incessant threats would begin.

New York
August 6, 1939

INDEX

Abad, *see* Garcia Abad
Addes, Bernard, 86
Agua Vita, 160
Albaceté, 11, 24-25, 28, 29, 33, 88, 229, 250; –Province, 25, 75
Albalaté, 188, 191-192, 222
Albarez, 108, 110, 114, 161
Alcañiz, 193, 208, 217
Alcorisa, 160
Alfambra, 164, 173
Alicanté, 232, 233
Altas Celadas, *see* Celadas, Heights of
Ambité, 108, 112, 114, 143-144, 161
Amlie, Hans, 76, 86, 96, 102, 114, 125
Amposta, 258
Anderson, Caspar, 85
Appleton, Owen, 137
Aragon, 73, 102, 160, 162, 167, 171, 183, 258; –offensive, 6, 112-139, 159, 227
Arganda, 37, 38
Argenté, 162-164, 167, 173
Arion, Ernest, 87, 96
Army of the North, 248
Arnold, Sidney, 56
Asco, 222, 258, 260

Associated Press, 296, 307
Asturians, 17, 248
Atalaya, 174-175
Azaila, 114, 123, 130-131, 187
Azuara, 131, 186-190

Balaguer, 240
Balearic Islands, 244
Barale, Louis, 56
Baratel, Ted, 292
Barcelona, 24, 25, 69, 84, 89, 102, 110, 112, 113, 122, 179, 182, 194, 195, 202-203, 240, 246, 248, 251-254, 277, 279, 286, 296, 300, 303, 306-308
Barsky, Dr., 60, 108, 161
Bartlett, Ephraim, 126
Basques, 90
Batéa, 201, 202, 206-209, 210, 216
Bates, Ralph, 62, 70, 109, 253
Bayne, James, 304
Beigelman, Eli, 36
Belchité, 6, 73, 84, 122-130, 131, 132, 183 *et seq.*, 239, 267
Belmonte, 173
Bender, Edward, 88
Benét, James, 87
Benicasim, 182, 196

INDEX

Benifallet, 258
Berkowitz, Norman, 240
Bessie, Alvah, 12, 218, 229, 278, 279, 284
Bevensee, Court, 108
Bianca, Joe, 240, 283-284
Biscay coast, 89
Block, Paul, 124
Boadillo de Monte, 92
Boehm, George, 11-12
Bourg-Madame, 311-312
Bradley, Carl, 119-120, 125-126, 128
Brandt, Joe, 208, 209, 213
Brihuega, 61
British Battalion, 28, 33, 38, 52, 53, 56, 63, 67, 69, 91, 96, 114, 119, 134, 138, 166, 175-176, 183, 186, 191, 198, 206, 208, 215, 243, 247, 269-270, 276, 278, 282, 283
Bronstein, Jean, 102
Brown, Archie, 272, 273
Bruneté, 87, 88, 91, 109, 110, 114, 117, 131, 172, 265; –offensive, 6, 89-106, 107
Burdick, Milton, 57
Burgos, 217, 255
Burns, Paul, 41, 46, 48, 96
Burton, Wallace, 86, 123
Busch, Dr. Irving, 108, 109

Caballero, Largo, 89
Cady, George, 291
Calaceite, 206, 208, 215
Campbell, Joseph, 57
Campesinos (Forty-sixth Division), 172-173, 177, 203; *see also* El Campesino *and* Gonzales
Campillo, 167
Cannon, Carl, 239
Capa, Robert, 307
Carlos, 62
Carlson, Arthur, 57
Caspé, 194, 196 *et seq.*

Castellon, 231
Castile, 5, 25, 100, 233
Castillejo, 108, 196, 272
Catalans, 23-24, 79, 164, 205, 232, 233, 308
Catalonia, 5, 83, 122, 159, 194, 201, 202, 219, 231, 234, 244, 248, 294, 300, 309
Cecil-Smith, Edward, 86
Celadas, 164, 178; Heights of (Altas Celadas), 164-166, 178, 181
Cervantes, 25
Chamberlain, Neville, 252
Cherta, 220
Chinchon, 30
Ciempozuélos, 37
Clark, Durward, 10-11, 87
Coad, Mark, 304
Cobert, Joe, 245
Codo, 122
Cody, Jim, 240
Cohen, Lou, 214
Cohen, Saul, 137
Collentine, Bob, 239
Concud, 167
Condor Legion, 9
Cook, Gerald, 239, 272
Cooper, Jack, 273-274, 295
Cooperman, Philip, 29, 47, 49, 59-60, 62
Copernico, 225
Copic, Vladimir, 68, 71, 96, 128, 181, 183, 196, 208, 249
Corbera, 7, 202, 203-207, 210-213, 220, 258, 270, 275, 284, 287
Cordoba front, 85, 88, 131, 250, 287
Corrigan, Jack, 202
Costello, Raymond, 304
Cuban, Joe, 245, 265
Cuévas Labradas, 164
Ciudad de Barcelona, 5, 84-85

Dadek, Stephen, 31

INDEX

Daily Worker (London), 278
Daily Worker (New York), 71, 240
Daladier, Edouard, 252
Dallet, Joseph, 83, 132, 135, 137, 155-157, 170
Darmos, 227 *et seq.*
Dart, Rollin, 131
Dash, Maury, 96, 108
Davidson, Jo, 301-302
de Armas, Rodolfo, 26, 27, 29, 36, 42
de Llano, Quiepo, 159, 194, 284
Detro, Philip, 76, 86, 136, 165, 170, 179
Deutsch, Jules, 240
Dimitroff Battalion, 38, 63, 91, 114, 116, 120
Dombrowski Battalion, 61, 63; *see also* Thirteenth Brigade, 8
Donnelly, Charles, 41, 73-74
Doran, Dave, 125, 127, 128, 152, 153, 154-155, 182, 183, 193, 197-198, 208, 210, 213-214, 215, 220, 255, 257, 270
Dorland, Norman, 96
Dougher, Joe, 137
Drill, Joe, 102
Drummond, David, 235
Dunbar, Malcolm, 182, 196, 208, 215, 255, 292, 310
Duncan, Norman, 108

Eaton, Henry, 125
Ebro Army, 11, 249, 258, 280, 298; —offensive, 7, 11, 12, 233-234, 238, 258-293; —River, 6, 12, 120, 133, 203, 207, 212, 224, 231, 243, 244, 258, 286, 288, 294, 296, 298
Edgar André Battalion, 206-207, 209
Edwards, Charles, 36-37
El Campesino, *see* Gonzales
El Muleton, 168-169, 174
Ellis, Bill, 208, 210

Engels, Dave, 124
English, Robert, 87
Epstein, Milton, 188-189
Estevas, Manuel, 255

Falset, 242, 258, 294, 297, 307
Fatarella, 7, 222, 258, 260-261, 274-275
Felsen, Milton, 14, 109
Field, John, 136
Field, Ralph, 136
Figueras, 23-24, 83
Fisher, Harry, 104-105, 237, 272
Fishman, Moe, 96
Flaherty brothers of Boston, 41
Flaherty, Eddie, 41-42
Flaherty, Frank, 41
Flix, 222, 223, 258
Ford, James W., 71
Franco, Francisco, 5, 8, 9, 16, 73, 77, 92, 114, 135, 159, 167, 184, 194-195, 201, 217, 235 n, 245, 247, 258, 264, 284, 291, 296, 299, 311
Franco, Victor, 137
Franco-Belge Battalion, 38, 52, 63, 99; *see also* Fourteenth Brigade, 8
Freidman, Jack, 87
Friedberg, Saul, 304
Fuencarral, 87
Fuentes Caliente, 162
Fuentes de Ebro, 10, 12, 120-121, 132-139, 142, 154, 159, 161, 172, 213
Fuqua, Colonel Stephen, 140, 143

Galan, Paco, 62
Galicia, 17, 259
Gall, General, 31, 67
Galleani, Major, 161
Gallo, Luigi, 196, 298
Gallup polls, 16
Gandesa, 7, 204 *et seq.*, 257, 258, 268 *et seq.*

315

INDEX

Garcia, 221, 229
Garcia, Abad, 235, 237, 260, 273
Garibaldi Battalion, 8, 61, 63
Garland, Walter, 86, 97, 99, 143
Gates, John, 85, 88, 187, 192, 201, 204, 213, 223-224, 225, 249-251, 254, 255, 270, 271, 286-287, 289, 291, 292, 301
Gayle, Lewis, 224, 236, 265
Geiser, Carl, 86, 137, 154, 216-217
Gellhorn, Martha, 70-71
Gibbons, Joe, 188, 190
Gittelson, Lester, 102
Gnepp, Louis, 304
Goddard, Howard, 123-124, 227, 255, 274-276, 292, 295, 311
Goldstein, Benjamin, 239
Goldstein, Murray, 233, 260-261, 265
Gomez, 48
Gonzales, Valentin (El Campesino), 62, 97, 172-173
Goodman, Kibby, 87
Gordon, David, 289
Gordon, Joe, 42-50, 190, 245, 256, 266-267
Gordon, Leo, 190, 256
Grachow, Leo, 87, 96
Graham, Sidney, 87
Grañen, 131, 161
Grant, Sam, 199
Greenleaf, Ralph, 48
Gross, Nat, 240
Guadalajara, 61, 77, 89, 160, 167
Guadarrama, 58; —River, 92
Guernica, 90

Hadley, William G., 85
Hakam, Harry, 80-83, 241-242
Haldane, J. B. S., 69
Halpern, Alvin, 303-304
Hampkins, Pete, 192
Hans, Colonel, 298

Hargrave, Roger, 13-14, 87, 102-103, 109-110
Harris, James, 29, 30
Haskell, Dan, 57
Hathaway, William, 57
Havins, Bernard, 304
Hawthorne, James, 71
Hecht, Joe, 224
Hemingway, Ernest, 70, 111, 130, 236, 241
Hendler, Max, 87
Hendrickson, 67
Hene, Dr. Julius, 295
Henry, Bill, 42, 43-44, 56
Herbst, Josephine, 70
Herndon, Angelo, 11
Herndon, Milton, 11, 137
Hijar, 114, 181, 183, 188, 193, 196
Hilario, 231-232
Hill, Jim, 239
Hinman, Luke, 218, 272, 282
Hitchcock, Douglas, 135
Hitler, Adolf, 9, 14, 16, 23, 128, 247
Hondorf, Michael, 85
Hoshooley, Jack, 87, 263, 291
Hourihan, Martin, 62-63, 70, 96, 108
Huesca, 183, 203
Hunter, John, 102
Hutchins, Evelyn, 87
Hutchins, Leslie, 87
Hutner, Daniel, 87, 126-127
Hutner, David, 87
Hyman, Isidore, 304
Hynes, Harry, 86, 102

I Was a German, by Ernst Toller, 279
Ibarurri, Dolores (La Pasionaria), 195, 231, 301
Ingot, John, 85
International Brigades, *passim*
Ivan, a Chicagoan, 213

INDEX

Jacobs, Deyo, 74, 75
Jacobs, George, 51-52
James, Weldon, 307
Jarama front, 6, 37 *et seq.*, 58 *et seq.*, 114, 132, 137, 141, 143, 190, 230, 235, 245, 264; —River, 30, 37, 40, 53; —Valley, 27, 30
Jelin, Maurice, 57
John Brown Artillery Battery, 17, 86, 88
Johnson, Allan, 63, 70, 143, 182, 195
Jones, Davy, 67

Kaplan, Joe, 189
Kaplan, Sam, 137-139
Kaufman, Al, 192, 222
Kaufman, Leo, 97
Kaufman, Ruby, 137, 240
Kay, George, 282
Keith, Irwin, 211
Keller, Fred, 111, 137, 154, 172, 179, 182, 196, 208, 210, 211, 213, 221-223, 262
Kerrigan, Peter, 29, 278-279
Kessner, Archie, 189, 239, 292
Kleber, General, 121
Kleidman, Larry, 169
Klein, Gabby, 272, 289, 300
Klimowski, Joe, 85
Kowalowski, Walter, 245
Krauthamer, Max, 102
Kurkuliotis, Nikolas, 235, 265, 273

La Mancha, 25-26
La Marañosa, 37
La Muela de Teruel, 168
La Pasionaria, *see* Ibarurri, Dolores
La Puebla de Alberton, 184, 186
La Puebla de Valverde, 173
La Sabiñosa, 284
Lackey, Fred, 57
Lamb, Leonard, 76, 85, 86, 98, 114, 125, 136, 161, 165, 170, 172, 182, 183, 196, 208-209, 210, 213, 220-221, 227, 235, 241, 259 *et seq.*, 276 *et seq.*, 296, 308, 309
Lancastria, 78
Lancer, Emanuel, 117, 283
Landetta, 49
Lardner, James, 236-238, 240, 243-244, 245, 263, 266, 267, 287-288, 289-291, 296-297
Laskowski, George, 57
Law, Oliver, 96
Lawrence, Bill, 88, 250
League of Nations Commission, 286, 294, 299, 308, 312
Lecera, 183, 187, 188, 191
Leider, Ben, 33
Leige, Clare, 57
Lending, Edward, 102
Lenoris, Jack, 51-52
Lenthier, John, 56, 239
Lenway, Clyde, 57
Lerida, 203, 240
Letucs, 183, 186, 188
Levante front, 86, 256
Levick, Lee, 239
Levine, Sid, 178
Levinger, Sam, 73, 125
Levinson, Leonard, 136, 172, 215
Lincoln-Washington Battalion, 6, 97, *et passim*
Lincoln, Abraham, Battalion, *passim*
Lister, Enrique, 62, 116, 122, 166, 177, 281, 299, 301
Listers, the (Eleventh Division), 101, 116, 122, 166, 177
Lloyd, Tom, 240
Lopoff, Aaron, 227, 235, 272-273, 284
Love, Vaughn, 240
Lukacs, 157
Lustgarten, Larry, 235, 265

INDEX

MacDonald, 41
MacEachron, Paul, 186, 202
Mack, Henry, 215, 272, 295
Mackenzie-Papineau Battalion, 11, 12, 13, 76-77, 88, 131 et seq., 155, 162 et seq., 183, 186 et seq., 243, 247, 260, 269-270, 272, 281-282, 286, 292
Madrid, 5, 7, 25, 30, 57, 70, 75, 77, 87 et seq., 96, 102, 103, 108 et seq., 123, 143, 144, 158, 159, 160, 182, 195, 251, 253, 279, 307, 311; —Valencia motor highway, 5, 37, 57; —Province, 173
Madrigueras, 75, 85
Maella, 201, 202
Makela, Nilo, 189, 190
Málaga, 89
Malgrat, 84, 85
Mallorca, 203
Malraux air squadron, 85
Manheim, 243
Manzanares River, 91
Maprahlian, Blackie, 224, 227
March, Juan, 65
Markovicz, Mirko, 76
Marlow, Inver, see Scott, John
Marlow, Sylvia, 75
Marsa, 242, 243, 245, 253, 256, 276, 294, 295, 297, 307
Martinelli, John, 199
Marty, André, 29, 299
Mas de las Matas, 160
Mataro, 279, 303
Mates, Dave, 76
Matthews, Herbert L., 67-69, 70, 71, 113, 236, 253, 307, 308
Mayer, William, 227, 235
Maynard, Lawrence, 102
McCrotty, John, 56
McDaniells, Eluard Luchell, 272, 304
McQuarrie, Roy, 86

Mediterranean, 5, 83, 84, 155, 182, 202, 232, 244, 258, 284
Mendelsohn, Wilfred, 263-264
Mequinenza, 258
Merino, Commander, 297-298
Merriman, Robert Hale, 9-10, 26, 29, 30-31, 33, 40, 47, 54-55, 62, 76, 111-112, 114, 131, 183, 186, 187-188, 192, 208, 210, 213-214, 220, 257, 270
Mesquite Crest, 94, 96; —Ridge, 92-94
Mickenberg, Morris, 95, 266-267
Minor, Robert, 71
Minuto, 275
Miravet, 258
Modesto, Colonel Juan, 11, 62, 298-299, 301
Mollerusa, 240, 243
Montblanch, 298
Monte Garabitas, 91, 110, 111
Mora de Ebro, 205, 215, 218, 258, 271, 275, 293
Mora la Nueva, 218, 226
Morandi, Lieutenant-Colonel, 85, 250
Morata de Tajuña, 30, 31-32, 35, 38-40, 52
Morse, Eugene, 42
Murcia, 196
Murra, John, 11, 88, 229, 238, 264, 304
Mussolini, Benito, 9, 16, 61, 89, 128, 247

Navalcarnero, 90, 107
Negrin, Premier Juan, 7, 231, 286, 287, 299, 301, 307
Nelson, Steve, 96, 103-105, 114, 125, 154, 155
Neuman, Sol, 87
Neure, Bill, 137
New Masses, 71

INDEX

New Republic, 87
New York *Herald Tribune*, 240
New York *Post*, 71
New York *Times*, 67, 255, 307
Niepold, Paul, 56
Nonaspé, 206, 207
Non-Intervention Committee, 27, 77, 246-247, 249, 254
Normandie, 18-20
North, Joseph, 240, 254, 267, 278-279
Norwood, Robert, 50-51
Nos Combats Contre le Fascisme: Le Livre de la 15ème Brigade Internationale, 75, 99
Nowakowsky, Anthony, 290-291

Offsink, Melvin, 211
Okin, Robert, 296, 307
Ornitz, Lou, 87
Osheroff, Abe, 239
O'Toole, Larry, 102

Pablo, a guard, 111-112
Page, Tom, 240, 264, 272
Pappas, Mike, 117, 235
Parales, 35, 114
Parker, Eric, 183, 187, 191, 202, 267
Patterson, John, 138-139
Paulo, Lieutenant, 263
Pedro, of Alicanté, 233
Penrod, Jack, 240
Perales, 162, 173
Perlman, Norman, 304
Perpignan, 23, 79
Peters, Roy, 102
Pick, Robert, 54
Pike, Dr. William, 29, 66, 295
Pinell, 224, 258
Pingarron Hill, 30, 38
Pinto, 30
Pintoca bridge, 37, 38
Pozo Rubio, 76, 86

Pozoblanco front, 250
Prago, Albert, 187
President Harding, 14
Prieto, 152
Puicgerda, 311-312
Purburell, 119; —Hill, 114-120
Pyrenees, 5, 23, 79-80, 81, 300

Quijorña, 91, 97
Quinn, Jack, 87
Quinto, 6, 112, 115-120, 121, 122, 130, 132, 140, 214

Raddock, Mike, 87
Raven, Robert, 59-61, 108
Red Star Over China, by Edgar Snow, 237
Regan, Charlie, 126
Rehill, Joe, 245, 246
Reid, Arnold, 267-268
Reiss, Dave, 183, 187, 191, 202
Renn, Ludwig, 298
Reuters, 240
Revere, Stephen, 102
Ribarroja, 258
Ripoll, 300, 302, 303, 308-312
Roach, Douglas, 71
Robbins, Al, 86, 96
Robbins, Dr., 101
Robinson, John Quigley, 114, 154
Rody, John, 269
Rogers, Bob, 240, 292
Rogers, Frank, 187
Rolfe, Edwin, 253-254, 278-279, 286-288, 296-297, 308-312
Romanillos, Heights of, 92
Roosevelt, Daniel, 277-279
Roosevelt, Pat, 240
Rose, Sol, 87, 88, 215
Rosenstein, Joe, 102
Rubin, Harry, 84
Rucker, Bunny, 87
Rusciano, Rico (Dick), 86, 236, 272

INDEX

Ryan, Frank, 208
Ryant, Ruby, 117

Sachs, Harry, 102
Sagaro, 110, 303
Sagunto, 253, 259
Sall, Bernard, 271
San Martin de la Vega, 30, 37, 38
San Pedro de Cardenas, 217, 255
Saragossa, 120-122, 123, 130, 131, 133, 168, 203, 217
Sastré, José María, 153, 183, 255, 298
Schechter, Rubin, 86, 102
Schrenzel, Isidor, 137
Schultz, William, 85
Scott, John, 26, 29, 36, 41-49, 56, 75
Seacord, Douglas, 21, 26, 29, 53, 56
Sears, Roy, 240
Segré River, 203, 231, 240, 307
Segura de los Baños, 6, 174, 179-180, 181
Seldes, George, 71
Seldes, Mrs. George, 71
Seligman, Joseph, 57
Service, Elman, 238, 297
Seville, 194
Shaffran, Jack, 240
Shapiro, 46, 48-49
Sheean, Vincent, 240-242, 297
Sheehan, Roy, 233, 241
Shenkir, Joseph, 233-234
Shepard, Harry, 304
Shirai, Jack, 29, 102
Shosteck, Sidney, 84, 131
Sierra Caballs, 7, 284, 292
Sierra de Lavall de la Torre, 287
Sierra Nevada, 17
Sierra Palomera, 174
Sierra Pandols, 7, 281, 284, 294
Sierra Pedigrossa, 174-175
Sigel, Paul, 10, 239

Simon, Dr. John, 244, 263-265
Smith, David, 87
Smith, Harold, 76, 265, 272, 273, 291
Smith, Owen P., 76, 86, 124, 255, 292, 295
Smorodin, Abe, 12-13, 189, 292
Sobol, Abraham, 303-304
Sollenberger, Dr. Randall, 101
Solomon, Herbert, 85
Spiller, Sam, 240, 272
Sramek, Martin, 239-240
Steck, Robert, 87
Steele, Ray, 102
Steward, Earl, 239
Stone, Al, 272
Stone, Hy, 86, 97
Stone, Joe, 86, 97
Stone, Sam, 86, 97
Stout, Frank, 269, 272
Stowe, Leland, 253
Strysand, Joe, 44, 49, 54
Stuart, Yale, 187, 235, 237, 262, 266-267, 272, 304
Sullivan, Martin, 237, 272
Sundsten, Tauno, 102

Tabb, Herman, 218, 229, 240, 263
Tajuña River, 30; —Valley, 58
Tanz, Al, 29, 48, 245
Tapsell, Walter, 208
Tarancon, 108, 196, 272
Tarazona de la Mancha, 76, 77, 88, 108, 131, 143, 196, 202
Tarragona, 202
Tarrega, 240
Taubman, Morris, 102, 240
Taylor, Douglas, 136
Taylor, Joe, 263, 266
Tchaikowski, 87
Tercio (Franco's Foreign Legion), 135-136, 216, 264, 268

INDEX

Teruel, 6, 158-180, 182, 183-184, 190, 196, 201, 205, 282
Thaelmann Brigade, 38, 169, 209
Thayer, Donald, 87, 240, 262, 263, 273, 295, 308
Thomas, Jack, 189
Thompson, David, 87
Thompson, Robert, 132, 137, 141
Tieger, Rudolph, 56
Tisa, John, 51-52, 75, 253
Titus, Bill, 178-180
Tivisa, 229
Toledo, 91; —front, 86
Toller, Ernst, 277-280
Toplianos, 48-49
Torre de España, 254, 259
Torreladones, 90
Tortosa, 194, 205, 210, 211, 215, 224, 244, 258
Tour de Carol, 312
Toutleff, John, 304
Trauslitz, Captain, 33
Two Wars and More to Come, by Herbert L. Matthews, 68 *n*

United Press, 307

Vaciamadrid, 30
Valdemorillo, 90
Valdemoro, 30
Valencia, 7, 24, 25, 69, 102, 114, 152, 159, 173, 182, 194, 195, 196, 232, 253, 256, 257, 259, 307
Valledor, José Antonio, 248-249, 255, 277, 289, 292, 298
Van den Berghe, 62, 114
Venta de Campesinos, 287
Vich, 303
Vidal, Lucien, 30
Villa Paz, 60, 108, 110, 196, 272
Villafranca del Castillo, 91
Villalba de los Arcos, 7, 205, 209, 210, 212, 219, 263, 268, 280

Villanueva de la Cañada, 91, 92, 96
Villanueva de la Jara, 26-28
Villanueva del Pardillo, 91, 99, 101
Volunteer for Liberty, the, 50, 70, 144, 246, 253, 279, 284

Walba, David, 102
Wallach, Jesse, 12-13, 292
Walsh, Bernard, 36, 86
Walter, General, 130, 190
Washburn, Griffith, 304
Washington, George, Battalion, 6, 17, 76, 77, 86 *et seq.*, 97; *see also* Lincoln-Washington Battalion
Washington, 21-22
Watson, Alonzo, 53
Watt, George, 213, 223-224, 225, 227, 235, 237, 262, 295, 308
Weinberg, Jerry, 104
Weiss, Jack, 96
Weissman, Irving, 286
Wellman, Saul, 86, 137, 170, 177, 189, 190-191, 216, 273, 279, 304
Wendorf, Paul, 58-59
Wheeler, Bill, 41, 43, 141, 245, 264, 273
White, David McKelvy, 100
White, Leigh, 240
Wickman, Morris, 86
Wild, Captain, 278-279
Wintringham, T. H. 76, 114
Witt, Arthur, 240
Wolff, Milton, 9, 76, 87, 100-101, 178, 182, 193, 196-197, 199, 204, 212, 213, 219-220, 221, 227, 235, 237, 255-257, 260, 262, 264, 271, 276, 277, 281, 285-286, 289, 291, 295, 301-303, 308, 309, 310
Wolk, Robert, 56

Yardis, 86

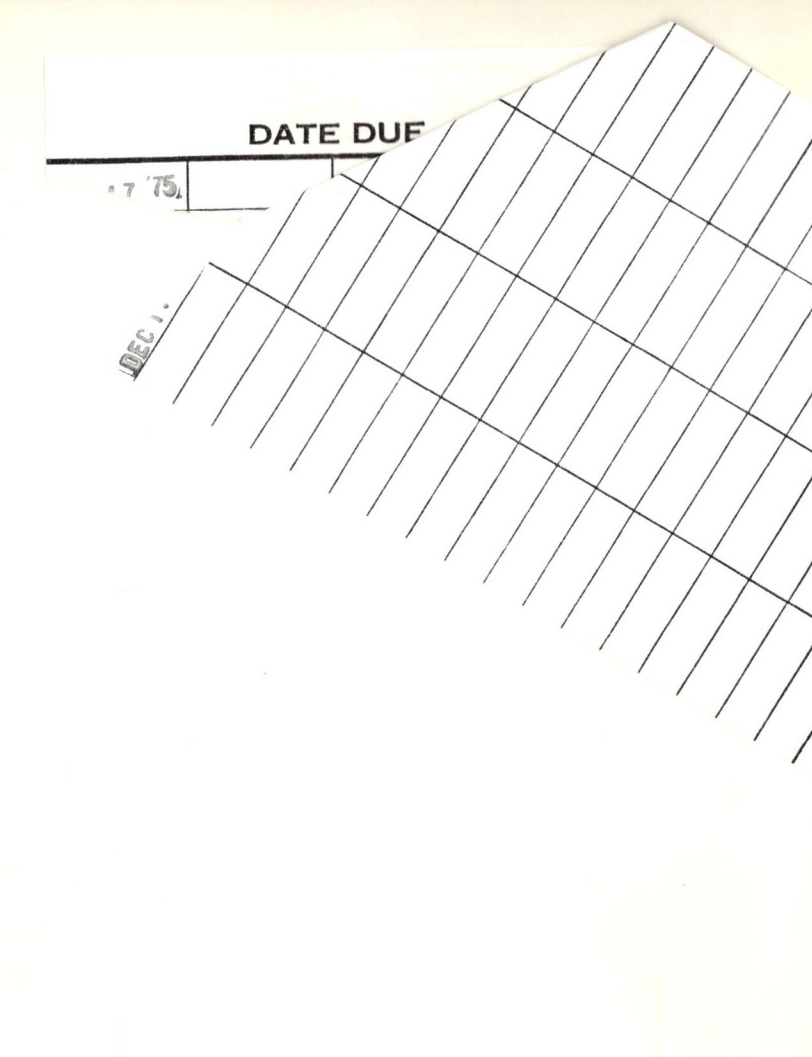